Aristotle, *Eudemian Ethics*

Philosophia Antiqua

A SERIES OF STUDIES ON ANCIENT PHILOSOPHY

Series Editors

Frans A.J. de Haas (*Leiden*)
Irmgard Männlein (*Tübingen*)

Advisory Board

Keimpe Algra, *Utrecht University* – George Boys-Stones, *University of Toronto* – Philipp Brüllmann, *University of Heidelberg* – Klaus Corcilius, *University of Tübingen* – George Karamanolis, *University of Vienna* – Inna Kupreeva, *University of Edinburgh* – Mariska Leunissen, *The University of North Carolina at Chapel Hill* – Sara Magrin, *University of Pittsburgh* – Marije Martijn, *Vrije Universiteit Amsterdam* – Christopher Moore, *Pennsylvania State University* – Noburu Notomi, *The University of Tokyo* – Pauliina Remes, *Uppsala University* – David Runia, *University of Melbourne* – Barbara Sattler, *Ruhr University Bochum* – Frisbee Sheffield, *University of Cambridge and Downing College* – Svetla Slaveva-Griffin, *Florida State University* – Carrie Swanson, *University of Iowa* – Katja Vogt, *Columbia University* – Christian Wildberg, *University of Pittsburgh*

Previous Editors

C.J. Rowe†
J.H. Waszink†
W.J. Verdenius†
J.C.M. Van Winden†

VOLUME 175

The titles published in this series are listed at *brill.com/pha*

Aristotle, *Eudemian Ethics*

Translated into English from the Oxford Edition of 2023, with Introduction, Notes and Appendix

By

Christopher Rowe

BRILL

LEIDEN | BOSTON

The Library of Congress Cataloging-in-Publication Data is available online at https://catalog.loc.gov
LC record available at https://lccn.loc.gov/

Library of Congress Cataloging-in-Publication Data

Names: Aristotle author | Rowe, Christopher editor
Title: Aristotle, Eudemian ethics : translated into English from the Oxford
   edition of 2023, with introduction, notes and appendix / by Christopher
   Rowe.
Other titles: Aristotelis Ethica Eudemia. English | Eudemian ethics
Description: Leiden ; Boston : Brill, [2025] | Series: Philosophia antiqua
   : a series of studies on ancient philosophy, 0079-1687 ; volume 175 |
   Includes bibliographical references and index. | Identifiers:
   LCCN 2025023065 (print) | LCCN 2025023066 (ebook) | ISBN
   9789004722071 hardback | ISBN 9789004722088 ebook
Subjects: LCSH: Ethics–Early works to 1800
Classification: LCC B422.A5 A75 2025 (print) | LCC B422.A5 (ebook)
LC record available at https://lccn.loc.gov/2025023065
LC ebook record available at https://lccn.loc.gov/2025023066

Typeface for the Latin, Greek, and Cyrillic scripts: "Brill". See and download: brill.com/brill-typeface.

ISSN 0079-1687
ISBN 978-90-04-72207-1 (hardback)
ISBN 978-90-04-72208-8 (e-book)
DOI 10.1163/9789004722088

Copyright 2025 by Christopher J. Rowe. Published by Koninklijke Brill BV, Plantijnstraat 2, 2321 JC Leiden, The Netherlands.
Koninklijke Brill BV incorporates the imprints Brill, Brill Nijhoff, Brill Schöningh, Brill Fink, Brill mentis, Brill Wageningen Academic, Vandenhoeck & Ruprecht, Böhlau and V&R unipress.
Koninklijke Brill BV reserves the right to protect this publication against unauthorized use. Requests for re-use and/or translations must be addressed to Koninklijke Brill BV via brill.com or copyright.com.
For more information: info@brill.com.

This book is printed on acid-free paper and produced in a sustainable manner.

Contents

Foreword VII
Preface IX
Acknowledgements XI

Introduction: a History of the Text of the *Eudemian Ethics* 1
1   The Early History of the *EE*   1
2   The Manuscripts   4
3   Modern Editions   7
4   Towards a New Edition   9
5   The Books of *EE*   13

Word List 18

***EE* Book I** 21
    Chapter 1   21
    Chapter 2   22
    Chapter 3   23
    Chapter 4   24
    Chapter 5   26
    Chapter 6   28
    Chapter 7   29
    Chapter 8   30

***EE* Book II** 35
    Chapter 1   35
    Chapter 2   40
    Chapter 3   42
    Chapter 4   45
    Chapter 5   46
    Chapter 6   47
    Chapter 7   49
    Chapter 8   50
    Chapter 9   54
    Chapter 10   55
    Chapter 11   59

EE Book III   61
- Chapter 1   61
- Chapter 2   67
- Chapter 3   70
- Chapter 4   71
- Chapter 5   72
- Chapter 6   75
- Chapter 7   76

EE Book IV   80
- Chapter 1   80
- Chapter 2   82
- Chapter 3   91
- Chapter 4   92
- Chapter 5   94
- Chapter 6   95
- Chapter 7   98
- Chapter 8   99
- Chapter 9   100
- Chapter 10   101
- Chapter 11   106
- Chapter 12   108

EE Book V   113
- Chapter 1   113
- Chapter 2   115
- Chapter 3   122

Appendix 1: *Phronêsis* and *sophia* in the *Eudemian* and *Nicomachean Ethics*   129
Appendix 2: On *EE* and the *Peri Ideôn*   145
Bibliography   156
Index of Terms   160
Index of Names   165

Foreword

With this commemorative text, we pay our homage to the author, Christopher Rowe.

Christopher Rowe (1944–2025) was a distinguished British classicist and among the most influential scholars of ancient philosophy worldwide over the past four decades. His translations of Plato and Aristotle, combined with his meticulous analyses and commentaries, have been extensively read by academics across various continents and philosophical traditions.

Christopher Rowe pursued Classics at the University of Cambridge, where he also earned a doctorate with a thesis on Aristotle's Ethics. Shortly before completing his Ph.D., he was appointed in 1966 by the University of Bristol, where he taught for nearly thirty years and served as Chair of Greek. In 1995, he accepted the Chair of Greek at Durham University, a position he held until his retirement in 2010. He continued his association with Durham as an Honorary Professor until his passing.

Christopher Rowe produced translations and commentaries on several Platonic dialogues (*Phaedo*, *Apologia*, *Euthyphro*, *Crito*, *Theaetetus*, *Politicus*, *Respublica*), as well as on the *Nicomachean Ethics* (2002, in collaboration with Sarah Broadie, who contributed the philosophical commentary). He also collaborated closely with Terry Penner on a volume dedicated to the *Lysis* (2005); his long-anticipated book on Plato followed in 2007 (*Plato and the Art of Philosophical Writing*). Both works were produced during a prestigious five-year Leverhulme Fellowship. Together with George Boys-Stones, he offered a complete translation of the principal sources on the Socratics (*The Circle of Socrates*, 2013). In a fitting return to his earliest research interests, he published a critical edition of the *Eudemian Ethics* for OUP (2023), accompanied by a comprehensive commentary in a separate volume (*Aristotelica: Studies on the Text of Aristotle's Eudemian Ethics*).

He was not only a stimulating scholar in ancient philosophy and an esteemed teacher but also played a significant role as co-editor of *Philosophia Antiqua* (Brill), overseeing an influential book series that has shaped contemporary scholarship in ancient philosophy, providing a platform for groundbreaking research and fostering dialogue among leading experts in the field. From 2007 to 2023 he was part of the editorial board of *Philosophia Antiqua* and curated more than 60 volumes for the series. He also contributed to the series as an author of chapters on Plato and Aristotle in the edited books of Christopher Bobonich and Pierre Destrée (Volume 106), Fiona Leigh (Volume 132), and Christelle Veillard, Olivier Renaut, and Dimitri El Mur (Volume 154). We are honoured to feature his newest translation of Aristotle's *Eudemian Ethics*, based on the 2023 Oxford-edition and complemented by an introduction, notes, and two appendices, in this Volume 175 of *Philosophia Antiqua*.

Christopher Rowe dedicated himself to making ancient philosophy a vivid discipline. He was one of the founding members of the International Plato Society, for which he also served as President. He also served as President of the Classical Association in the UK, and in 2009 he was awarded the Order of the British Empire for his scientific achievements.

We hope to have captured the most significant achievements Christopher Rowe realized as a teacher, scholar, and leader in the academic community. His vision, scholarly rigor, and unfailing generosity shaped not only the character of the *Philosophia Antiqua* series but also the collaborative spirit behind it. Christopher was not merely an editor – he was an active contributor and set a standard of excellence that inspired everyone involved. He will be deeply missed by colleagues, students, and friends worldwide.

Irmgard Männlein-Robert and Frans de Haas (editors)

Preface

This annotated translation is based on my 2023 Oxford Classical Text Edition of the *Eudemian Ethics* (*EE*). It is the companion, in effect, of my translation of the *Nicomachean Ethics* (*NE*) written to accompany Sarah Broadie's commentary (= Broadie-Rowe 2002), and for the most part it uses the same translations for key words. It also looks back to the Broadie-Rowe *NE* in another way. Three of Aristotle's books (originally papyrus rolls) on ethics are handed down in the manuscript tradition only as part of the *NE*, with indications in some manuscripts of the Eudemian text that they belong there too, so that *NE* IV–VII also becomes *EE* V–VIII. Whether or not Aristotle really wrote these three books to be part of two separate treatises is a highly controversial matter, but it is more and more the norm to behave as if they were and print an *EE* with eight books. The present volume does not do so, and this requires an explanation. My chief reason for leaving out the so-called 'common books' (hereafter 'CB1–3') is that the fit between them and the undoubtedly Eudemian books is considerably less than perfect, as I argue, in relation to the treatment of wisdom (*phronêsis*) and 'intellectual mastership' (as Broadie-Rowe renders *sophia*) in Appendix 1 below. This is not in itself a decisive argument, since *NE* itself has its own anomalies if the 'CB' are included, most obviously that it will have two ample discussions of pleasure, one in 'CB3' and another in *NE*, the latter apparently written as if the former was not there. It is, I think, a matter of the balance of the argument, and in my view that balance is against taking the equation *NE* V–VII = *EE* V–VIII as fixed. So I leave out the 'CB.' But my version of the three books is there in Broadie-Rowe 2002 for anyone who wishes to include them after all. My position on the 'CB' is summed up in my numbering of the fifth book of *EE* in the present volume exclusively as V. Appendix 1 will give readers a taste of some of the kinds of issues involved and perhaps give them an opportunity to make up their own mind on a topic ('the problem of the common books') that continues to cause the spilling of much ink, and will almost certainly never be resolved.

Appendix 2, for its part, is ultimately concerned with a tool in Aristotle's analytical toolbox ('focal meaning') that helps allow Aristotle to come to terms with his most significant predecessor in ethics, Plato. The *EE* engages with Plato to a much greater degree than the *NE*, particularly by way of repeated references, whether implicit and explicit, from the first book through to the last, to Socrates, where 'Socrates' is usually, if not exclusively, the Socrates of the Platonic dialogues. But I propose that the *EE* uses focal meaning as a way of reaching a kind of compromise with Platonic metaphysics, a central topic in *EE* Book I on which the *NE* shows him dismissing Plato's views, by name, as 'empty'. The use *EE* makes of focal meaning is integrated into its argument, as I argue in my notes on the relevant passages, and meanwhile there appears to be more than one reference to the *Peri Ideôn*, '*On Ideas*', an evidently specialised, 'esoteric' work that may well have been one of Aristotle's earliest works, and in which he may well have first developed the groundwork for, if not the actual idea of, 'focal meaning'. Appendix 2 introduces the relevant parts of the evidence we have of this lost early work, partly with the aim of injecting a live sense of the possibility that Aristotle is not merely referring back to another work but actively continuing a discussion begun in it; that this should happen, if it does, in the *EE*, as it does not in the *NE*, may give us additional reason for supporting a view that I tend to hold on other grounds, namely that the *EE* is a relatively early treatise of Aristotle's, written before the *NE*. (The sharper tone against Plato in the *NE* is at least consistent with a greater lapse of time since what will surely have been a cooling of Aristotle's personal connection with his teacher after the establishment of his own school in the Lyceum and the gathering of his own students around him). If this were to be the case, it would raise significant further questions about the common, understandable, but ultimately unhelpful practice of trying to interpret the *EE* from the *NE* (why would Aristotle bother to write out again the same things that he had already said?).

The aim of the translation itself, with its notes, is to bring out the full significance of the novelties revealed by the new text. Others will of course continue to dispute the decisions and choices underlying the new text where they see fit, but I shall proceed on the basis that the fundamental work is done, following complete collations of all the primary MSS, to whose number I have added a fourth.

Durham University/Hebden Bridge
February 6th, 2025

Acknowledgements

The bulk of the translation was done after an adverse medical diagnosis in early autumn 2024, following which the care and support I received from both the Leeds Teaching Hospitals NHS Trust, and more locally from the Calderdale and Huddersfield NHS Trust, has been exemplary.

But first I wish to acknowledge the huge support given me in this project, as in everything else, by my wife Heather, my marriage with whom happens to have begun in the very same year, 1965, as my encounter with the Eudemian Aristotle: a wife who not only continues to read and correct everything I write, her sharp mind and eyes saving me from countless errors, and who has always gracefully conceded space, at whatever cost to herself, for my ongoing conversations with 'Ari' – although in fact those conversations are typically four-way, with Heather herself as much part of the process, so familiar has she become with the material, not to mention the four decades when Aristotle retired into the background only to be replaced, first by Socrates, and then by Plato.

The book is dedicated first to Heather, then to our children Daniel and Sarah, and to our grandchildren Sadie and Micky Short and Mia Rowe, whose beautiful presence, whether actual or virtual, has been a vital part of what has carried me through. May they carry on their steady path to 'fine-and-goodness' (see *EE* V.3).

A key figure in my whole, career-long, project on the *EE* has been Tony Kenny, with whom I have corresponded, lunched, and corresponded again ever since he first attempted to recruit me – then a struggling junior lecturer – to project 'Aristotelian Ethics', with the 'CB' installed in the *EE*, by sending me the tables from Kenny 1978. I fear that my lack of enthusiasm for the cause has proven a disappointment to him, but I record here that one of the very greatest pleasures of my own project has been in our friendship, born in disagreement but also, as is the way with scholars and philosophers, warmly nurtured by it.

In textual matters Dieter Harlfinger, of the Freie Universität Berlin, has been my mentor and guide; I thank him warmly for all his help and encouragement, and for technical assistance provided through his student Matthias Krobbach.

But lastly – and lastly only because it is only at the last that I fully recognise how important a role he has played in my professional life, I thank Terry Penner, of Madison, Wisconsin. It was Terry who first taught me how to read Plato, by teaching me how to read Plato's Socrates; I now realise (and this will surely be as much of a surprise to him as it is to me), that in the process he was simultaneously teaching me how to read Aristotle. My first lesson, which had to be repeated many times, was that Socrates' denial of *akrasia* was never intended as a mere paradox, something said for the sake of provoking us into thinking: rather, it was something that Socrates actually held; and not only held, but held for a good reason, – namely that it is actually true, in real life, that it is impossible for us to act contrary to what we conceive to be the best thing for us, once we have grasped what the best for us is, to be 'dragged around like a slave' by something else – least of all a desire for what is actually bad for us; the cause, when properly understood, is always ignorance (this is a rough paraphrase of *NE* VII.3, a.k.a. 'CB' 3, 1145b21–7); it is the same concession to Socrates that Aristotle makes at the end of *EE* V.1. But let us be clear about exactly what Aristotle concedes: not that there are no such people as acratics: for him, there certainly exists an acratic type, and he is at pains to work out how *akrasia* is, despite Socrates' arguments, still possible. But what he insists on is that even the acratic person need not be as he is: *akrasia* is itself something that is up to us (we no more *have* to be acratic than we *have* to be vicious and bad); for after all we can acquire wisdom, *phronêsis*, 'than which there is no stronger thing'. If acratic actions, for Aristotle, are always a matter of intellectual error (bad decisions made in the heat of the moment, for example), then wisdom will be our best guardian. The difference, ultimately, between Socrates and Aristotle is that Socrates will deny that anyone can truly desire what merely appears to be good for us and is actually not, while Aristotle thinks that a step too far: by nature we always desire what is truly good for us, but we do not always remain true to our essential natures as human beings. Aristotle's position here is a concrete expression, and example, of that other familiar Socratic saying, 'An unexamined life is unliveable for a human being' (Plato, *Apology* 38a5–6), which too, in effect, Aristotle adopts as his own, when he insists – as he does, in my reconstruction of the text of the *EE*, that philosophy is not an optional extra but an intrinsic part of a full human life (see especially V.3, in conjunction with the introductory Book I).

In short, it was Terry who helped me find the joy of ancient philosophy, whether working together to unlock a text (see Penner and Rowe 2005), or working with a Socrates, a Plato, or an Aristotle to investigate the way things are. For that I thank Terry from the bottom of my heart.

Introduction: a History of the Text of the *Eudemian Ethics*

The *Eudemian Ethics* (*EE*) has for the larger part of its existence been the poor relation of the *NE*, surviving at around the beginning of the 13th century CE perhaps in a solitary manuscript, the ancestors or ancestor of which may well at some point have become separated from the rest of the corpus. Byzantine Sicily and then Renaissance Italy saw a brief surge of interest in the work, with that single manuscript giving birth, eventually, to twenty or so more, until it then again sank into obscurity, accompanied by doubts about its authenticity; only in the last half-century has it begun to receive anything like the full philosophical attention it deserves in its own right. Because of the vicissitudes in its transmission, the text of the *EE* is often in a poor, sometimes very poor, state. I myself completed a full new collation of the four main manuscripts (P, C, B and L) – including one (B) locked away in a private collection until the 1970s – as well as examining their descendants, in order to produce a new and usable text,[1] believing it possible to improve substantially on the available editions, which have been founded either on an incomplete understanding of the manuscript tradition, or on inaccurate and incomplete collations, or more usually both, and so provide a better basis for the philosophical understanding of this tantalising work.

1 The Early History of the *EE*

Few things are certain about the history, not just of the *EE* but of Aristotle's writings on ethics as a whole. Two of these, the tiny *De virtutibus et vitiis*, '*VV*', and the *Magna Moralia*, '*MM*', are in my view spurious: that both are included in the traditional corpus of Aristotelian writings tells us nothing by itself, since the corpus can include pseudo-Aristotelian productions (e.g., *Problems*). In the Byzantine period, and in the Italian Renaissance, *MM* was regarded as Aristotle's (why would it not be?). There it was, waiting to be copied, along with everything else, typically placed before *EE*; some continue to think it authentic.[2] What we do know for sure is that Aristotle wrote at least fifteen books on the

---

1 = Rowe 2023a: the new Oxford edition/OCT ('Oxford Classical Text'), with the companion volume Rowe 2023b.
2 See Rowe 1975.

subject of ethics, if we restrict ourselves to the constituents of those assemblages that we label respectively 'Eudemian' and 'Nicomachean': that is, what we count as the seven undisputed 'Nicomachean' books, five similarly undisputed 'Eudemian' books, three more that are either both 'Nicomachean' and 'Eudemian' or one or the other (i.e., the 'CB', were they to be actually shared by both works, '*NE* V–VII' '=' '*EE* IV–VI'). A 'book' in this case will correspond to the length of a papyrus roll,[3] the end of each typically coinciding with the end of a treatment of a particular topic or collection of topics, so that each can be separately labelled as 'about *x*' or 'about *y*'. There are clear signs that Aristotle intended to cover not just individual ethical topics but the subject of ethics as a whole, both because he talks about such a subject, and because the end of one book may be explicitly connected with the beginning of another, or a book will explicitly look forward or backward to one or more other books. It is also clear that he covered a large number of subjects twice, but – unless some books were lost, early on, and disappeared without trace – dealt only once with some topics: including most, but not all, of the topics of the 'common' books,[4] together with (e.g.) the treatment of *eutuchia* we find in what we call *EE* V.2.

It is thus reasonable to say that among Aristotle's writings there were the elements of two general treatments of ethics, neither of which could have included all the topics discussed in the other unless the discussions of some topics were shared. What we cannot say with certainty is that two such overall treatments were fully conceived, let alone realised, by Aristotle himself. But at some point two ethical works did emerge, one with the label 'Eudemian', perhaps because it was put together by Eudemus of Rhodes (*physically* put together, even, with the assembling of books in a certain order?), and another with the label 'Nicomachean', perhaps because it was put together by Aristotle's son Nicomachus. Both labels, we may suppose with reasonable safety, were attached after Aristotle's death, since so far as we can tell he is happy in other works to refer to ethical discussions (books) as 'the/my ethics', *ta êthika*, *hoi êthikoi logoi*, and so on, without distinction. It would, I think, in any case be a category mistake to suppose that such expressions, in cross-references by Aristotle himself, would necessarily refer to an *Ethics* like our *Eudemian* or

---

3 The question 'how long is a papyrus roll?' is a little like asking about the length of the proverbial piece of string, except that beyond a certain length a roll would be unwieldy, while at the lower limit a roll would not be a roll without a certain bulk.
4 'Not all': to take the best known example, pleasure: discussed not only in the third 'common' book but in (what we call) *NE* X.

Nicomachean; as I shall argue, those are not necessarily the terms in which he operates.

It is notoriously difficult to find our *EE* and *NE* in the ancient catalogues of Aristotle's works.[5] This is no doubt partly a matter of accident, of what happened to arrive in the particular collection or library that was being catalogued, but also a matter of the way in which they arrived: however much 'editors', those responsible for dealing with the master's *Nachlass*, may have encouraged readers to read certain 'books' together, those books will still have been physically separate from each other, and unless they were somehow very clearly marked as a connected group cataloguers would naturally tend to list them separately. In the three ancient lists we have, or for which we have evidence, there are only two substantial groups of books on ethics listed, one of five and one of eight. The group of five might be the five undisputed Eudemians, that is, excluding the 'common' books, but it might not; the group of eight, which apparently once appeared in a catalogue by Andronicus of Rhodes, is actually there labelled 'Eudemian'. On one plausible account, *both* references are to the *EE*, the five-book version being without the three 'common' middle books, the eight-book with them;[6] in which case our *NE*, as such (i.e., as a single entity), would not appear at all. Yet Cicero seems to know of a 'Nicomachean' *Ethics*, Plutarch is surely quite familiar with what is certainly our *NE*, and Aspasius writes a commentary on it. 'In Aspasius' writing', comments Kenny, 'we find the situation with which we have been familiar for centuries: [*NE*] is the undoubted treatise of Aristotle, [*EE*] is the problematic treatise whose attribution fluctuates, regarded now as authentic Aristotle, now as the work of his disciple Eudemus.'[7]

---

5 See Moraux 1951; Kenny 1978/2016, 39–46; Barnes 1997: esp. 57–9.
6 See Primavesi 2007: 70–73. The style of the numbering of the books of our *EE* is later than that of the rest of the corpus (*Problems* apart), indicating – so Primavesi argues – that the three middle books were a later addition. But that does not rule out the possibility, indeed, I would add, the near certainty, that *EE* had been in eight books before. Eudemus would have laid claim to those middle books surely as much as Nicomachus; why would either of them have left a great hole in the middle of his *Ethics*? So now *EE* has eight books, now five, now eight again; and that, as we shall see, is the pattern from the Byzantine and Renaissance periods on.
7 Kenny 1978/2016: 29. Interestingly, Aspasius seems to write as if the middle books belonged to *EE*, and to Eudemus; Alexander of Aphrodisias reads them as part of *NE* (see preceding note).

2   The Manuscripts

The situation as thus described is no doubt the chief reason for the dire state of the transmitted text of *EE*, at least in many of its parts. Since all of the extant manuscripts are descended from a single archetype (the lost ω in Fig. 1), the failings of a single copyist have a disproportionate effect, and there is evidence, for one part of *EE*, that one markedly incompetent copyist did in fact intervene in the tradition not so long before the earliest of the surviving Greek manuscripts of the *EE*, namely P and C, which were written in the late thirteenth century BCE. There exist Latin translations, probably by William of Moerbeke, of the last two chapters of *EE*, v.2-3, that evidently rely on a lost Greek manuscript (the lost ψ) that was significantly less corrupt than any Greek manuscripts deriving from the archetype ω; editors including myself have made extensive use of these versions in restoring the Greek text. The Latin *EE* v.2, preceded by a translation of the corresponding chapter of *MM*, constitutes the *Liber de bona fortuna* ('*BF*'), which still survives in more than 140 manuscripts;[8] in one case it is followed by the Latin version of v.3. If we may extrapolate from the obviously much better state of these two chapters in the manuscript used by the Latin translator(s), there was greater deterioration in the transmitted text in the century before our first extant Greek copies than in all the preceding fifteen.[9] But then, perhaps partly because of the dissemination in Latin of what is surely its most distinctive chapter (v.2),[10] there is a modest growth of interest in *EE*, as evidenced by the commissions for copies, first – so

---

[8]   As compared with the 20+ Greek manuscripts we have for *EE* as a whole, dating from the end of the thirteenth century (one, i.e., C, is precisely dated by the copyist himself to 1279) to the beginning of the sixteenth.

[9]   There is general agreement that the text of the 'common' books as they appear in manuscripts containing *EE*, or in *EE* itself, derives from the Nicomachean tradition. This is entirely consistent with the fact that they are in a much better state than at least *EE* II, III, IV and V better, even, than *EE* I, which is for the most part the least problematic, textually, of the undisputed Eudemian books, perhaps because – until the final chapter – it is less technical than the rest, and has a marginally more flowing style.

[10] Cf. the suggestion by Aldo Manuzio, in the dedication of the fifth volume of the Aldine edition of Aristotle to Alberto III Pio, Prince of Carpi, that the *ad Eudemum moralia*, included in the volume, "will offend both your and others' most learned ears". Does this perhaps reflect the notoriety of the theological turn in the chapter (on which see further below, in Section 5, 'The Books of *EE*')? That, in any case, was surely the motive for the commissioning of the translation of this particular excerpt, along with the chapter of *MM*, which pretends to correspond to it while puzzlingly managing to omit nearly all the original theology. (Did the author of the *MM* chapter just not understand it, or did he too find it too much?).

INTRODUCTION: A HISTORY OF THE TEXT OF THE EUDEMIAN ETHICS 5

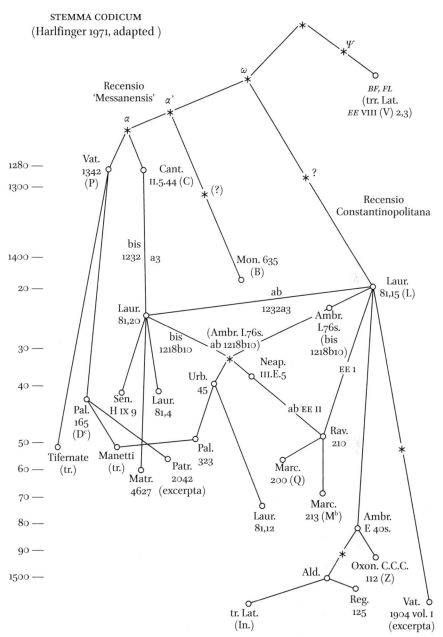

FIGURE 1   A diagram which shows the *stemma codicum* derived from the work of Dieter Harlfinger, 1971.

far as our evidence goes – in Messina in Sicily (where two of our four primary manuscripts, P and C, were copied), then in Byzantium, and subsequently in Renaissance Italy. From there, for *EE*, it is downhill pretty much all the way[11] until modern philological engagement with the text[12] begins in the nineteenth century CE, and philosophical interest in it gradually grows in the twentieth.

The *stemma codicum* printed above (Fig. 1) derives almost entirely from the work of Dieter Harlfinger,[13] the main change being the displacement of Harlfinger's hyparchetype α in favour of a new one, α', in consequence of the discovery that B (= Mon. gr. 635) is closer to the archetype, ω, than P (= Vat. gr. 1342) is, and *a fortiori* closer to it than P's twin, C (= Cantab. gr. 11.5.44).[14] These, together with L (= Laur. gr. 81,15), constitute our primary manuscripts; all the others are secondary or *descripti*; that is, they are descended from these four.[15] P, C and B, together with their descendants (though B in fact has none), constitute one family, as deriving from one hyparchetype, and sharing its errors, while L and its descendants – L being itself a hyparchetype, at the same distance from ω as α' is – constitute another. Neither family is 'better' than the other, nor is any single manuscript among the four primary ones 'better' than the others: one or more will often supply what another gets wrong, and each has its own moments. But all four primary manuscripts, because primary, have precedence over the *descripti*, in the sense that we need only to take the latter into account when P, C, B and L fail us. Usually, the secondary manuscripts will reproduce the same failings as their sources, but sometimes, whether by

---

11   But see the notes by Sylvester Maurus (Rome, 1668) on the whole Aristotelian corpus, including *EE* in vol. 2.
12   For which a model is provided by 'Victorius', i.e., Pier Vettori (1499–1585), whose corrections and conjectures are preserved in his copy of the Aldine, accessible online in the Bayerische Staatsbibliothek, Munich (https://inkunabeln.digitale-sammlungen.de/Exemplar_A-698,1.html, Teil 2). He is the first scholar to set out, apparently over many years, to improve the text by comparing different manuscripts, in his case evidently the three available to him in the Laurentian library in Florence. Not only does he correct obvious errors, including many made in the typesetting of the Aldine, but his work on the text as a whole stands comparison with the best of modern scholarship (See Rowe forthcoming a.).
13   Harlfinger 1971: 30.
14   In 1971 B was inaccessible; shortly thereafter the Bayerische Staatsbibliothek bought it. It was Harlfinger himself who suggested to me that it needed closer examination: it had been proposed that it was a copy of C, but a full collation (on which see below) shows beyond doubt that it is an independent witness, in the same family as P and C, later in date but stemming from an earlier source.
15   It should be noted that 'B', 'P', 'C' and 'L' are all short for '*EE* in B', '*EE* in P', and so on; in each case the codex will contain one or more other works, which may but may also not be copied from the same source as the text of *EE*.

luck or (very occasionally) by judgement they will get something right, or will propose a reading that deserves consideration. Any such proposal, however, has no greater standing, in itself, than a conjecture made by a nineteenth- or twentieth- (or fifteenth-) century scholar: that is, that Marc. 213, say, reads y rather than x (x being read by one or more of P, C, B and L) is of no consequence, by itself, for the reconstruction of the text, and is not worth even recording *except* where there are problems about what the primary manuscripts offer us.

3   Modern Editions

It should immediately be plain from this how much it matters to get the stemma right; that is, to understand the true relationships between the manuscripts, and which of them deserves to be prioritised over others. Thus Immanuel Bekker, for his edition of 1831 (the first properly critical edition of *EE*), mainly used only two manuscripts, Marc. 213, which is his 'M^b', and P, his 'P^b', i.e., one of what we know – but Bekker did not know – are the four primary manuscripts (P), and a descendant of another (Marc. 213, descended from L). Now since, as it happens, the two he relied on, and collated, represented the two sides of the tradition, one emanating from one hyparchetype, the other from the other, this allowed him to produce a text that despite its many faults remains hardly less usable, in many respects, than its nineteenth and twentieth century successors. One of these, Susemihl 1884,[16] recognised that P and C ('C^c' in Susemihl) were gemelli, that they were older than any of the other manuscripts, and that Pal. 165 (his 'D^c') belonged to the same family. On the other hand, the Aldine edition ('Ald.') and what to Susemihl was its lost source, together with Marc. 213 and Oxon. C.C.C. 112 (his 'Z'),[17] were attributed to a different and for the most part inferior family. If one is looking for an understanding of the manuscript tradition, this represents simultaneously a step forward and a step backwards from Bekker 1831. Even Walzer and Mingay 1991, twenty years after Harlfinger's intervention, looks rather more like Susemihl 1884 – and indeed like Bekker – than it should do. The consequence of Harlfinger's recognition of L's importance (despite its somewhat later date) should have been to deprive all other manuscripts apart from P, C, and L of their status as witnesses, whereas in fact the

---

16   Two earlier editions, *EE* in the Didot edition of Aristotle (vol. II, 1850), and the edition by Theodor (A.T.H.) Fritzsche (1851), were both based on Bekker's collations of the manuscripts, and can therefore be passed over in the present context.

17   This Oxoniensis, which is on my counting independent on only a single occasion, was known to and sometimes used by Bekker too.

apparatus in Walzer and Mingay 1991 regularly records their readings alongside those of the primary manuscripts as if they were on a par with them,[18] in many cases copying them directly from the Teubner.[19]

Once the stemma is established, much then depends on the accuracy of editors' reporting of the manuscripts. Despite taking account of more manuscripts, Susemihl appears to have done less actual collation than Bekker, re-collating P for himself, but taking little notice of C except to establish its relationship to P, and relying both for C and for any new insights into Marc. 213 on reports from others; similarly with Pal. 165 and the Oxoniensis. It seems that L was fully collated for the Walzer-Mingay edition;[20] the position with regard to P and C is less clear. Mingay reports that the Oxford Press gave Walzer the conjectures and readings left behind by W.D. Ross, who 'had collated all the codices[21] shortly before his death', and also that Walzer himself had also collated many of them in his youth.[22] The apparatus in Walzer and Mingay 1991 gives clear evidence of these re-collations, providing information that was not available from Susemihl 1884, particularly about C. My own prolonged encounters with the manuscripts demonstrate that there are severe shortcomings in the new collations (or at least in the reporting of them) – severe enough to prevent the apparatus in Walzer and Mingay 1991 from performing its two proper functions, namely, first, of giving us an understanding of the differences between the primary texts, and second, of bringing to our attention the most important material – conjectures, corrections, etc. – available to editors for the restoration of what all are agreed is a highly corrupted text. The text printed in Walzer and Mingay 1991 also includes lacunas, adopts wrong-headed

---

18   Which of course they were for Susemihl, although he prizes P, and in principle C, above the others (they are 'the best and most ancient codices of the *Eudemian Ethics*', he says on p. 1 of his preface).

19   Walzer and Mingay 1991 is also recognisably still Susemihl 1884 in other respects – in its overall presentation, and its punctuation; it seems that it was delivered to the press in the form of a marked-up copy of the Teubner.

20   By Brian Hillyard, using photographs supplied by Dieter Harlfinger (Walzer and Mingay 1991, Preface, v n. 3: i.e., presumably, from the microfilm in the Aristoteles-Archiv at the Free University in Berlin; cf. n. 27 below). L is reasonably easy to read, and my own autopsy of the codex turned up few surprises – that is, in comparison to my experience of it online; Hillyard's photographs are unlikely to have been markedly less readable than the digital version.

21   "All the codices, with the exception of *v* ... were collated by Ross not long before his death", Preface, p. xi. '*v*' here is the 'codex Victorii', so named by Susemihl as the mysterious ("codex nescio quis [some codex or other]", p. 1) source of Vettori's marginal corrections and conjectures; in fact that source was the three Laurentian MSS (see n. 13 above), all of which, apparently, Ross did collate.

22   Mingay in Walzer and Mingay 1991: Preface, xi.

conjectures, and sometimes even fails to offer any sense at all,[23] thus tending to inhibit rather than encourage ongoing philosophical discussion of EE. In short, for all the work done by Victorius,[24] by Bekker, by Susemihl, by Walzer and Mingay themselves, and by the numerous other scholars and critics whose conjectures they report, the task of restoration, by 1991, was far from complete.

4   Towards a New Edition

Some might think – perhaps on reading Jonathan Barnes's review of the Walzer and Mingay edition[25] – that EE has suffered just too much damage in transmission, and that its history stops more or less here. But my own experience of the text shows that this is not the case. With the stemma fixed, and full collations of the primary manuscripts completed, I claim to have established a usable text: one that is necessarily to some degree speculative in a number of places, but which is in every other part defensible as being either what Aristotle wrote or as close to it as makes no difference.[26]

The chief reason, in my view, why so little progress had previously been made with the text of EE is that the job of restoration had been attempted with far too little attention paid to Aristotle's *argument*. The best illustration of this is the large-scale commentary on EE by Dirlmeier (the most substantial commentary to date),[27] which includes enough conjectures and corrections virtually to count as a new critical edition. Dirlmeier's restored text has been criticised for its 'conservatism, visible in its obstinate and at times excessive defense of the manuscript tradition':[28] to be clear, a proper respect for the

---

23 See, for example, Barnes 1992; or Donini 2005, where the Walzer-Mingay text is printed opposite a translation of what is quite often a different text, that text being given and defended in the Notes.
24 See n. 13 above.
25 "MSS are not enough: the text of EE is in a vile state – hideous corruption on every page", Barnes 1992: 28.
26 We sometimes need to choose between two or more alternative restorations that give us exactly the same outcome in terms of the sense and the argument; in such cases it would be absurd to pretend that one had restored Aristotle's actual phrasing.
27 Dirlmeier 1962.
28 Donini 2005: xxv. Donini's judgement (*ibid.*) that the text presupposed by Dirlmeier's translation "is nevertheless by a long way the best available" is hard to accept: for all its weaknesses, the Walzer-Mingay text is still considerably more usable than Dirlmeier's (as is Rackham's Loeb, which Dirlmeier dismisses with contempt as "practically worthless") – which is not to deny that the latter makes many important contributions, in a sense *malgré lui*.

tradition is a virtue, and quite indispensable, in a textual critic;[29] Dirlmeier just goes too far, attempting to defend some of the worst messes left by the copyists.[30] But the overriding weakness of Dirlmeier's reconstruction is that it evinces so little of Aristotle's own primary interest in systematic argument. The plain fact, too often ignored by textual critics working on EE, is that in the case of a philosophical author of Aristotle's calibre the run of the argument is itself part of the evidence.

The scribes who copied our manuscripts are more often than not working mechanically, rather than with an eye to the sense of what they are endeavouring to reproduce: that is why there are so many standard errors, and so many gaps.[31] It is also why they will, on occasion, reproduce nonsense, or create it for themselves – or indeed, sometimes, where they are paying at least some degree of attention to what is being said, invent a new sense altogether. In such cases the traditional methods of the textual critic (comparing different manuscripts, identifying standard errors, and so on) will take us only so far. While it is of course imperative, indeed the only possible course, to start from the manuscript tradition, that tradition cannot and should not always have the last word. In other words, while we should not diverge unnecessarily from it,[32] it is sometimes perfectly obvious that it cannot be preserved. In such cases we may be able to detect how the corruption of the text occurred, but we may also be unable to do so except in general terms (quite often reducing to plain inattention). It is then that a sense of the overall argument in the context, and of how a particular sentence will connect with the one preceding and the one following, properly comes into play.

This approach was fundamental for my new critical edition of EE.[33] The edition is accompanied by a substantial separate volume of notes[34] explaining the reasoning behind every editorial decision, providing additional information about the manuscripts that cannot reasonably be accommodated even

---

29 See further below.
30 Or, alternatively, assuming them to be explicable, e.g. as the consequence of mistakes in the transition between majuscule and miniscule, when most errors are plainly the result of simple carelessness (and anyway later than that transition). Paradoxically, the outcome is often conjectures that are anything other than conservative.
31 P, C and B are generally more 'gappy' than L (but the L copyist too has his own weaknesses, which often can be repaired from the others).
32 This is an especially important principle in the case of EE. Much of EE is written in an extraordinarily concise style, and it is often tempting to regularise its Greek. The temptation should be resisted. The stylistic brevity of EE is one of its singular features and not something to be ironed out; see below.
33 Rowe 2023a.
34 = Rowe 2023b.

INTRODUCTION: A HISTORY OF THE TEXT OF THE EUDEMIAN ETHICS

in the ample *apparatus criticus* attached to the text itself, and – in particular – discussing rather than merely reporting alternative solutions.[35] My general observation, however, is that the reputation of EE as a corrupt text has tended to work against it, inviting intervention when none is needed: finding the way to a solution to a problem often starts with looking to see whether there actually is a problem at all, and then scraping off the layers of successive editorial interventions, quite often themselves developments or refinements of the proposals of previous critics. In a large majority of cases, my own restoration of the text involves either reinstating what one or more of the primary manuscripts gives us, or, in those relatively few cases where the manuscripts themselves fail us completely, working out – from all the evidence, which includes corrections/glosses in those manuscripts – what they would allow us to reconstruct, with the fewest possible changes, in order to produce a good and appropriate sense: that is, a good *argument*.[36] In short, the manuscripts are not in such a desperate state as has generally been suggested.[37] The proof of the pudding, of course, will be in the eating. But the notes accompanying the new edition ought to provide a full enough account of the ingredients for anyone wishing to question the mix.

A further principle of the new edition is that it never relies on parallels with NE. Such reliance was understandable at a time when, as in Susemihl's case, there was not even a presumption that Aristotle was the author of EE,[38] but hardly acceptable in the 20th and 21st centuries, when not only is the question of authorship settled, but the precise nature of the relationship between EE and NE is quite the opposite of settled. It being clear[39] that EE sometimes shows significant differences in content from NE, it is hardly a plausible strategy to try to use what Aristotle says in the undisputed books of NE in order to establish what he is saying in the undisputed books of EE. Perhaps, where he wrote two versions on the same topic, one 'Eudemian' and one 'Nicomachean',

---

35 Of which there are frequently many, and their relative advantages and disadvantages need to be assessed as part of the case for any particular solution.

36 That is, a good argument for and in the context. This is probably an example what is sometimes called 'philosophical charity', although 'charity' sounds too grudging: the question is, what – given the surrounding context – would Aristotle be *likely* to be saying here? (After all, how often, in a piece of continuous argument, does he lose his thread? He may go off at surprising tangents, but that is another matter, and one we may easily observe.)

37 See Barnes as cited in n. 26 above; the restoration of the text "ultimately requires nothing short of divinatory powers", Harlfinger 1971: 29.

38 'Aristotelis Ethica Eudemia', it says on the outside cover of the 1967 reproduction of the 1884 Teubner, '[Aristotelis Ethica Eudemia] Eudemi Rhodii Ethica' on the title page.

39 See, e.g., Kenny 1978/2016, chs 7 and 8.

he was writing them for different audiences. That is one possible reason for their being two versions, but there is no pretending that in every case, or even in most cases, he is simply saying the same things in a different style. Nor, if it was a matter of Aristotle's addressing different audiences, did that mean making things *simpler* for one audience than for the other. No one has to my knowledge ever been inclined to describe the differences between Eudemian and Nicomachean material in terms of greater and lesser simplicity; they are differences of substance and content, pure and simple, or else of emphasis, and they are enough in themselves to rule out arguing about the shape of the one set of material from the shape of the other.

If it is simplification we are looking for among ethical works in the corpus, the prime candidate would surely be *MM*, 'the *Great Ethics*', apparently written as a kind of compendium of Aristotelian ethical ideas and arguments[40] (notwithstanding that there are individual flourishes, especially in the form of sometimes curious dialectical interludes). I have already mentioned my view that it is not by Aristotle.[41] However, given that, as many have observed, it tends to follow the shape and pattern of *EE* rather more than it does that of *NE*, it could in principle still be called in aid in the restoration of the former, as the product of what must surely have been a very early reader of Aristotle. In fact I shall so use it in one case, but only on a larger scale;[42] at the detailed level it appears to me that the quality of the discussion in *MM* is so much lower than

---

40   This seems to me already a sufficient explanation of its being described as 'great', if we compare the work with an *EE* or an *NE*: the reference would be not so much to the physical bulk of the two books of *MM* – as suggested to Cyril Armstrong by Henry Jackson (see the introduction to the Loeb *EE*); in fact *EE* IV, by itself, at about 11 Bekker pages, is not so much shorter than *MM* II, at about 14 – as to what they managed to contain: the whole of the subject of ethics, covered in a space equivalent to about half an eight-book *EE*, or a third of a ten-book *NE*. (The latter may be the more apt comparison, given that in the tradition *MM* sometimes appears as the *Great Nicomachean Ethics*, and the title *Great Ethics* is apparently not attested before *NE* had become *the* Aristotelian *Ethics* [see above].)

41   The relatively good state of the text of *MM*, compared with that of *EE*, tends to suggest that *MM* was the more widely read (so too the fact that, in the codices that contain both, *MM* comes first; that the *Liber de bona fortuna* gives precedence to *MM*'s account of *eutuchia*, or at least has it come before *EE*'s, is perhaps a consequence of this). But that no more demonstrates the authenticity of *MM* than the fact that the so-called 'common' books were preserved with *NE* gives us the answer to the question about their original home – if they had one. This is the question with which this introduction started, and the one to which it returns in the next section.

42   See below, on *MM*'s reversal of the order of the subjects treated in *EE* IV and V.

in *EE*, and the author misses so much, that it is quite useless for the purpose of restoring any individual sentence in *EE*.[43]

5 The Books of *EE*

One large issue faces any editor of Aristotle's *EE*: how many books does it have? One answer to the question, and perhaps the right one, is that it does not have any at all, because '*EE*' was not strictly Aristotle's creation, but someone else's (I suppose, Eudemus). But let us suppose that the modern editor's task is to put together what history, at least, recognises as 'the *EE*'; and the present chapter, after all, announces itself as 'a history' of the text of *EE*: what then? There appear to be two different *EE*s, one with five books and one with eight, if the 'common' books are included.[44] There is also, however, a third *EE*, which has four or seven books instead of five or eight: thus Bekker makes *EE* VIII into a continuation of VII, Susemihl in the Teubner subtitles VIII.1–3 '(VII.13–15)',[45] while Walzer-Mingay announces VIII as VIII but then mysteriously numbers the individual chapters as VII.13–15. Bekker was in fact following Marc. 213, in which the new book (or new chapter, as Bekker has it) begins on the same line that the last one ends, with only six or seven characters between them. But the situation in Marc. 213 is the consequence of a simple, accidental omission in L. The previous seven books in L all begin with the title on a separate line above the first line of the book, and with the initial letter of the book written larger, in the margin, and coloured in; at the beginning of the eighth there is a blank line where the title should be, and the initial letter of VIII is missing. Plainly the *intention* was to include a title, not just because of the missing letter but because the space left between the new section and the last is exactly the same as that left between all the preceding books. The copyist seems to leave titles to someone else (they are in a different hand from the text), perhaps the same person responsible for any illustration or use of colour; in the case of *EE*

---

43 Contrast Dirlmeier 1962, which is peppered with references to *MM*; Dirlmeier thinks it "[Aristotle's] first sketch of the field of the ethical virtues ..." (Dirlmeier 1966: 147; a complete reversal of his views about *MM* since Dirlmeier [1939]).

44 For a judicious overview of the *status quaestionis* (in 2014), see Jost 2014; for a new defence of the Nicomachean origins of *NE* V–VII, Frede 2019.

45 If only as a gesture to what he calls the "inferior family of codices", in which VII absorbs VIII; it happens that in just this one instance the family *is* inferior (Solomon, in his Oxford Translation, which generally follows Susemihl's text, here diverges from it and follows Bekker's numbering without giving a reason).

VIII this someone else failed to do his job.[46] *EE* VIII remains a puzzle, because of its abrupt beginning (so abrupt that some hands attempted to make it continuous with the preceding treatment of friendship, which it is not), its strange ending, and its unusual shortness for a 'book', but according to the tradition, at least until L,[47] it is undoubtedly a separate document or book.

So if VIII is a separate 'book' (however fragmentary), the remaining question, for an editor, is whether to print a five-book or an eight-book *EE*, i.e., an *EE* without or an *EE* with the middle books. The short answer is that, from the perspective sketched at the beginning of the present chapter, *EE* without the middle books would not be 'Eudemian': after all, from that perspective *EE* as conceived by Eudemus (if it was indeed he) was conceived as a complete treatment of the subject of ethics, and that it would not be without the middle, 'common' books, any more than *NE* would be Nicomachean without them. Whether the middle books are Eudemian in a stronger sense,[48] for example because originally written at the same time as the undisputed books of *EE*, is a different question. One complication is that I think *EE* already contains material that overlaps with the second 'common' book,[49] in which case this book would sit in *EE* as it stands with something of the same uneasiness with which the third 'common' book sits in *NE* because of the resulting duplicate treatment of pleasure: see below. But no sensible copyist, one would have thought, would put himself to the trouble of writing out the same material twice (and a publisher would jib at printing it, as the Oxford press has done, reasonably, in my own case).[50] And that generally reflects the practice of the copyists of our Greek manuscripts of *EE*. Where *NE* has preceded in a codex, the middle books of *EE* are not generally copied out (so in P, C, Pal. 165, Marc. 213, Oxon.);[51] they are copied out where there is no *NE* preceding (L, Laur. 81,20, Laur. 81,4, Neap., Urb., Pal. 323, Matr., Laur. 81,12, Ambr. E 40s). But not in all. Most importantly, codex B does not include an *NE* and still has only five books, which moreover are labelled straightforwardly as I–V. Rav. also fails to reproduce the middle

---

46   See Laur. 81,20, the second half of which is a direct and accurate copy of L: its copyist had no doubt at all about the intention in L, VIII being introduced with full title and a beautifully decorated marginal alpha.
47   See Section 4 above.
48   As Kenny argues (see n. 11 above, and further below).
49   A view I argue for in Rowe forthcoming b.
50   Not so the Aldine, the first printed edition of *EE*, which has the full eight-book *EE* after a ten-book *NE*. OUP would have allowed eight books if the middle ones had been re-edited; that task I was and am unwilling to take on.
51   I have mentioned one of the exceptions, the Aldine; the other, Reg. 125, is a manuscript copy of the (printed) Aldine.

books despite not containing an *NE*, and Marc. 200 lacks them even though in its case *NE* follows *EE*.

The key to this mixed picture is contained the marginal notes in Rav. and its two offspring, Marc. 200 and 213, which tell us us that the three missing books – the next in all three being labelled VII – have been left out, and are "similar in everything and in expression" to *NE* V–VII: evidently the commissioning in these cases will have included the instruction 'leave out Books IV–VI'. But 'similar in everything and in expression' does not mean 'the same', i.e., identical, as becomes clear from a comment in Par. 2042 by the original source of the marginal note, Cardinal Bessarion, which tells us that *Aristotle* actually left out – i.e., did not write? – the counterparts of *NE* V–VII when writing *EE*: "at least, I have never yet encountered them". In short, according to Bessarion, *NE* V–VII are just borrowed by *EE* from *NE*. And there are some signs that that is actually the typical view of them in the Byzantine and Renaissance period. There is (i) the hand in the margin of Rav. that writes "*fifth* book of Aristotle's *EE*" where VIII should begin; (ii) the behaviour of the copyist of Laur. 81,12, who not only announces an *EE* with five books and then gives eight, numbering the first five I–V, but after the fifth says, with a flourish, "end of Aristotle's *EE*" and then gives each of the last three books the simple title "Aristotle's"; (iii) that the five-book Marc. 200, despite the note in the margin that three middle books have been left out, still numbers its five I–V, with the final flourish "end of the five books of *EE*";[52] (iv) that the five-book Oxon. numbers its *EE* VII as VII only after having announced it as IV at the foot of the preceding page; and (v) the way Pier Vettori writes "V *êthikôn* ad Nicom." against the beginning of *EE* IV in his Aldine,[53] crossing out the original title along with part of the first page, "VI *êthikôn* ad Nicom. " against *EE* V, "VII liber ad Nicomachum" against *EE* VI. Thus, when we find B with just five books and no mention of any more, that is not because the reference to *NE* V–VII has been left out, but rather because the five books reproduced constitute the whole of *EE* as handed down. It is still, of course, obvious that this *EE* is incomplete; but why – a Bessarion, or anyone, might well have asked – would we expected *Aristotle* to have filled in what was missing by borrowing chunks of another work? *EE* follows the same sort of pattern as *NE* in the parts that are present (except in VIII); he just failed to write the Eudemian equivalents of *NE* V–VII.

---

52 On the other hand, while the beginning of V (VIII) is clearly marked as such, i.e., as V, the heading of Book IV (VII) seems to read 'Book IV of the *seven* of Aristotle's *Eudemian Ethics*'.

53 That is, in one of his Aldines; he had two, both now held in the Bayerische Staatsbibliothek in Munich.

But was it right for Bessarion, and is it right for us, to think of Aristotle in this way? It is hard to stop supposing that Aristotle dealt in *treatises*, even when we have the evidence staring us in the face that he did not: the *Metaphysics*, everyone knows, is a ragbag collection of bits and pieces on the subject; the *Physics* does a bit better, and the *Politics*, but even they lack the real unity that characterises every single work of Plato's, from the shortest to the longest (even, in its own way, the *Laws*). Aristotle can manage short treatises on smaller subjects, and as both the undisputably Eudemian and the undisputably Nicomachean books show, he can also look forwards and backwards among larger aggregations. With *NE* and 'its' ten books established, historically, as a finished – if not so finished – 'Aristotle's *Ethics*', the temptation then was naturally to regard *EE* in the same way. And so arose 'the problem of the common books', because there is a set of discussions of apparently required topics that will be needed by both. Bessarion's solution, it seems, was to suppose that the Eudemian counterparts of *NE* V–VII were never written; our modern solution, until recently, was to suppose that the 'common books' belonged to *NE* and were borrowed by Aristotle himself for *EE*, and that has perhaps been the most commonly accepted solution of all, over the centuries. Now, since the advent of Kenny's statistical and other arguments,[54] the general view has tended to swing in the other direction, in favour of identifying *EE* as the original home of the three books in question. But the flaw in all of this is that neither *NE* nor *EE* is, actually, a fully organic whole even with them. "[O]ur [*NE*] is an absurdity, surely put together by a desperate scribe or an unscrupulous bookseller and not united by an author or an editor": this judgement by Jonathan Barnes,[55] starting from the presence in *NE* of two treatments of pleasure, may be overstated,[56] but the basic point is surely right, namely that no one would have *planned NE* that way. But then neither would anyone have *planned* to finish the 'treatise' we call *EE* with the fragment that is 'Book VIII' – that is, anyone who was seriously in the business of treatise organisation.

Here is a hypothesis: that, with both *NE* and *EE*, we are dealing with what were originally looser assemblages of 'books' than the titles '*Nicomachean Ethics*' and '*Eudemian Ethics*' would suggest. The author of *MM* worked mainly from a collection of books that had something of the shape of what we call

---

54 I.e., in Kenny 1978/2016; see n. 1 above.
55 Barnes 1997: 59.
56 Pakaluk 2011 makes the best attempt yet to defend the compatibility of the two treatments of pleasure, treating the Book VII treatment as being about non-rational pleasures, the Book X treatment as being about the pleasures of our rational part. But Pakaluk himself admits that there are arguments against such an interpretation, and there is a general sense in his essay that he is testing the limits of the unity thesis.

EE. But there is a difference: the topics of *EE* VIII are placed, in *MM*, before instead of after the treatment of friendship, and after the treatment of *akrasia* and pleasure. That, I suggest,[57] is where the *MM*-writer found, or himself placed, our VIII. This is tangible evidence of the contingent nature of the ordering of ancient collections of books (i.e., papyrus rolls), and in truth it is a matter of indifference whether 'VIII' comes before or after 'VII', given that, because of its fragmentary nature, 'VIII' is problematic wherever it comes. But because of the way it abridges the content of *EE* VIII.2, and also of *NE* VI '=' *EE* V, *MM* additionally avoids an anomaly which, in my view, is apparent in an *EE* that includes both a Book V ('=' *NE* VI) and VIII.2: that is, that such an *EE* would first introduce something called *nous* that 'perceives' what is to be done in a particular case, and then (in VIII) introduce something very like it that is not called *nous*, in a context where *nous* and its derivatives are actually used but with a different reference.[58] This is a problem of the same type as, if on a smaller scale than, the one about the double treatment of pleasure in '*NE*'.

We resolve such problems, I propose, not by smoothing them over, or explaining them away, or by shifting books from one 'treatise' to another. There is a collection of books that we can usefully refer to as 'Eudemian', and that differ in interesting ways from another collection we can label 'Nicomachean'; there are also three other books that may perhaps be more 'Eudemian' than 'Nicomachean',[59] but most of whose contents would be required, in some form or other, by any general treatment of the subject of ethics as Aristotle clearly conceives of it. But he himself, I take it, did not write two fully organised treatises on ethics, or indeed even one. There are clear signs, not least in the forward and backward references that we find among the two sets of books, that he had thoughts in that direction. But those thoughts were not translated into reality, I propose, until Eudemus and Nicomachus intervened – both of them laying claim to the three middle books, as they had to if both were to construct (more or less) complete works on ethics.[60]

---

57 Following Dirlmeier and others before him.
58 See Rowe 2023a.
59 I refer here to the statistical arguments in Kenny 1978 (on which see Preface above).
60 One consequence of all this is of course that my own new edition of *EE*, by only including five books, will not be the full work, as put together (I am proposing) by Eudemus; unfortunately, the title too will be misleading, if it calls the work Aristotle's *EE*. But there is no way out of the latter problem, and the former will only be resolved, for OUP, when someone (else) re-edits the middle books.

Word List

Note: this is not, nor is intended as, a complete list of key words, merely a list of translations preferred in the present work for key words that tend to be rendered differently by different translators and interpreters of Aristotle's ethical treatises.

adikêma	unjust action
aisthêsis	perception, sense (i.e. sensory capacity)
akolastos	self-indulgent
akousios, *akôn*	counter-voluntary
akratês	lacking self-control, uncontrolled, un-self-controlled
akribês	precise
alazôn	impostor
anankazein	constrain (in the context of voluntary agency)
aneleutherios	avaricious
archê	beginning, origin, principle, source, starting-point
areskos	obsequious
aretê	excellence ('virtue')
asôtos	wasteful
athlios	miserable
bia	force
boulêsis	wish
diathesis	disposition
dianoia	thought
dianoêtikon	intellectual, having to do with thought
dikaiôma	just action
doxa	judgement, opinion
dunamis	capacity
eirôn	self-deprecating
eleos	pity
eleutherios	open-handed, civilized, worthy of a free man
endoxa	received opinions, existing view
energeia	activity, actuality
enkratês	self-controlled
eph'hêmin	dependent on us, in our power
epichairekakia	malice
epieikês	decent, respectable; reasonable
epistêmê	knowledge, scientific knowledge, systematic knowledge

epithumia	appetite
ergon	function, work, product
êthikos	to do with character
êthos	character, character-trait
eudaimonia	happiness
eupragia	acting well, doing well
eu prattein	do well, act well
êutuchês	fortunate
eutuchia	good fortune
gnome	sense (as in 'good sense')
haireisthai	to choose
hairetos	desirable
haplôs	without qualification
hekousios, hekôn	voluntary
hexis	disposition
kakia	badness ('vice')
kalokagathia	fine-and-goodness, refined excellence, nobility
kalos	fine, beautiful
kata sumbebêkos	incidentally, coincidentally
kath' hauto	in/for, as itself, for what it is
kinêsis	movement, process
kolasis	forcible correction, punishment
kolax	ingratiating
krinein	to discriminate, discern, judge
lupê	distress, pain
megaloprepes	munificent
megalopsuchos	great-souled
mesos, mesotês	intermediate
metameleia	regret
mikoprepês	shabby
mikropsuchos	little-souled
mochthêros	bad, of bad character, depraved
nous	intelligence
ôphelimos	beneficial
orexis	desire
orthos logos	correct reasoning
pathos/pathêma	affection, affective state, emotion
phaulos	bad, inferior
phronêsis	wisdom
phthonos	grudging ill will, envy, jealousy

pleonektês	grasping
ponêros	bad
praos	mild
prohairesis	decision, choice, power of decision (cf. *haireisthai, hairetos* [sometimes 'intention' is a better match]
psogos	censure
skopos	target, goal
sophia	intellectual accomplishment
sophron	moderate
spoudaios	excellent, serious
sumpherein	to be advantageous
sunaisthanesthai	to perceive concurrently
sunesis	comprehension, acumen
sungnômê	sympathy
suzên	to live with, share life with
ta pros to telos	what forwards the end, what leads to the end
technê	technical expertise, skill
teleios	complete, perfect ('end-like?')
tharros	boldness
theios	godlike, divine
theôrein	reflect on, observe; have regard to, V.3)
theôrêtikos	reflective, purely reflective, theoretical
thrasus	rash
thumos	temper, rage
tuchê	luck, chance, fortune

EE Book I

EE Book I, Chapter 1

1214a1 Someone wrote up in Delos in the presence of the god,[1] revealing his own judgement, on the propylaeon of the temple of Leto,[2] and dividing the good and the fine and the pleasant from each other, as not belonging to the same thing, using the lines 'Finest is what is most just, but best is to be healthy, / and most pleasant is the getting of what one loves.' But as for us, let us not agree with him, for happiness, being finest and best of all things,[3] is also most pleasant.

a8 There being many matters for reflection that in relation to each thing and in relation to the nature of each[4] present difficulty and demand inquiry, some point towards the acquisition of knowledge and nothing more, while others have to do both with the [*sc.* ways of] acquiring the thing [*sc.* knowledge] and with the actions that come with it. Well then, as for those matters that involve a pursuit of knowledge[5] for the sake of reflection alone, we must speak about them as the proper occasion arises, in whatever way is[6] germane to the inquiry, but first [*sc.* here and now] we must [*sc.* embark on the second sort of investigation[7] and] investigate what it is that brings living well with it, and how it is to be acquired – whether all those who fulfil the designation in question [*sc.* 'happy'] become [*sc.* happy] by nature in the way that tall people become tall, short people short, and some differ from others in skin-colour? Or is it through

---

1 When we reach Book v/viii.2, we might wonder whether 'the god' in question could refer to something other than Apollo, god of Delos (though 'the god' can also refer to gods in general, so that the inscriber could just be being described as being conscious of the presence of divinity: a solemn declaration, then, if someone else's words [Theognis]).
2 Presumably a graffito; a modern parallel might be someone inscribing some lines from the Bible that he particularly liked?
3 Could there perhaps be an implicit reference to nobility/fine-and-goodness here (see v/viii.3. 1249b11–12, with note)?
4 Reeve rightly says (n. 3) that *phusis* can be used as a way of referring to an entity of some sort (Plato uses it regularly like this), but that would mean construing the Greek as 'in relation to each thing and in relation to each thing', which hardly looks attractive.
5 'Pursuit of knowledge' here renders *philosophia*.
6 Following a suggestion by Christopher Strachan on the basis of a Platonic parallel, I treat the imperfect tense *ēn* like a 'gnomic' aorist (i.e., the translation is not simply cavalierly substituting a present).
7 Which, we should recall, has been said to have a 'theoretical' and a practical side (where 'theoretical' = 'for the sake of reflection alone'). Aristotle is about as far as he could be from advocating a hard and fast distinction between the two.

learning, on the basis that[8] happiness is some sort of knowledge – or through a sort of training? For people possess many of their [characteristics] neither through [sc. their] nature nor through learning but through habituation, bad ones in the case of those habituated badly, good[9] where the habituation has been good. **1214a21** Or [sc. do people become happy] in none of these ways, and is it one of two things, either that it is through the inspiration of some sort of divine entity,[10] as if in the grip of possession, like people possessed by nymphs or gods, or that it is through fortune/chance – for many say that happiness and good fortune are the same thing. It is not unclear, then, that happiness belongs to people by virtue of the presence either of all of these [sc. factors], or of some particular ones among them, or of one particular one; for pretty well everything that happens to or with people goes back to these beginnings – since one can group all those deriving from thought, too, with actions deriving from knowledge.[11] **a30** But being happy and living a blessed and fine life will lie most of all in three things that seem most desirable: for some say that wisdom is greatest of goods, while others say it is [ethical] excellence, and still others, pleasure. Again, **1214b1** some dispute the weight of the three things in relation to happiness, asserting that one of them contributes more to it than another, some on the basis that wisdom is a greater good than excellence, others reversing the order, while others say pleasure is a greater good than either. Again, some think that living happily comes from all three things, others from two, others that it lies in just one of them.

EE Book I, Chapter 2

So: after having begun by positing that everyone capable of living in accordance with their own choice sets out some sort of target for living finely, either honour or reputation or wealth or education, by reference to which they will perform

---

8   Another reference to Socrates (if the excellences are forms of knowledge, and happiness lies in excellence [as Socrates also holds], then happiness will be all about knowing).
9   Here *chrêstos*, another synonym of *agathos*.
10 *Daimonion ti*: surely an implicit reference to the 'divine sign' (*daimonion sêmeion*) that Socrates says intervenes regularly to stop him from doing something he would otherwise have done. Some version of this explanation of the cause of happiness will be taken with full seriousness in *EE* V/VIII.2–3, in a complex combination with the following option, here treated as quite separate. (There could hardly be clearer evidence of the connectedness of at least the undisputed books of the *EE*: see Appendix 2 above, and 'the problem of the common books'.)
11 I.e., broadly speaking ('one can'), as a way of including them.

all their actions – not to have one's life coordinated in relation to some end is a sign of great foolishness, **1214b12** most of all it must be our first [business] in the matter to distinguish, neither too quickly nor lazily,[12] in which aspect of our existence living well lies, and what are the things without which human beings cannot live well. For being healthy is not the same as the things without which health becomes impossible, and this holds similarly in many other [spheres]; so neither is living finely [the same] as the things without which it is not possible to live finely. Some of the things in question[13] are not peculiar to health or life but are common to practically everything, including dispositions and actions; for example, without our breathing and being awake and sharing in movement, nothing either bad or good would happen to us, while others, to which we must pay attention, tend to be more peculiarly related to a particular nature, as for example meat-eating and after-dinner walks are pertinent to good physical condition in a different way from the things just mentioned. [It is important to make this distinction] because these are the things that cause the dispute about being happy, about what it is and through what things it is that it comes about: some people suppose that the things without which it is not possible to be happy are parts of happiness [itself].

EE Book I, Chapter 3

1214b29 Now to consider all the views that different sorts of people hold is superfluous, since there are many things that even young boys, the sick and the mad suppose, about which no one with intelligence would [bother to] raise an inquiry/any difficulties; for what they require is not arguments, but either to reach an age when they will change [their ideas] or else medical or civic correction (medication is no less a matter of correction than a beating). In the same way neither [need one consider] the views held by the many, for they speak anyhow/say whatever occurs to them about almost everything, and most of all about the things we are discussing now, about which we should restrict consideration to the views of respectable people;[14] for it is out of place to apply

---

12   *Pace* e.g. Reeve, the structure of the sentence seems to me indicate that this warning is for us as investigators, not people in general; clearly people generally will need to make the distinction in question (it is fundamental), but that is not the point here, and would in any case seem to be demanding an unexpectedly high degree of intellectual awareness on the part of ordinary agents.
13   I.e., the necessary conditions.
14   I.e. *epieikeis*, fairly indeterminate classification, the main element in which is the contrast with 'the many'; sometimes, as below in a12, 'decent' is more appropriate rendering, the

argument to the sort of people that have no need of argument, just suffering.[15] But since there are difficult issues for investigation that are peculiar to each area of inquiry, it is clear that they exist too in relation to the highest life and the best way of living. So it is a fine thing to examine the views held in the area we are discussing, for the refutation of the disputant is a proof of the opposing view that he is disputing. And further, that we pay attention to such things is of advantage especially towards [answering the questions] to which all inquiry [sc. in the area we are discussing] is aimed, namely **1215a9** what those things are in consequence of which we partake of life well and finely – if perhaps 'blessedly' is too presumptuous for one to say,[16] and in relation to the [degree of] expectation that would accrue to decent people[17] of acquiring whatever it was that was needed. For if living finely is to be found among the things that come about through fortune/chance, or those that come about through nature it would be something many could not hope for, for [if those are the source] its acquisition is not through concerning themselves with it, nor is it up to them; it is not something they can busy themselves with. If on the other hand it is to be found in one's being, oneself, of a certain sort, and likewise the actions one performs oneself, the good would be more widespread and more divine, more widespread in that it would be possible for more to participate in it, more divine by virtue of happiness' lying there for those that make themselves and their actions be of a certain sort.[18]

EE Book I, Chapter 4

1215a21 Most of the things that are disputed and that we are raising difficulties about will be clear once one has appropriately defined what we should suppose happiness to be: whether it lies simply in the soul's being of a certain sort, as some of the older philosophers[19] thought, or whether to be happy one must indeed be of a certain sort oneself, but it is more a matter of one's actions being

---

reference being to ethical quality (as it probably more normally is in Aristotle) than to intellectual capacity, though they will still not be unthinking like 'the many'.
15   I.e., a beating.
16   'Blessedness', *makariotês*, being associated with gods.
17   Perhaps, as we might say, 'ordinary decent people'?
18   Divinity, presumably, being associated here with active causation.
19   Just *sophoi* in the text, not *philosophoi*; Broadie-Rowe generally prefers 'intellectually accomplished' for *sophos*, but the choice of Anaxagoras as an example (1215b7) confirms that it is the particular accomplishment of doing philosophy that Aristotle has in mind here.

of the right sort. When lives are distinguished – with some not even making a claim to constitute such well-being,[20] for example those concerned with the vulgar skills, those with making money, and the banausic ones ('vulgar' skills here being those aiming at nothing more than acquiring or improving one's standing in society, 'banausic' skills those of sedentary fee-earning, money-making ones those concerned with retail buying and selling) – and there being just three things that are reckoned as counting towards a happy existence, namely the ones we spoke of before,[21] too, as greatest goods for human beings, namely excellence, wisdom, and pleasure, we see that there are also three lives [between] which all who have the opportunity to choose will choose, namely a political life, a life of philosophy, and a life devoted to enjoyment. Of these the philosophical life aims to concern itself with wisdom and reflection on the truth, the political with those actions that are fine, and these are the ones that derive from excellence, and the life of enjoyment with the bodily pleasures. This is why x will call one person the happy one, y another, as we also said before:[22] **1215b7** [for example] Anaxagoras of Clazomenae, when asked who was happiest, said 'None of those *you* suppose; he will appear to you a strange sort to choose. He gave this answer because saw that his questioner supposed that it was impossible to fulfil the designation 'happy' without being tall and beautiful or wealthy, while perhaps thinking himself that it was the one who lived painlessly and without blemish in regard to justice, or partook in some way in reflection like a god,[23] that was as close to being blessed as a human being could be.

---

20 Reeve makes unnecessarily heavy weather of *euêmeria* here, translating it as 'joy', but the logic of the sentence suggests that it ought to be just a substitute for happiness, *eudaimonia*, which is quite in line with its usage elsewhere.
21 See 1214a30–b6.
22 I.e., in 1214a30–b6.
23 'Some sort of divine contemplation' (Reeve) is a literal translation of the Greek; my rendering presupposes a particular interpretation of what the Greek phrase is actually saying, namely that the person Anaxagoras has in mind is doing what god(s) do most of all (the Aristotelian god [the first mover], at any rate), i.e., reflecting, on whatever subject. Reeve's is the easier choice, in so far as it fits with the usual understanding of Aristotle's idea of the philosophical life as involving higher-level, probably metaphysical investigation, but the way the sentence ends surely suggests that the point has something to do with the difference between men and gods, and if that does not exclude metaphysics, it does not obviously bring it in either, unless we suppose a reference to the objects of the prime mover's thinking being restricted to himself – which is a feature of the prime mover only, not of (Aristotelian) gods in general.

EE Book I, Chapter 5

Well now, there are many other things too on which judging well is no easy matter, but the most difficult is the subject that seems to everyone to be easiest, and one that any and everyone is capable of knowing, namely which among the things involved in living is desirable, and which, if one acquired it, one's appetite would be filled, **1215b18** for there are many things [*sc.* in life] that turn out to be such that people throw it away because of them, like diseases, severe pains, or storms; so that it is clear that even from the start, if one had the choice, the prospect of things like that would make it desirable not to have been born at all. In addition to these [*sc.* undesirable lives] there is the life we live while still children, for no right-thinking person would tolerate a reversion back to *that*. And again, many of the things that bring no pleasure or pain with them, and of the things that do bring pleasure, but not of a fine sort, are themselves such as to make not existing preferable to living. **b26** And in general if one were to gather together all the things that people do and have done to them, with none of them done or suffered voluntarily, none of them being for its own sake, and added in an unlimited extent of time, would anyone choose to live rather than not to live? But then again neither would anyone who was entirely slavish put value on living for the pleasure of food or that of sex if one took away all the other pleasures that knowing and seeing or one or other of the other senses provide. For clearly, for anyone making this choice, it would make no difference at all whether they had been born a wild animal or a human being: at any rate in Egypt the bull **1216a1** they honour as Apis has ample supply of more such things than many monarchies. In the same way no one would choose [*sc.* living over not living] because of the pleasure we enjoy in sleeping, for what difference is there between sleeping an uninterrupted sleep from one's first day to one's last for a thousand or whatever number of years and living life as a plant? Certainly that seems to be sort of life plants live, as do babies, for babies when they first come into existence inside their mothers continue in their formed state but sleeping all the time. So it is clear from such [*sc.* considerations] that the answer to the question about what constitutes [*sc.* living] well and the good that lies in living eludes people **a10** when they look for it.

11216a11 So they say that Anaxagoras replied to someone raising problems about some things of this sort and asking what it was for the sake of which one would choose to have been born rather than not. They report that he said it was 'For the sake of reflecting on the heavens and the way the whole universe is ordered.' So *he* thought the choice to live rather than not was for the sake of a sort of knowledge, while those who call Sardanapallus blessed, or Smindyrides of Sybaris, or some other representative of the life of enjoyment, all *these* appear to be locating happiness in the taking of pleasure. But others would not choose any sort of wisdom or the bodily pleasures over the actions that derive from [ethical] excellence; at any rate some people choose them not only for the sake of reputation but even if they are not going to gain repute. **1216a23** As for statesmen, most of them do not truly deserve the title, for the are not statesmen in truth, the statesman being the one who typically chooses fine actions for the sake of those actions themselves, whereas most actual 'statesmen' take on this sort of life for the sake of money and advantage over others.[24] **a28** So from what we have said it is clear that everyone relates happiness to three sorts of life, the political, the philosophical, and the life of pleasure. Taking these in turn, it is clear enough what physical pleasure is, what its quality is, or what its sources are, and so we do not need to look into them, but rather whether they contribute anything towards happiness or not, how they do, and whether, if we should attach pleasures to living well it is these that we should attach, or whether rather we need to partake in these in some other way, and the pleasures people have in mind when they think, reasonably enough, that the happy person lives pleasantly and not just painlessly are different. Well, we must discuss these questions later on; let us reflect first about excellence and wisdom, both about what the nature of each is, and whether these are parts of a good life, either themselves or the actions that derive from them, **1216b1** since even if not everyone attaches them to happiness, certainly all people worth taking into account do so. An example is Socrates, I mean the old one,[25] who thought the goal was to acquire knowledge of excellence, and would go off searching out what justice is, what courage is, and so on with each of its parts. That he did this was reasonable enough, because he thought that all the excellences were [*sc.* forms of] knowledge, so that both knowing [*sc.* what] justice [*sc.* was] and being just would come about at the same time; after all, we learn geometry and house-building and at the same time we are house-builders

---

24 The sentiments here echo some of the main conclusions of Plato's *Statesman*; is there an allusion here, supporting what are otherwise bare statements?
25 The familiar Socrates is here perhaps being distinguished from a younger one mentioned at *Metaphysics* 1036a25 as an expert mathematician. I owe this proposal to Kenny 2011: 151. I add the point that there is no decisive reason against supposing that it is this younger Socrates that Plato portrays in conversation with his older namesake in the *Statesman* (cf. preceding note), who trains with Theaetetus, pupil of the geometer Theodorus; he might well have been known to Aristotle's immediate audience in the Lyceum, or even been one of them; no one, even mathematicians, is exempt from the study of ethics, and it may not be insignificant that geometry figures as an example in the present context.

and geometers. That is why he sought after what excellence is but not how it is acquired and from where it stems. This is what happens in the case of [*sc.* forms of] knowledge that are concerned with reflection alone, for there is nothing more to astronomy or natural philosophy or geometry than coming to recognise the nature of the things that form their subject-matter, although there is nothing to prevent them, incidentally, from being useful to us in relation to many of the necessities of life. But in the case of the productive sorts of knowledge the end is different from the knowledge and the knowing, for example health in the case of knowledge, good order or something else of such a sort in the case of statesmanship. **1216b19** It is, certainly, a fine thing to come to know each and every thing that is fine, too; even so, in relation to *excellence* what is most valuable is not to know what it is, but knowing the things from which it arises. For what we want is not to know what courage is but to be courageous, and not to know what justice is but to be just, even as we want to be healthy rather than to know what being healthy is and to be in good physical condition rather than to know what being in good condition is.

EE Book I, Chapter 6

1216b27 In all these things we must try to seek for conviction through arguments, using what appears to people by way of evidence and example. Best would be if all humankind were in plain agreement with what we are going to say, but failing that everyone in some sort of way, which if we shift them they will do. For each individual has something of their own to contribute towards the truth, from which we must somehow make our demonstrations about the things in question. It is through our moving forward from things that are truly said but unclearly that clarity too emerges, if people are hearing all the time what is more recognisable to them instead of things that are usually said in a jumbled way. There is a difference in every sphere between arguments made philosophically and those made unphilosophically. This is why one should not suppose that even for those in the political sphere there is anything superfluous about this sort of reflection, through which not only the what [*sc.* is to be done/is the case] but the why. Such is the philosophical way with each sphere. But this [*sc.* area] needs to be approached with great caution, for **1217a1** there are some that think that it belongs to a philosopher to say nothing without giving a reason/argument for it often fail to notice that they are offering arguments that are alien to the treatment in hand and empty. This they do sometimes out of ignorance, sometimes because they are impostors, and it can be that they catch out even people that are experienced and capable doers while they themselves neither possess nor are capable of possessing any constructive or practical way of thinking. They are like this because of a lack of culture, for a lack of culture, in relation to anything, is a matter of not being capable of judging between reasons/arguments that belong to the matter in hand and those that are alien. It is a good thing, too, to judge what is being demonstrated separately from the account being given of the reason for it, both because of what we said just now, that one should not always pay attention to arguments and their outcomes, but often rather to what appears to be so and so to people. As it is, if people are unable to dismantle [*sc.* an argument], they are compelled to believe what has been said, and because, **a15** often, what seems to have been demonstrated by the argument is true, but not for the reason that the argument claims. For a truth can be demonstrated through a falsehood, and that is clear from the *Analytics*.

EE Book I, Chapter 7

1217a19 With all this by way of preface, let us begin the discussion by starting, first, as we said, from those first, unclear statements of the matter, seeking all the time to find clarity about what happiness is. Well, it is agreed that it is greatest and best of human goods. I specify human because there could perhaps also be a happiness that belonged to some superior entity, for example a god. None of the other animals that are inferior to humans in nature have any claim to being called happy. A horse is not happy, and neither is a bird or a fish or any creature there is that has no portion of something divine, as the [*sc.* formation of] the word *eudaimôn* [*sc.* 'happy' = 'with a good *daimôn*'] proposes. One sort of such creatures will live a better life than another by sharing [more] in goods in some other way [*sc.* other than the way that sharing human goods brings us happiness]. But that this is the case is something we must look into later; for now, let us say, of goods, that some of them fall within the range of action by human beings while others fall outside it (I restrict the point to humans because some entities do not partake in movement at all, and therefore not of goods either, and these entities are perhaps the best natures of all), while some are achievable by action, but only by beings superior to us. But since 'achievable by action' has two senses, referring as it does both to the things for the sake of which we act and the actions we perform for the sake of these – for example, we count not only both health and wealth as achievable by action but also the things we do for their sake, healthy things in the one case, financial in the other – it is clear that happiness too is achievable by action by human being, indeed as best such thing.

EE Book 1, Chapter 8

1217b1 So we must inquire into what the best is, and in how many different ways 'the best' is talked about as being. It appears to be identified with three views in particular: people say that best of all things is the good itself, and that it belongs to the good itself to be first of goods and cause by its presence in the other goods of their being good; both they say belong to the [*sc.* Platonic] idea of the good (by 'both', I mean being first of goods and being cause by its presence in them of their being good), for they claim both that 'the good' is said most truly of it, the other goods being good by sharing in or resemblance to it, and that it is first **1217b11** of goods; for if the good that is being shared in is taken away, so too are those sharing in the idea that are called good by virtue of sharing in it, and the first stands in this relation to what comes later. **b14** The conclusion is that the good itself is the idea of the good; for, they say, it is separate from the things that share in it, just like the other ideas.

To look in detail at this view is a matter for a different discussion, and one that is necessarily more logical in nature.[26] Still, one should make a summary statement on the issues in question, and if so, let us say, first, that to saying that there are ideas not only of the good but of anything else, whatever it may be, belongs to the sphere of dialectic[27] and is empty of meaning. But we have examined many different aspects of the subject both in our exoteric works[28] and in those written in accordance with the requirements of philosophy.[29] Then again: **1217b24** even if the ideas absolutely[30] do exist, including an idea of good, there is no way in which it is of use in relation to a good life or in relation to actions. For 'good' is said in many ways, in fact in the same number of ways as 'being'; for as we have laid out in detail in other works,[31] not only does this [*sc.* use of 'being'] indicate the what [*sc.* a thing] is/its essence, but that use indicates what sort it is/its quality, another the how much, another the when/the time,

---

26   I.e., what Aristotle calls dialectic (*Topics* 101b2), the task of which is to expose the weaknesses in arguments as presented, in the context of any discipline, for the destructive arguments that have common application are not found in any other discipline.
27   See preceding note.
28   These included dialogues, which by itself suggests that they were more accessible than the treatises.
29   I.e., presumably, first of all the treatises, but also surely including the lost *Peri Ideôn* (see Appendix 2), from which the following arguments against forms may well have been borrowed, given that the build-up to these arguments makes reference (i.e., the reference now under discussion) to the group of works to which it plainly belonged (from what we know of it, it was as specialised and 'philosophical' (b24) as any of the treatises.
30   Literally 'as much as possible'.
31   The reference is perhaps to the *Categories* above all.

but in addition to these [uses] there is the being in being moved/changed and in moving/changing; b30 and 'good' is there too in each one of the categories in question: in that of essence, it is [for example] intelligence or god, in that of quality the just, in that of quantity the proportionate, in that of time the right moment, and teaching and being taught in the case of movement/change. So just as being is not some one thing over and above the things just mentioned, so neither is the good, nor is there a single discipline covering either 1217b36 being or the good; indeed there is no single discipline whose business it is to have reflected even on things called 'good' in different but similar categories;[32] for example the right moment or the proportionate, but rather one discipline reflects on the right moment here, another there, and so with the proportionate, as for example in relation to diet it is medical and gymnastic expertise that reflects on the right moment and the proportionate, whereas with action in warfare it is generalship, and so on, with a different discipline always going with a different [sc. sphere] of action. 1218a1 So it will hardly be the business of a single expertise to have reflected on the good *itself*. Again, where there is a prior and a posterior,[33] there is no common thing over and above these that is separate from them. For if there were there would be something prior to the first – the common, separate thing would be prior because with the removal of the common thing the first thing would be removed too: thus for example if the double is first of the multiples, it is not possible for the multiple that is predicated of all of them in common to be separate, for it will turn out to be prior to the double, [sc. which was first]. Or else it turns out that the common thing is the idea, as for example if one were to make the common thing separate, [sc. as the supporters of forms seem actually to do]. For they say, if justice is a good thing, and courage is too, then there is some good by itself. The 'itself' is added to the common account, and what could this be adding but that it[34] is eternal and separate? But what is white for many days is not the least bit whiter than what is white for a single day. So neither, then, is the common good the same as the idea, for a thing that is common belongs to everything.[35]

---

32 At best a loose translation, but it must be what Aristotle is saying with *homoioschêmonôs* – apparently a hapax legomenon, perhaps even invented for the occasion.

33 I.e., *x* is related to *y* among the things concerned in such a way that there can be *x* without *y* but not the other way round.

34 Presumably the common thing that constitutes the 'account'.

35 Aristotle is not here suggesting any commitment on his own part to the idea of a 'common' good, it being incompatible with 'good' being 'said in many ways'; 'the common good' came in and remains on stage only as part of the dialectical refutation of the Platonists; cf. the clear statement, in the parallel treatment of the Platonic form of the good in *NE* 1.6, that 'it is clear that there will not be some common and unitary universal in this case;

1217b15 They[36] should also demonstrate the good itself in a way that is the reverse of the way they presently attempt it. As things stand, they try to demonstrate that the things agreed to be good are good from things not agreed to possess the good – 'demonstrating' from numbers that justice is a good thing and health is a good; for justice and health are ordered structures – numbers, they say, on the basis that good belongs to numbers and units, because the One is good itself. They should instead be demonstrating from things agreed to be good, like health, strength, and moderation, that the fine[37] is to be found to an even greater degree in unchanging things, for these all represent order and stability, and if they do, then so too do health, strength, etc., for order and stability belong to them to a greater degree. There is a recklessness, too, about the demonstration that the One is the good itself because numbers aspire to it, for neither is it said clearly how numbers 'aspire' (they just say it, too simply; and how could one suppose that there is desire in things that are not alive? They ought to pay close attention to this, and not take seriously, without argument,

for otherwise good would not be said in all the categories, but only in one' (1096a27–9). However, while such a 'common and universal' good is equally out of question for him in *EE*, he clearly does not think, and could scarcely think, that 'good' is predicated of different goods by mere homonymy. But then he has something up his sleeve that will allow 'good' to be predicated neither by homonymy nor non-homonymously, so that there is a commonness or relatedness in play even if not an actual 'common *thing*' – i.e., 'focal meaning' [on which see Appendix 2], even if this does not surface explicitly as such in the present chapter (but see following note), only in IV.2, on friendship (1236a8–24), albeit there with sufficient indication that he thinks it will help with 'good': see my notes *ad loc.* What results – if 'focal meaning' is indeed in the background in the present chapter – is a kind of compromise with the Platonist position, rather than the outright rejection we find in the overlapping *NE* context, as summed up in the medieval maxim attributed to Aristotle, Plato amicus, magis amica veritas ('Plato is a friend, truth the greater friend'). This is an illustration of the attitude Aristotle recommended at the beginning of the present book: 'Best would be if all humankind were in plain agreement with what we are going to say, but failing that everyone in some sort of way, which if we shift them they will do' (1216b29–31), only in relation to his friend and teacher Plato. In a moment like this, the idea that *EE* could have been written by someone else (e.g., Eudemus: cf. Susemihl 1884), if anyone were still to be tempted by it, seems to become pointless, or 'empty', *kenon*, as Aristotle would call it: it looks so much like him that we do not need to bother with the possibility that it is someone else imitating him. The account of non-homonymy to be given, allowing the compromise in question, is as certainly Aristotle's as it is that the *Peri Ideôn* is his (see below with Appendix 2). Plato is, as usual in Aristotle, not mentioned by name (*NE* I.6 is an exception in this respect); it is his successors, in any case (evidently Aristotle's contemporaries), that are the main targets of the counter-arguments in *EE*. All this may, I think, betoken a lesser distance in time between Aristotle and his friend and teacher than at the time of writing of the *NE*.

36   Sc. the Platonists.
37   Or 'beautiful', *kalon*.

things that it is not easy to believe even with it. And to say that all entities aspire to some One Good is plain false; each thing aspires to a good of its own, an eye to sight, a body to health, and so on with everything else.

1218a33 So, as for there not being some good existing by itself, it is difficulties of the sort we have gone through that are involved, and there is the point that it is not useful for statesmanship, which has its own good, like other forms of expertise, as for example gymnastic expertise has good physical condition.[38] Again, it is not achievable by action. And in the same way the common good is neither good in its essence,[39] because then it would belong even to an insignificant good, nor is it achievable by action. For it is not the business of medical expertise to see to it that what belongs to anything whatever will be brought about, but that health will, and similarly with each of the other expertises too.

But the good [is said] in many ways, and some of it is fine; and some of it is achievable by action, some not. The sort of good that is so achievable is that for the sake of which, and that does not exist in unchanging things [sc. like numbers].

b8 So it is clear that neither the form of the good nor the common good is the good by itself that we are looking for, for the one is unchanging and not achievable by action, while the other is affected by change but not achievable by action; **1218b11** it is that for the sake of which is best, as end, and cause for the things under it,[40] and first of all things.[41] So it is this that will be 'the good itself', the final end of things achievable by action by human beings. And this falls under the expertise that controls all others – and this is political expertise, and economic, and wisdom; for these expertises/dispositions[42] differ in

---

38 The manuscripts give us a sentence here that I think is a later insertion, and not Aristotle's, which runs (a36–7) 'Furthermore there is also the argument in the/?my? written text, to the effect that the form of the good is either useful for no discipline or useful to all of them in the same way.' If we kept the sentence, we could possibly take it as a direct reference to the *Peri ideôn*; what better text to refer to than one dedicated to the subject in hand? However, a similar form of reference at 1244b31 cannot be explained in this way, and Aristotle could just have just been referring back to, and misremembering, an earlier part of the present discussion. Some think of Aristotle lecturing to students with some sort of circulated handout, or fourth-century equivalent of a blackboard, but that is surely an anachronistic thought. In any case I exclude the sentence as extraneous.
39 Aristotle uses the same unusual adjective, *autoagathon*, 'itself-good', at *Metaphysics* 996a28 ('there could not be something *autoagathon*', referring to the form of the good).
40 Kenny translates 'the things that lead to it', which is tempting.
41 Sc. all things that are good. 'First of all things': as the focus in cases of focal meaning is: 'What is sought in all [such] cases is what comes first', 1236a24.
42 Aristotle writes just 'dispositions', *hexeis*, presumably only because of the mention of wisdom; I take it that politics and economics remain expertises.

relation to all others by their being things of such a sort [*sc.*, controlling]; as for whether they differ at all from each other, we must talk about that later.[43]

1218b17 But that the end is cause of the things under it is shown by the practice of teachers: they start by defining the end/goal and then demonstrate the goodness of each of the other things involved, that for the sake of which being cause, as in the following example: 'Since being healthy is *this*, *that* must be what is advantageous towards it; the healthy is cause of health, i.e., efficient[44] cause, by which I mean it is cause of its being/coming about, not of health's being something good. Again, no one ever *demonstrates* that health is a good thing – unless they are a sophist rather than a doctor, for sophists typically bring in alien/inappropriate arguments – any more than anyone demonstrates the goodness of any other starting-point.

1218b25 We must now examine the good for human beings as end and the best of things achievable by action, to see in how many ways 'best of all things' is said, given that this *is* best.

---

43 See the 'common book' *NE* VI '=' *EE* V.8; this is one reference that appears to justify the 'common' in 'common' books, but it remains a live possibility that *EE* originally contained different material, now lost.

44 'Moving' in the Greek.

EE Book II

EE Book II, Chapter 1

Next, taking a new starting-point, we must discuss the following questions. All goods are either external or in [the] soul, and those in the soul are more desirable, as we also say in the exoteric works,[1] when we make the distinction: wisdom and excellence and pleasure are in the soul, of which either some or all seem to everyone to be the end. And of those in the soul, some are dispositions or capacities while others are activities and movements.

Let us then postulate these things to be so, as a basis for our discussion; also, on the subject of excellence, that it is **1219a1** the best condition or disposition or capacity of anything that has some use or work.[2] This is clear from induction: we take this to be so in all cases. For example, there is an excellence of a cloak, because it has a certain work and use; and similarly there are excellences respectively of ship and a house and everything else. So soul has an excellence too, for it has a particular work that it does. And let the better disposition have the better work to do; and [in general] as the dispositions relate to each other, so let the works issuing from them relate to each other too. And the end of each thing is its work/what it does. From these [points] it follows that the work of a thing is better[3] than its disposition, for the end is best, as end, given that our assumption was that an end is the best and the last,[4] as end, namely that for the sake of which everything else is. It is clear then that what a thing does is better than its disposition and its condition; but 'what it does' is used in one of two different senses, for with some things the work is some separate [product] over and above **1219a15** the use of the thing, as for example a house in the case of building expertise is the work, not the building process, and the work of medical expertise is health, not the making healthy or the doctoring. But in other cases, it is the use that is the work: seeing, or example, in the case of sight, the reflection in that of mathematical knowledge.[5] So, necessarily, where it is the use that is the work, the work is better than the disposition. With these

---

1   I.e., works written for a less specialist audience than the treatises.
2   I.e., *ergon*, usually translated as 'function'; but 'work' gets the basic sense, 'what *x* does', better.
3   'Better', here, presumably, = more end-like, or more constitutive of the end.
4   I.e., last in the series that includes the actions leading to it; is of course still first in an explanatory context.
5   'Reflection': *theoria* again; and again, surely not just 'contemplating' e.g., the beauty of a theorem, but thinking discursively, working things out. On the whole issue of 'the rendering of *theôrêtikos*', see especially Broadie (unpublished).

things distinguished in this way, we say that the work of a thing is also that of its excellence, only not in the same way. For example, a shoe is the work of expertise in shoemaking and of the process of making shoes; if, then, there is an excellence that belongs to shoemaking and the good shoemaker, its work is a good shoe. And it is the same way with everything else. Further, let the work of soul be **a25** making a thing be alive, and the active, living [part] of living, for sleeping is a sort of idleness and leisure. So, since the work of the soul and its excellence must be one and the same, the work of the excellence will be a good life. It is this, then, that is the final and complete[6] good, which is what we said[7] And it is clear from **a28** the assumptions we have made, for we said that happiness was best, and that the ends, the best of goods, were in [the] soul, and that these were either dispositions or activities: since the activity is better than the condition [from which it flows], the best activity is also that of the best disposition; but then since excellence is a best disposition, the best of [goods] will be activity of the excellence of the soul; but we said happiness too was the best: happiness, then, is activity of a good soul. But since happiness, we said, was something final and complete, and since life can be either complete or incomplete, so too with excellence, for it can either be excellence as a whole or it can be some part of excellence, and the activity of incomplete excellences[8] is an incomplete activity, happiness will be activity of a complete life according to excellence complete.

1219a40 That we are giving a good statement of its kind and its definition is witnessed by the things that all of us think:[9] **b1** we think that both doing well and living well are the same thing as being happy, either of which is a using and an activity, as is life and action, for the life of action is one of using: the bronze-smith makes the bridle, but it is the expert horseman that uses it. Then there is the fact that neither is anyone 'happy' just for a single day, nor is a child, or a person of just any age, which means that Solon spoke well when he said we should 'call no one happy while they are living, only when [their life] reaches an end'; for nothing incomplete[10] is happy if it is not whole. Again, we

---

6   One word, *teleon* in the Greek, which in the context is both 'as *telos*', i.e., end, goal and 'complete', and complete because final, and 'last': there is nothing further in the chain.
7   The imperfect is 'philosophical': it is not wholly clear that 'we' said exactly that, but certainly something like could be inferred from what has been said, especially if we add in the fact that we are beginning from, and trying to make clear, what people say.
8   I.e., of some single particular excellence on its own.
9   Literally 'the things we all think are witnesses', where 'witnesses' renders the word *marturia*, used of court evidence.
10   The word is *ateles*, '*telos*-less', where *telos* surely plays on the ambiguity between 'end' as an actual ending and as goal.

praise excellence because of its products,[11] and encomia are of these too; and it is those who win that are crowned with laurels, not those capable of winning but not actually winning. Our judgement on what sort of quality someone has, too, is based on what they do. Again, why is it that happiness is not an object of praise? It is because everything else is praised because of it, by virtue either of their being referred back to it or of their being parts of it. This is why calling a person happy is a different thing from praising them or offering them an encomium: an encomium describes a particular thing done, while praise concerns someone's being such-and-such in general; calling someone happy relates to ends.[12] These [considerations] also bring clarity to something people puzzle about sometimes, namely how it can be that the good are no better than the bad for half of their life, **1219b20**, for everyone is alike when they are sleeping, and the reason is that sleep is idleness of soul and not activity. This is also why, if there is some other part of the soul, like the nutritive part, the excellence of this is not part of excellence. As a whole, just as bodily excellence is not, either; for in sleep the nutritive is more active, whereas the perceptive and desiring [parts] are incomplete in sleep; although to the extent that they do in a way participate in movement in sleep even the images that appear to the good are better,[13] unless brought on by illness or deformation.

1219b28 Next we must reflect on the subject of soul, since excellence belongs to the soul, and not just coincidentally.[14] Since it is human excellence we are looking for, **b30** let it be our assumption that the parts of soul sharing in reason are two, but that both do not share in it in the same way: one shares in it by giving commands, the other by being by nature such as to obey and listen; if there is something that is non-rational in a different way, let this part be discarded for our purposes now. It makes no difference whether the soul is divisible[15] or whether it is[16] without parts; in any case it has diverse capacities, i.e., the ones just mentioned. Just as in the curved the convex and the concave are inseparable, so too are the straight and the white; however, the straight is not white except coincidentally, not by virtue of its own essence. If there is some other part of the soul, like the vegetative, that too we have put to one

---

11   I.e. *erga*, 'works'.
12   Sc. chosen and achieved?
13   v.2 will have something to say about better dreams and dreamers.
14   I here borrow Kenny's rendering of *mê kata sumbebêkos*.
15   I.e., whether the parts are located separately in the body.
16   Sc. in this sense.

side, for the parts we have mentioned[17] are peculiar to a human soul,[18] which explains why the excellences of the nutritive and generative [part] do not count as human excellences[19] either.[20] For if [we are considering a human being] as a human being,[21] then reasoning[22] must be inherent as starting-point,[23] and action too,[24] and reasoning is in control 1220a1 not of reasoning but of desire and of affective states;[25] necessarily, then, a human soul has these parts.[26] And just as good bodily condition consists of a combination of the excellences of individual parts, so too does excellence of soul as end.

1220a5 There are two kinds of excellence, one ethical,[27] the other relating to thought – for we praise not only people that are just but people possessed of acumen, and the intellectually accomplished;[28] a7 for we said we were assuming that either the excellence or its work/product were an object of praise, and

---

17 I.e., the two that share in reason.
18 Sc. which is why we are concerned with them, our inquiry being into the human and not any other sort of soul.
19 I.e., because they are shared with other animals.
20 Aristotle's argument is laid out, as so often in *EE*, with a succinctness that hardly helps the reader. My own inference from this is that while Aristotle may well have read out his texts to an audience, – itself, surely, involving logistical issues: are we to imagine piles of wax tablets next to him as he read them one by one? Surely not: wax tablets are designed to be erased, so that their contents would have had to be transferred to papyrus (presumably) as soon as possible; the resulting scrolls would then be stored, and taken out when necessary, whether for revision, consultation, or for reading out in the Lyceum, his main purpose was to get his arguments down; in other words, his priority was not the requirements of a live audience (though he has them in mind too: see note on 1220b37 below), but rather just getting his arguments straight, for himself in the first instance.
21 See preceding note: all Aristotle gives us is 'as/*qua* a human being'.
22 Or 'calculation', *logismos*.
23 The 'as' ('as starting-point') is one reading of what is normally plain 'and', *kai*, (but can also mean 'that is'; it is important to be aware of this, because we are about to get into a passage that apparently introduces a starting-point/first principle that is not reasoning, even if it has *some* sort of rational aspect; but Aristotle is in any case here setting out what is typically human, not telling us what is the case with every action.
24 Only human beings are capable of action (*praxis*); other animals, or plants, just *do* things (*poiein*, which carries no implication, as *praxis* does, of prior reasoning of *some* sort; but in their case too, as with any movement there would have to be some sort of starting-point; on balance, then, 'inherent *as* starting-point' it is. (It is the very fact that other animals do not reason before their 'doing what they do that constitutes the reason why they are not said to partake in *praxis* [EE II.1, 1219b39–1220a2].)
25 I.e., *pathêmata* or *pathê*, distinguished from *hexeis*, 'dispositions': anger, fear, etc. (see ch. 2, 1220b6 *ff*.)
26 I.e., the. two parts marked off as rational in their different ways at b31–2.
27 I.e., relating to the *êthê*, 'character-traits'.
28 I.e., those with *sophia*: see Appendix 1 below.

while the things in question are not activities themselves, there are activities *of* them.[29] And since the excellences relating to thought involve reason, such excellences belong to the [part] whose possession of reason is a matter of giving commands, while the ethical excellences belong to the [part] that does not have reason but tends by nature to follow the lead of the one that does have it; when saying what sort of person someone is in relation to their character traits, we do not say that they are intellectually accomplished or clever but that they are mild or rash.

1220a14 Next after these things we must first investigate ethical excellence, asking what it is, what sorts of parts it has (for this is a question the discussion has now reached). We must seek our quarry just like everyone in in everything else, with something already in hand, so as always to try, through things that are truly but not clearly said, to catch the clearly *and* clearly said. For as things are in a similar position to the one we would be in if we were hunting for health and had in our hand just that it is the best disposition of the body, or that Coriscus is the darkest-skinned **a21** among the people in the market-place: in neither case do we actually know the thing we're looking for, but having what we do have is nevertheless a step towards knowing it.

a23 Let us assume, first, that the best disposition comes about from the things that are best, and that the actions that are best in any field derive from the excellence proper to that field; so for example it is the exercises and the diet from which good physical condition comes about that are best, and it is being in good condition that allows people to exercise best; again, let us make it our assumption that every disposition comes about from the same factors, only applying to the situation different ways, in the way that health comes about from diet, exercise, and climate. **1220a29** These things are clear by induction. Excellence too, then, is the sort of disposition that both comes about through the movements that are best in relation soul and produces the best things done and the best affective states; it also comes about from the same things, [applied] in one way, as it is destroyed by [when they are applied] in another way. **a34** And in addition to this let us assume that its use is in relation to the same things by which it is both increased and destroyed and in relation to which it disposes its [possessor] in the best way.[30] And an indication of this is that both ethical excellence and badness relate to pleasant and painful things, for punishments, which are ways of curing people, and have their effect through [the application of] opposites, work by means of these.[31]

---

29 I.e., relating to/associated with them.
30 *beltista diatithêsin*, i.e., provides them with the best disposition, *diathesis*.
31 I.e., pleasure and pain.

EE Book II, Chapter 2

a39 That excellence of character[32] is concerned with pleasant and painful things, then, is clear. Since character is just as even its name (*êthos*) **b1** indicates, namely that what progress it makes[33] comes from habit (*ethos*),[34] and what is [changed] under the influence of something not inborn is habituated by being moved many times over in a certain way, that is how there is already something capable of acting [in accordance with the appropriate character-trait];[35] which is something we do not see in the case of inanimate things – even if you throw the stone upwards any number of times, it will never do it without being forced. **b5** So let character be this: a quality[36] belonging to [the part] of soul capable of following in accordance with command-giving reason. So we must spell out what it is in the soul that makes our character-traits be of a certain kind: it will relate both to our capacities for the affective states in question when people are said to be 'emotional', and to the dispositions by reference to which we are described in relation to these affective state as experiencing them in a certain way or as being emotionally unaffected. [After this [comes] the division in the [works] between affective states, capacities and dispositions][37] **1220b10** [After this, the division in the things removed,[38] of the affective states,

---

32   I.e., *êthikê*, 'of *êthos*', 'having to do with character-traits'.
33   For the expression *echein epidosin* see e.g. Plato, *Theaetetus* 146b5.
34   Aristotle is probably right about the etymological connection.
35   Another extraordinarily laconic piece of writing (but not so extraordinary for *EE*).
36   *Poiotês*, apparently an invention of Plato's (*Theaetetus* 182a9).
37   The sentence is 'intrusive' (Barnes 1991: 29), in one way or another, but since it is there in the text, even in square brackets [here signalling to the reader 'No need to linger here!'], I translate it (which is already enough to show that it is problematical).
38   Kenny 2011 translates 'Here comes the division, made elsewhere ...', Reeve has 'Next, is the division, made in separate contexts [i.e., in Aristotle's works] ...', relying on the fact that the division in question does in fact appear in several different works. Both translators read *apêllagmenois*, as do I, but neither of the senses they supply can actually be got from the verb in question; both versions are simple inventions. But now it happens that the natural meaning (if there is such a thing, under the circumstances) of *ta apêllagmena* is 'the things removed' (see, e.g., Montanari 1995, *s.v.*, giving 'remove' as the first use of the active verb, and citing 'Plat. *Prot.* 354d etc.') My own proposal, is that perhaps Aristotle, or his copyist, in the writing up from the wax-tablets first written by the scribe, made a significant error and consequently had to erase a portion of the text; that erasure, I speculate, would have been visible, somehow, to at least some in the live audience, and Aristotle, knowing this, writes out an acknowledgement of the erasure and what exactly was erased, namely the division we now find in b12–20. So (a) nothing has been lost, (b) the sentence is not 'intrusive' in quite the way Barnes suggests (i.e., with the implication that it was written by someone other than Aristotle), just intrusive for the reader, who does not need the information Aristotle is providing (as I propose) to the live audience. Of course this

our capacities [for them], and the dispositions.][39] 'Affective states' are these sorts of things: anger, fear, shame, appetite – in general, the things that are accompanied for the most part by sensual pleasure or pain. These do not make a person of a certain quality, rather the person [merely] experiences them; it is with the potentialities [for them] that a person's quality comes into question. **1220 b16** By 'potentialities'[40] here I mean those by reference to which those actively experiencing the affective states are described, for example as irascible, impassive,[41] amorous, bashful or having no shame. Dispositions, for their part, are the states that are responsible for these states' occurring either in accordance with reason or in opposition to reason: for example, courage, moderation, cowardice or self-indulgence.

---

is highly speculative, not least in that it presupposes a scenario for which there is only slim evidence (but evidence it is: see n. 42 below on the reference to *'the hupographê'*) apart from what is needed to make my proposal work – plus that attested meaning for *ta apêllagmena*, though that is far from insignificant: why *would* he be referring to things 'removed' which, according to the best evidence of the MSS, he did)? Here I envisage two possibilities, one distinctly less likely than the other, namely that Aristotle would have been reading from a papyrus roll holding it partially unrolled and in a position, aloft, such that it could be at least partially seen from the audience side, so working in principle somewhat like the running captions in a modern theatre or opera-house. The second possibility (on which see the Introduction above), is that there was a second copy of the text circulating in the audience even as Aristotle spoke, and if that was his normal practice, he might well have felt that a large erasure should be acknowledged. What is surely true is that Aristotle's argument, even at its most expansive, is so dense that an audience would be likely to be grateful for any extra help they might get in following it. Simpson 2013 proposes that the reference is to the *De virtutibus et vitiis*, a work widely regarded as not by Aristotle that Simpson suggests is a kind of 'abstract': this would be convenient, but there is no evidence beyond that either to confirm or to reject the suggestion.

39 I follow my normal practice of translating even intrusive (bracketed) material, because it is printed (in those square brackets) in the text; the reader needs to be aware that something was once there, whatever its origin and however difficult it may be to make sense of. In the present case, if there is any substance to my speculation, a reader that skips the sentence as instructed by the square brackets [n. 36 above] will not have missed much, or indeed anything relevant to the argument of the chapter.

40 'Potentialities' (borrowed here from Kenny 2011) renders *dunameis*, more usually ('powers' or) 'capacities', which *pace* Reeve and others will not fit here; Aristotle has no reason in the present context to be interested in people's capacity to feel angry, for example, but every reason to be interested in *this* person's tendency, e.g. to lose their temper.

41 *Analgêsia* is originally insensitivity to pain, *algos*, particularly pain from insult or injury received.

EE Book II, Chapter 3

1220b21 With these distinctions made, we must grasp the point that in everything continuous and divisible there is excess, deficiency, and a mean, all of these either in relation to each other or in relation to us, as for example in the sphere of gymnastics, medicine, house-building, in steersmanship, and indeed in any practical activity whatever, whether falling under some form of expertise or none, whether involving some skill or not; for movement is a continuum, and activity is movement. But in all of these it is the mean in relation to us that is best. For this is as knowledge bids us, and reason. Everywhere, too, it is this that brings about the best disposition. And **1220b30** this is clear from induction, and from argument: for opposites destroy each other, and the extremes are opposites are opposite both to each other and to the mean; for the mean is either of the extremes to the other, as the equal is greater than the less and less than the greater. Necessarily, then, ethical excellence is concerned with certain means and is itself a mean state of a certain sort. In which case we must find out what sort of mean excellence is and what sort of means it is concerned with. **b36** So let us suppose some things to be taken for the sake of an example.[42] and let us reflect on each item from the [following] summary:[43]

---

42   'Let us suppose ...', because we don't *know* yet that they are examples.

43   The word *hupographê* is typically translated as 'diagram'. The same formula, *theôreisthô ... ek tês hupographês*, appears (at least) three other times in the Aristotelian corpus (*De int.* 22a21–2 *Mete.* 346a31–2, and *Hist an.* 510a29–30; in the latter two cases 'diagram' is certainly meant (what follows *is* a diagram), but in *De int.* it is more 'summary', 'outline', 'list'. What we have here in *EE* is more like the latter case than the other two, not because it *looks* more like an outline or summary than exactly a 'diagram' (for which the scribes may well have been responsible, not Aristotle (all our MSS, I believe, give us 14 trios, not in columns; how Aristotle arranged the material we cannot tell), but because all that is needed is a list, which is what it is. It must somehow be visible to an audience: 'the' outline, said to a live audience, requires it (though one wonders how much use it would be to them; if they succeeded in seeing it in any detail, they would hardly need to remember much about it when each pair is going to be identified, and discussed, in the immediate sequel); my explanation (see n. 18 above) is that in such a scenario Aristotle would have held up the scroll he was reading and pointed to the relevant part of the text – probably, then, arranged in columns, since otherwise it would hardly stand out. The main point about the *hupographê*, whatever it is, is that it gives us 14 *pairs* of vices between which we are invited to find the mean – not, I think, supplied by Aristotle – which is why everything in the third column in the Greek text is in square brackets – but rather by an editor, from the following pages; 'and let us reflect on each item from the [following] outline' is 1220b37 is pointing us towards what follows the *hupographê*, which is where the 'reflection' is done; the outcomes ought not to be in the *hupographê* itself.

irascibility	impassivity	[mildness]
boldness	cowardice	[courage]
1221a1 shamelessness	bashfulness	[modesty]
self-indulgence	insensitivity[44]	[moderation]
envy	nameless	[indignation[45]]
profit	loss	[just]
a5 wastefulness	avariciousness	[open-handedness]
imposture	dissembling[46]	[truthfulness]
sycophancy	surliness	[friendliness]
obsequiousness	self-centredness	[dignity]
softness[47]	hardiness	[endurance]
1221a10 conceitedness	little-souledness	[great-souledness][48]
extravagance	shabbiness	[magnificence][49]
cunning	simple-mindedness	[wisdom][50]

1221a13 These affective states and others like them[51] come the way of souls, and all of them get their names from being cases of either excess or

---

44 To be distinguished from 'impassivity' in that 'insensitivity' relates specifically to physical pleasure (1231a37–b2).
45 Specifically at the unmerited good or bad fortune of others.
46 *Eirôneia*, Socratic 'irony', pretending to ignorance (Aristotle surely has Socrates in mind).
47 'Pampered', perhaps.
48 The 'great souled' here, the *megalopsuchos*, is possessed of greatness; the key element of *megalopsuchia*, 'great-souledness' ('great-spiritedness', might be marginally better, given that '-souledness' is not English, but there is no English equivalent]) is provided by the contrast with 'little-souledness', *mikropsuchia* ('diffidence', which is a matter of behaving as the insignificant, unambitious, person one actually is but need not be/have been?).
49 I.e., in expenditure, so 'munificence', but 'munificence' misses the *megalo-* in *megaloprepeia*.
50 There could be no clearer signal of intrusion in the list than this entry (and there is competition enough, especially perhaps from the trio 'profit, loss, just' – we will be told how to understand these in terms of character-traits, or whatever it is that the list is of (see next note), but as its stands the trio is no more than shorthand (if Aristotle was responsible for it, he presumably knew what he meant, but he gives True, *phronêsis* could reasonably be considered as something between cunning and simple-mindedness, but (a) Aristotle is explicitly talking about ethical virtue (1220a14), and (b) he shows no interest anywhere else in the *EE* in making the intellectual excellences as means or intermediates.
51 Even when the third item in every trio is bracketed, there is some residual difficulty in treating the list as being exclusively of affective states (*pathê*): paltriness (sc. in expenditure), for example, looks more like a disposition than an affective state, as these were distinguished in 1220b12–20. But perhaps it can be either, and 1221a13 is telling us to take it as the former.

deficiency.⁵² An irascible person is the one who is angry more than he should and more quickly and at more people, while an impassive person is the one who is defective with respect to the people he should be angry at, when and in what way; a bold person is the one that neither fears the things he ought to fear nor when nor in what way, while a cowardly person is the one who fears both the sorts of things he should not and when he should not **a19** and in a way he should not. Similarly, a self-indulgent person is the one who is characterised by appetite and goes to excess in every way possible, while an insensitive person who is deficient in this respect, and lacks appetite even for as much as is better [for anyone] and is in accordance with his [human nature], being as unaffected as a stone. An acquisitive⁵³ person is the one who claims more than he is due from every source, while the loser⁵⁴ claims nothing or little from anywhere. An impostor is the one who pretends to have more than he has, **1221a25** a dissembler to have less. A flatterer is the one who praises more things than is fine, the surly person less; trying too hard to give pleasure is obsequious, while doing it om few occasions and with reluctance is self-centred. Again, the person who will put up with no pain at all, even if **a29** it would benefit him is soft; the one who will put up with any pain, whether small or great without distinction strictly speaking has no name, but is described metaphorically as hard, long-suffering and hardy. A conceited person is one who thinks himself worthy of greater things, the little-souled of lesser. Again, a **a32** wasteful person is one who goes to excess in relation to any sort of expenditure, an avaricious person one deficient in any expenditure. Similarly with the shabby and the ostentatious, for the one exceeds what is fitting while the other falls short of it. The cunning person maximises what he gets in every way and from every source, while the simple-minded person does not even get from the sources he should. **a37** An envious person is one who is more often distressed by the successes of others than he should be – for the envious are distressed by those who deserve to do well, when they do; his opposite is somewhat lacking a name, but there is someone who goes to excess in not being distressed even by the undeserving when they do well, but is easy-going about it, like a glutton, who [will tolerate anything] as long as it is food, unlike his opposite, who is disagreeable in his envy. It is superfluous to specify that none of these are as they are [merely] by

---

52   This then finally rules out any possibility that 'These affective states and others like them' in a13 includes the third column, no single item in which connotes either excess or deficiency.
53   Here is the information we need to decipher 'profit', *kerdos*, in the list (the adjective is *kerdaleos*].
54   The *zêmiôdês*, characterised by (perhaps 'attuned to'?) loss, *zêmia*.

coincidence,[55] **1221b5** for no [sort of] knowledge, whether primarily reflective[56] or productive, either says or does it, making this additional specification in its terms of definition; it is no more than a guard against verbal quibbles infecting the productive expertises. So let that stand as our broad definition for now, and be more precise when we talk about the opposing dispositions.

b10 Kinds of these affective states themselves[57] get their names from their differing in respect of excess in relation either to time or to intensity or to one of the things producing the states. I am saying, for example, that a short-tempered person gets his name from being affected more quickly than they should be, while the hot-tempered too is bad-tempered[58] by reference to intensity, a bitter person because of the way they nurse their anger, aggressive and abusive by reference to the punishments they hand out in their anger, **1221b16** gourmands and gluttons and drunkards by reference to whether it is food or drink that their affective capacity finds its enjoyment contrary to reason. But one should be aware that some of the states we are talking about are not to be understood in terms of something's being done in a certain sort of way – for example a philanderer is not called such because he sleeps with other people's wives more than he should, because there is no such thing, – philandering itself is already a [form of] badness, the state being talked about with its badness bound up in the name itself. Similarly with assault. This is why people dispute the charges against them, claiming that they did sleep with the woman but it was not adultery because they did it out of ignorance or because they were forced into it, and that they did punch their opponent but it was not an assault – and similarly with everything like that.

EE Book II, Chapter 4

1221b27 With these things noted, the next thing is to say that since two parts of the soul and excellences relating to each have been distinguished, some of these intellectual excellences belonging to the [part] possessed of reason, whose **1221b30** work is truth either about how things are or about how

---

55   I.e., plainly, because of some chance combination of factors rather than because of the way the person is, himself.
56   *Theôrêtikos*: so, again, an *epistêmê* with no product outside the reflection itself and its outcomes.
57   Again, clearly just the first two items in each trio.
58   'Bad-tempered': *chalepos*, which takes over in III.3 as the opposite of *praos*, 'mild'.

things come about,[59] the others belonging to the [part] that is irrational but has desire, for it is not just any part of the soul that has desire, if indeed the soul is divisible into parts, necessarily a character-trait will be bad or good by reference to whether it pursues or avoids these or those pleasures and pains. This is clear from the distinctions we make about the affective states, the capacities[60] and the dispositions, for the capacities and the dispositions belong to the affective states, and the states are distinguished by their relation to pain and pleasure; in consequence both of these considerations and our preceding assumptions it follows that every excellence of character relates to pleasures and pains. For the sort of things that naturally make any disposition of soul worse and better are also the things it relates to and is concerned with; and we say that we are bad because pleasures and pains, that is, either by pursuing and avoiding them as one should not, or pursuing and avoiding the ones we should not. This is why, too, everybody is ready to identify the excellences as states of insensibility and lack of concern in relation to pleasures and pains, and the [different sorts of] badness as coming from the opposites of these.

EE Book II, Chapter 5

1222a6 Since we have made the assumption that excellence is the sort of disposition from which people become doers of the best actions and in accordance with which they are best disposed in relation to the chief good, and that best and chief good is what is in accordance with correct reason[ing]; and since this is the mean between excess and defect relative to us, **b10** it will necessarily be the case that excellence of character is, each of them, in itself a middle or concerned with certain means in pleasures and pains and pleasant and painful things: the middle will sometimes be in pleasures, for there is excess and defect there too; sometimes it will be in pains, sometimes in both pleasures and pains; for the person who goes to excess in enjoying himself excessively is going to excess in the pleasant, and the person who is excessively pained is going to excess in the opposite – and this either without qualification or in relation to some standard, **1222a16** as for example when it is 'not in the way the many do it'; but the good person does it as they should. And since there is a disposition that makes its possessor such as to accept the excess of the same thing on one occasion and a deficiency of it on another, then necessarily, as these are

---

59 'How things come about': the 'things' here will – in the present context – be practical ends more than anything, though the formula will also naturally include investigation of causation more widely.
60 'Susceptibilities', Kenny, helpfully.

opposed to each other and to the mean, **a21** so the actions are opposed to one and to excellence. However it can happen that in one case all the opposites are rather clear, in another the ones to do with excess, and in yet another the ones to do with deficiency. The reason for the discrepancy is that **1222a25** they are not always at the same levels of inequality or similarity with respect to the middle, but sometimes one gets more quickly from excess to the intermediate trait, sometimes more quickly from the deficiency, and he who is further away from it seems to be more opposed to it. For instance in the case of the body too, when it comes to exercise, the excess is healthier than the **1222a30** deficiency and nearer the middle, whereas when it comes to food, the deficiency is healthier than the excess; so also the decision-making traits characteristic of those who favour gymnastics will favour health when it comes to making these two choices: in the one they favour exercise, in the other they favour dieting. And opposed to the measured person, i.e., the person who does as reason dictates, is in the one case **a35** the lazy person and not both extremes, in the other case the sybarite and not the one going hungry. This happens because our nature is not right away in all cases at a similar distance from the middle, but we favour training less and tend to be more sybaritic. Things are similar with the soul. We take the opposite **1222a40** trait to be the one in whose direction we, along with most people, err more, but the other escapes our notice as though it were not there, for it goes unseen because of its rarity. For instance, anger gets opposed to mildness, and the irascible person **1222b1** to the mild person, although there is also excess in being meek and in being conciliatory and in not getting angry when slapped. But such people are rare and everyone inclines towards the former. This is also why spirit is no flatterer.

1222b5 A list of the traits has been given for each type of feeling, i.e. the excesses and deficiencies, including also the opposing traits because of which people are in line with correct reason[ing] (what such correct reason[ing] is, and what standard we should look at in saying what the middle is, must be examined later.) So it is clear that all ethical excellences and [forms of] badness concern **b10** excesses and deficiencies of pleasures and pains, and that pleasures and pains come about from the aforesaid character-traits and affective states. Yet the best state really is the one that is the middle concerning each thing. Therefore it is clear that the excellences, either all or some of them, will be amongst the middles.

EE Book II, Chapter 6

1222b15 Let us then take another starting-point for the current investigation. All substances are in their nature origins of some sort, e.g. a human produces humans, and speaking generally, an animal produces animals and a plant plants. In addition to this, it is humans who, alone **b20** among animals, are also an origin of certain actions, for we should not say of any other animal that they act. Among origins, those which are the primary sources of processes are said to be controlling, and this is most of all correct for those from which comes what cannot be otherwise. Perhaps god originates things in this way. But among the origins for things which are not moved, e.g. among the mathematical ones, there is not a controlling item, although something is at least said to be that **1222b25** through similarity. But there, if an item is changed, everything proven from it would change, but it is not that they change themselves, with one destroying the other (except in the case of destroying a hypothesis and thereby proving something). But a human is an origin of a different kind of process. For action is a process. Since **1222b30** just as in other matters the origin is a cause of things which are, or happen, because of it, we should think likewise in demonstrations. For if the fact that triangles contain two right angles necessitates that quadrilaterals contain four right angles, it is clear that the fact that triangles contain two right angles is the cause of that. But then if triangles change **b35** quadrilaterals too must change, e.g. if they contain three right angles, quadrilaterals must contain six, if four, eight. And even if they do not in fact change, they are still like that, and that consequence is still necessary. It is clear from the *Analytics* that what we are attempting to show here must be so, but in the present context it is not possible to affirm it or deny it in sufficient detail, except this much: if nothing else is a cause of triangles being so, that fact would be an origin and a cause of the facts posterior to it. So since some of the things that are can be opposite to the way they are, necessarily their principles too are of that sort. **1223a1** For what follows from things which hold of necessity is itself necessary, but what comes from these other things can turn out in the opposite way, and the things which are up to humans constitute a large part of things of this sort, that is, human are origins of things of that sort. So it is clear that the actions which a human is **a5** an origin of, and which they control, can both happen and fail to happen, and that the things whose happening or not is up to someone are the things such that humans are in control of their being or not being. And whatever is up to someone to do or not do, are the things of which that person is a cause. And the things they are a cause of are the ones that are up to them. Both excellence and badness and the accomplishments that come from **1223a10** them are praiseworthy and blameworthy, for the things that are praised and blamed are not the things that hold by necessity, chance, or nature, but those things we ourselves are the causes of, for when someone is the cause of something, they get both the blame and the praise for it. Therefore, it is clear that both excellence and badness concern the things of which someone **a15** is a cause and an action-origin. Therefore we must grasp of what things one is a cause and an action-origin. Everyone then agrees that whatever is voluntary and stems from each person's decision is something that person is a cause of, and whatever is counter-voluntary the person is not a cause of. Clearly everything someone has decided to do they also do voluntarily. It is clear therefore that excellence and badness are in the domain of the voluntary.

EE Book II, Chapter 7

1123a23 We should therefore grasp what the voluntary is and what the counter-voluntary is, and what decision is. And given that excellence and badness are delimited by them, we should first examine the voluntary and the counter-voluntary. They would seem to be one of the following three: either what stems from desire or from **a25** decision or from thinking things through, the voluntary being what stems from one of these, and the counter-voluntary being what goes against one of these. But desire is divided up into three kinds, wish, spirit, and appetite, so that we should make the following divisions, beginning with what stems from appetite.

1223a29 Everything that stems from appetite would seem to be voluntary. For **a30** everything counter-voluntary seems to be forced, and what is forced is painful, as is everything that people are compelled to do or undergo. Just as Evenus says, 'Everything compelled is by nature grievous.' So if something is painful, it is forced, and if forced, it is painful. And everything that goes against appetite is painful (for the object of appetite is the pleasant), so that **a35** it is forced and counter-voluntary. Therefore what stems from appetite is voluntary, since these are opposites to one another. Furthermore, every [sort of] badness makes a person more unjust, and lack of self-control seems to some to be a case of badness. Now the uncontrolled person is the kind of person who do actions that stem from their appetite and go against their reason[ing]. And someone acts uncontrolledly whenever their activity stems from that appetite. But acting badly is voluntary. So, the **1223b1** uncontrolled person will act unjustly by doing an action that stems from appetite. Therefore they will not act voluntarily, and what stems from appetite is voluntary. For it would be especially strange if by becoming uncontrolled people will more just.

1223b3 Based on these considerations it would seem that the voluntary is what stems from appetite, but **b5** one might draw the opposite conclusion from the following. For everything that someone does voluntarily they do from a wish, and what they wish for, they do voluntarily. And nobody wishes what they think to be bad. However, the person who acts uncontrolledly does not do what they wish, for acting uncontrolledly is to do what goes against what one thinks best, because of appetite. Hence it will turn out that the same person **b10** acts voluntarily and counter-voluntarily at the same time; but this is impossible. Furthermore, the self-controlled person will act well; for self-control is an excellence more than lack of control is, and excellence makes people better. And someone acts with self-control when they do what stems from their reason[ing], against their appetite. Hence, if acting well is voluntary, as is also acting badly (for both of these seem to be voluntary, and if one of them is voluntary then necessarily so is the other), and what goes against appetite is counter-voluntary, then the same person will at the same time do the same thing voluntarily and counter-voluntarily.

1223b18 The same argument applies to spirit as well. For there seems to be lack of control and control over spirit too, just as there is over appetite. And **b20** what goes against spirit is painful, and restraint is a case of being forced, so that if what is forced is counter-voluntary, everything that stems from spirit would be voluntary. Heraclitus too seems to say with a view to the strength of spirit that it is painful to stop it: 'It is difficult to fight against spirit; for the price it pays is life.' And if it is impossible **b25** for the same person to do the same thing voluntarily and counter-voluntarily, at the same time and with respect to the same aspect of the matter, then what stems from wish is more voluntary than what stems from appetite and spirit. There is evidence for this; for we do many things voluntarily in the absence of anger and appetite.

1223b29 It remains, then, to investigate if what is wished for and the voluntary are the same. **b30** This, too, appears impossible. For we have assumed, and it is held, that badness makes people worse, and lack of self-control appears to be a case of badness; but the opposite will then follow. For no one wishes things they think to be bad, but people do such things when they become uncontrolled. So if acting badly is voluntary, and the voluntary is what stems from wish, then when **b35** a person becomes uncontrolled, they will no longer act badly, but rather they will be better than they were before they became uncontrolled; but this is impossible.

1123b37 It is evident, then, that the involuntary is not action that stems from desire, nor is the counter-voluntary what goes against desire.

EE Book II, Chapter 8

1223b38 That it is not what stems from decision, either, is in turn clear from the following. For it has been demonstrated that what stems from wish is **1224a1**

not counter-voluntary, but rather everything that one wishes is also voluntary. All that has been shown is that it is possible to act voluntarily even when one does not wish to. And we do many things all of a sudden, while acting on our wishes, but nobody decides on something all of a sudden.

1224a5 If it was necessary for the voluntary to be one of these three, either what stems from desire, or what stems from decision, or what stems from thinking things through, but two of these it is not, it remains that the voluntary lies in action that is in some way based on thinking things through. Pursuing our discussion a little further still, let us complete the task of delimiting the voluntary and the counter-voluntary. For it seems that doing something by force and a10 not by force is related to what has been discussed. For we say both that the forced is counter-voluntary and that everything counter-voluntary is forced. In consequence, we should first examine that which is forced, what it is and how it relates to the voluntary and the counter-voluntary.

1224a15 It seems that what is forced and compulsory, and force and compulsion, are opposed, in the domain of action, to the voluntary and to persuasion. In general, we speak of what is forced and of compulsion also in the case of inanimate things, for we say both that a stone is moved upwards and that some fire is moved downwards by force and under compulsion. But when these things move in a way that stems from their natural and intrinsic impulse, they are not said to be moved by force nor for that matter voluntarily, but the opposed case is without a name. Still, when they are moved in a way that goes against that impulse, we say that it is by force. Likewise in the case of both inanimate beings and animals, we see that they both undergo and do many things by force, when something external moves them in a way that goes against their internal impulse. While the origin is simple in the inanimate beings, it is multiple in the animate beings, for desire and reason are not always a25 in harmony. In consequence, what is forced is simple in the case of the non-human animals, just as with the inanimate beings, since they do not have reason and desire opposed to each other, but live by desire; but in the human being both are present, i.e. at a certain age, at which we also attribute action. For we do not say that the child acts, nor that the animal does, but the person a30 who acts already does so because of reason[ing]. It seems, then, that everything that is forced is painful, and no one does anything by force but does it gladly.

That is why there is a great deal of controversy about the self-controlled and the uncontrolled person. Each acts while their own impulses are opposed to them, so that the self-controlled person drags himself away by force, as people say, from their appetites 1224a35 for pleasant things (for they even feel pain as they drag themselves away by force against their reason[ing]). But the latter seems to be pained less, for the object of appetite is the pleasant, which they follow gladly. In consequence, the controlled person acts more voluntarily and not by force, since their action is not painful. On the other hand, persuasion is opposed to force and compulsion, and the **1224b1** self-controlled person is led to what they have been persuaded to do, and proceeds not by force but voluntarily. Appetite, by contrast, does not lead by persuasion, for it does not share in reason.

1224b4 It has been said, then, that only these, the self-controlled and the uncontrolled, seem to act by force and voluntarily, and for what reason, namely that it is because of a certain similarity with the force that is spoken of also **b5** in the case of inanimate objects. However, if one adds in the addition that is present in the definition, the topic of discussion is resolved. For whenever something external causes movement or rest against the internal impulse, we say that it is by force, but whenever there is not, we say that it is not by force. But in the uncontrolled and the self-controlled it is their intrinsic and internal impulse that leads them, **1224b10** for they have both; as a result, neither acts by force, and therefore they would act voluntarily, and not by compulsion, either. For we call compulsion the external origin that either obstructs or effects movement against this impulse, e.g. if someone were to grab someone's hand so as to strike another, with the person resisting both by wish and by appetite, but whenever **1224b15** the origin is internal, the action is not by force.

Still, both pleasure and pain are present in both. For the self-controlled person is both pained, so that they are already acting against their appetite, and they enjoy the pleasure of anticipation that they will benefit later, or they are already benefiting by being healthy. And the uncontrolled person is pleased in that, while they act uncontrolledly, they obtain **b20** the object of their appetite, but on the other hand they suffer the pain of anticipation, for they think that they are doing something bad. As a result, there is some reason to say that each of them acts by force, and that each sometimes acts counter-voluntarily because of their desire or because of their reason[ing]. For each of these two is separate and they can force each other out. People transfer this to the **1224b25** whole soul because they see that the parts of the soul undergo something like this. So whereas one can say this in the case of the parts, the whole soul both of the uncontrolled and of the self-controlled person acts voluntarily, and neither of them acts by force, though something internal to them does, since it is by nature that we have both. For reason will be present as a natural originator, **b30** if development is allowed to proceed and is not stunted, and so will appetite, because it accompanies us, i.e. is present within us, right away from birth. And what is by nature is pretty much delimited by these two, i.e. by what accompanies things right away from their generation, and by what comes to belong to us when our development is allowed to go forward, e.g. grey hair, old age, and other things **b35** of this kind. As a result, in a way each person's action does not stem from nature, but without qualification each person's action does stem from nature, though not from the same nature. These, then, are the difficulties about the self-controlled and the controlled person, about whether both, or one or the other, act by force, so that either they act not voluntarily, or at once by force and voluntarily, and at once voluntarily and counter-voluntarily, if what is by force is counter-voluntary. **1225a1** From what has been said it is pretty clear how these difficulties should be met.

a3 However, there is another way in which people are said to act by force and compulsion, without their reason and their desire being in conflict, whenever people do something that they take to be painful or bad, but if they do not do it there will be a beating, imprisonment or death. For people say that they do these things under compulsion. Or is that not so, but everyone does even these things voluntarily? For it is possible not to do them, and to endure the suffering. Furthermore, perhaps someone would say that some of these actions are voluntary while others are not. For in all cases of **a10** this kind in which it is up to one whether the outcome does not come about or does come about, whenever one does what one does not wish to do, one acts voluntarily and not by force. But those things of this kind that are not up to us are in a way done by force, although not unqualifiedly so, because the person does not decide on the thing done, but on the goal for the sake of which it is done. In fact, in these cases there is a distinction to be drawn. For if someone kills someone else in order not to get caught in a game **a15**, it would be ridiculous if they claimed to have acted by force and under compulsion, but there must be something worse and more painful that they will suffer if they do not do the thing in question. For in this way the person will act under compulsion and by force, or not by nature, whenever they do something bad for the sake of something good or for the sake of avoiding something worse, and in any case counter-voluntarily. For these things are not up to the person.

For this reason **1225a20** many regard sexual desire, too, as counter-voluntary, and some cases of anger and natural conditions, because they are strong and beyond the person's nature. And we pardon such things on the grounds that they are of such a nature as to overpower our nature. And a person would seem to act more by force and counter-voluntarily when acting in order to avoid strong pain than mild pain, and in general, when acting in order to avoid pain than in order to **a25** enjoy oneself. For what is up to one, in terms of which everything is explained, is this: what one's nature is able to bear. What it is not able to bear, and what is not naturally in the domain of one's desire or reason[ing], is not up to one. For this reason, even though those who are inspired and who make prophecies come up with intellectual accomplishments, we nevertheless deny that it is up to them either to say what they said or to do what they did. But this is not due to appetite, either. As a result, there are both thoughts and affective states that are not up to us, nor are the actions that stem from such thoughts and reasonings, but as Philolaus said, some things said are more powerful than us.

1225a34 Thus, if it was necessary to examine the voluntary and the counter-voluntary, and their relation to what is by force, **a35** let these things be distinguished in this way. For the accounts that most impede the voluntary are those according to which people act by force and not voluntarily.

EE Book II, Chapter 9

Since the discussion has reached its goal, and the voluntary is delimited neither by desire nor by decision, it remains, **1225b1** then, to delimit it as those things that stem from thinking things through. **1225b2** It seems, then, that they are opposites – namely (a) the voluntary to the counter-voluntary, and (b) acting with knowledge of whom one acts on, or with what one acts, or what one acts for the sake of – for sometimes someone knows that this is one's father, though one acts not in order to kill, but in order to save him, just as did the daughters of Peleus, or one knows with what one acts, that it is a drink, but **1225b5** takes it to be a potion or wine, whereas it was hemlock – to acting in ignorance of who one acts on, with what one acts and what one is doing, and doing so because of ignorance, non-coincidentally. **b7** But what is because of ignorance, of what one is doing, with what, and on whom, is counter-voluntary. The opposite, therefore, is voluntary. All those things, then, that someone does while it is up to the person not to do them, not in ignorance and because of themselves, those things are necessarily voluntary, and **b10** the voluntary is this. On the other hand, all those things that a person does in ignorance, i.e. because of his ignorance, they do counter-voluntarily.

Given that understanding and knowing are twofold, having understanding being one thing and employing it is another, there is a way in which someone who has understanding but fails to employ it could justly be said to act in ignorance, but there is also a way in which they could not be, e.g. if the failure to employ it was due to carelessness. And likewise even a person who does not have it **1225b15** could be blamed if the knowledge in question was easy or required, and they lack it because of carelessness, pleasure or pain. These distinctions, then, must be made in addition.

Let the voluntary and the counter-voluntary be distinguished in this way, then; and

EE Book II, Chapter 10

Let us next discuss decision, after first thinking through some difficulties for an account of it. For one might be unsure about 1225b21 what kind it naturally belongs to and in what grouping it should be placed, and about whether or not the voluntary and the object of decision is the same. Above all, decision is said by some people, and would seem to an inquirer, to be one or the other of two things, either opinion or desire. For both of these evidently accompany it. Now it is clear that it is not desire. 1225b25 For it would be either wish, or appetite, or spirit; for no-one desires without experiencing one of these. Spirit and appetite, then, belong to the brutes as well, but decision does not. Furthermore, appetite and spirit are always painful, whereas we make many decisions without feeling pain. However, wish and decision are not the same thing either. For people knowingly wish for some things that are in fact impossible, e.g. to be king of all human beings and to be immortal, but no one decides on something impossible b35 unless they are ignorant of that fact, nor in general on something possible, when they do not think it is up to them to do or not to do. As a result, one thing is clear; that the object of decision is necessarily something that is up to that person. 1226a1 Likewise it is clear that it is not opinion, either, that is to say, if someone thinks anything, without qualification. For the object of decision is something that is up to the person, whereas we opine many things that are not up to us, e.g. that the diagonal of a square is commensurable with its side. 1226a4 Furthermore, decision is not true or false. Therefore, it is not even the type of opinion that concerns practicable things that are up to us, by which we end up thinking that we should do or refrain from doing something.

This applies jointly to opinion and wish: for no one decides on any goal, but on those things that contribute to the goal. I mean, for example, that no one decides to be healthy, but to walk or be seated for the sake of health, nor to be happy, 1226a10 but to pursue wealth or run a risk for the sake of happiness. And in general, it is clear that a person always decides both on something and for the sake of something,[61] where there is on the one hand that for the sake of which

---

61 Translating the text in Walzer and Mingay 1991, Inwood and Woolf construe 'In general a decision shows what one decides to do, and that for the sake of which one decides to do it'. But as I propose in Rowe 2023b, (a) there are no grounds for such a claim, and

something else is decided on, and on the other hand that which is decided on for the sake of something else. But it is most of all the goal that is the object of wishing, and one opines that one should be healthy and that one should do well. 1226a15 Thus it is clear through these considerations that decision is different both from opinion and from wish. For wishing and opinion pertain very much to the goal, whereas decision does not.

It is clear, then, that decision is neither wish, nor opinion, nor supposition without qualification. But how does it differ from them, and how a20 does it relate to the voluntary? At the same time it will also be clear what decision is. Now among the things that can be and not be, some are such that it is possible to deliberate about them, while about other things this is not possible. For some things can be or not be, though their coming into being is not up to us, but some of them can come to be because of nature, whereas others come to be because of a25 other causes, and about none of these things would anyone even attempt to deliberate, except in ignorance. By contrast, things that are not only capable of being and not being, but that it is possible for human beings to deliberate about, these are all the things that are up to us to do or not to do. This is why we do not deliberate about matters in India, or about how to square the circle, a30 for the former are not up to us, while the latter is completely unpracticable. Nor do we deliberate about all the things that are practicable for us, by which it is also clear that decision is not opinion without qualification. But the objects of decision and action are among the things that are up to us.

This is why someone might raise the difficulty why it is that doctors deliberate about the things that fall under a35 their expertise while grammarians do not. The reason is that mistakes arise in two ways, either in reasoning, or, when we are doing the thing, in a way that stems from perception. While in medicine it is possible to err in both of these ways, in grammar mistakes stem from 1226b1 perception and action, and if they investigate *that* they will go on *ad infinitum*.

So, given that decision is neither opinion nor wish individually, nor both together (for no one decides all of a sudden, but people do seem to act and wish that way), it therefore is from both, for both of these belong to someone who decides. But it must be investigated how it is that decision is from these. In a way the name itself indicates it. For decision is a choice, though not

---

(b) *dêloi* here is not 'shows' but an example of *dêloun* in a different use, i.e., 'it is clear that [the subject] is doing [whatever it is]': thus Woods 1979, 'a man evidently always chooses something, and chooses for the sake of something' – which actually (although Woods acknowledges no changes here to the Walzer/Mingay text, which he is generally following) anticipates, and accurately translates, the text I print.

without qualification, but of one thing before another. And this is not possible without investigation and judgement. This is why decision is from deliberative opinion.

Now no one deliberates about the goal, which is, rather, laid down for all, but people do deliberate about the things that bear on it, whether this or that is conducive, or, once a decision a judgement has been reached, how this will be. And we all deliberate about this until we refer to ourselves the origin of coming into being. Thus if no one decides without preparation or deliberation b15 about whether something is worse or better, and one deliberates about these things that are up to us among the things that contribute to the given goal, which are things that can be and not be, then clearly decision is a deliberative desire for things that are up to oneself. For we wish for all the things that we decide on, although we do not decide on all the things we wish for. By 'deliberative' I mean that whose origin b20 and cause is deliberation; one desires because of having deliberated. For this reason there is decision neither in the other animals, nor at every age, nor in a human being who is in just any condition. For neither is deliberating, nor supposition about the reason why. Many may well form the opinion that something should or should not 1226b25 be done, but not so with the opinion being formed through reasoning.

For it is the part of the soul that grasps a certain kind of cause that is deliberative. For the cause for the sake of which is one of the kinds of causes, for the reason why is a cause. For example, the cause of walking is collecting money, if the person walks for the sake of that. This is why those for whom no aim is laid down b30 are not deliberators. Now if someone does or refrains from doing something that is up to them to do or not to do, and does so of one's own accord and not because of ignorance, then they voluntarily act or refrain from acting. But we do many things of this kind without having deliberated or having engaged in forethought. It is necessary, therefore, that every object of decision is voluntary, while the voluntary is b35 not the object of decision, and that everything that stems from decision is voluntary, whereas not everything that is voluntary stems from decision. At the same time it is also clear from these considerations that legislators do well in distinguishing, among bad conditions that come about, those that are voluntary, those that are counter-voluntary, and those that depend on forethought. 1227a1 For even if they are not completely precise, nonetheless they latch on to the truth to some extent. We will discuss these things in the investigation about justice. But as for decision, it is clear that it is neither without qualification wish nor opinion, but opinion and desire together, whenever a5 they arise as a conclusion from deliberating.

Given that anyone deliberating always deliberates for the sake of something, and there is always an aim for the deliberator in relation to which they examine that which is conducive, no one deliberates about the goal, but it is a principle and postulate [*hypothesis*], just like the postulates in the reflective forms of knowledge. (These things a10 have been discussed briefly at the beginning, and with precision in the *Analytics*.) Everyone's inquiry, whether with or without specialised skill, is about those things that promote the goal; for example, whether or not to go to war, this is a topic for those who deliberate. But that because of which, i.e. that for the sake of which, e.g. wealth, a15 pleasure, or some other such thing that may be the goal, will rather depend on something prior. For what a deliberator deliberates about, if they have considered things from the goal, is how to refer to themselves what conduces to the goal, or what they are capable of in relation to the goal.

By nature the goal is always good, as are also the things people deliberate about in particular cases, e.g. a doctor might deliberate about whether to give a20 a drug, or a general about where to set up camp. It is the unqualifiedly best goal that is the good in question for them. However, against nature and because of corruption the goal is not the good but the apparent good. The reason for this is that while some among existing things cannot be employed except in relation to what they naturally relate to (e.g. sight, for it is impossible to see something that is not a25 an object of sight, nor can one hear something that is not an object of hearing), it is possible, by contrast, to produce from an expertise something that is not an object of the expertise. For health and disease are not in the same way objects of the same expertise, but it stems from nature that the expertise is of health whereas it is of disease against nature. Likewise, wish by nature relates to the good, but against nature it also relates to the bad, and while by nature what one wishes for a30 is the good, against nature and because of corruption people also wish for the bad.

However, the destruction and corruption of each thing does not proceed into just anything, but into the opposites and what is intermediate. For it is impossible to depart from these, since even error does not come about into just anything, but into the opposites in the case of what has opposites, and into a35 those of the opposites that are the opposites in line with the relevant expertise. It is necessary, therefore, that both error and decision come about from the intermediate to the opposites. And it is the more and the less that are opposed to the intermediate. What causes this are the pleasant and the painful. For they are such that the pleasant appears good to the soul a40 and the more pleasant better, and the painful bad, and the more painful 1227b1 worse. So that it is clear also from these considerations that excellence and badness concern pleasures and pains. For as it turns out, they concern the objects of decision, and decision concerns the good, the bad, and the apparent good and bad, and pleasure and pain are by nature such.

b5 Given, then, that excellence of character is both an intermediacy and as a whole concerned with pleasures and pains, and that badness lies in excess and deficiency and concerns the same things as excellence, it is necessary that excellence of character is a state that decides on the intermediacy in relation to us in those pleasant and painful things with respect to which someone is said to have a certain quality **1227b1** of character, if they enjoy them or are pained by them, for someone who favours sweet or bitter flavours is not said to have a certain quality or character.

EE Book II, Chapter 11

Now that we have made these determinations, let us say whether excellence makes decisions unerring, i.e. whether it makes the goal correct, in such a way as to decide for the sake of what one should, or whether, as some think, it makes reason **b5** correct. But this is self-control; for it does not corrupt reason. However, excellence and self-control differ from one another. They must be discussed later, since this is the reason why some people think that excellence makes reason correct: self-control is of this kind, and it is one of the praiseworthy traits.

Let us discuss this after first testing a difficulty. For **1227b20** it is possible for one's aim to be correct, but to go wrong in those things that contribute to the aim; it is also possible for one's aim to be mistaken, but to be right about the things that promote that aim. And it is possible for neither to be correct. Does excellence produce the aim or the things that contribute to the aim? We affirm, then, that it produces the aim, because of this there is neither reasoning nor **b25** argument. Well, then, this is postulated just like a principle: for neither does a doctor consider whether or not one should be healthy, but whether or not one should take walks, nor does a trainer consider whether or not one should be in good bodily condition, but whether or not one should wrestle. Likewise no other expertise considers the goal. For just as the postulates are principles for the reflective forms of knowledge, so for the productive expertises **b30** the goal is a principle and a postulate: given that this person should be healthy, what must be in place if this is going to be, just as in the realm of the reflective realm, if the triangle is equivalent to two right angles, then such-and-such must be the case. The goal, then, is the origin of thinking, and the conclusion of thinking is the beginning of action.

If, therefore, the cause of all correctness is either reason or excellence, them, if it is not reason **1227a35**, it would be because of excellence that the goal is correct, but not the things that contribute to the goal. But it is the thing for the sake of which that is the goal. For every decision is of something and for the sake of something. Now, it is the intermediate that is the thing for the sake of which, whose cause is excellence, in that it decides for the sake of what one should. Decision is not of this, but of the things that are for its sake. Correctly identifying all those things that one should do for the sake of the goal 1228a1 is the task of another capacity. On the other hand, excellence is what causes the goal of the person's decision to be correct.

And because of this we discern what someone is like from their decision: that is to say, from what they act for the sake of, not from the action itself. And similarly, badness makes the person's decisions be for the sake of goals that are opposite. 1228a5 So if it is up to someone to do fine things and refrain from doing disgraceful things, but they do the opposite, then clearly this person is not in possession of excellence. As a result, both excellence and badness are necessarily voluntary. a9 For there is no necessity to do bad things. For these reasons badness is blameworthy, and a10 excellence praiseworthy. For people are not blamed for disgraceful and bad things that are counter-voluntary, nor are they praised for good things that are counter-voluntary, but for voluntary things. Furthermore, we praise and blame everyone with a view to their decisions rather than to their accomplishments, since people do bad things under compulsion too, without anybody's making a decision. Nevertheless, the activity of excellence is more choiceworthy. Furthermore, because it is not easy to see what someone's decision is like we are compelled to judge what the person is like from their accomplishments. The more choiceworthy thing, then, is the activity, but what is more praiseworthy is the decision. These are results of the things we have laid down, 1228a20 and furthermore they agree with the appearances.

EE Book III

EE Book III, Chapter 1

1228a24 That there are intermediates among the excellences,[1] then, that these have to do with decision, as are the opposing forms of badness, and what these are, has been said in general terms; now let us take each separately and talk about them in succession.

And first let us talk about courage. Practically everybody thinks that a person's courage has to do with fears, and that courage is one of the excellences. In our outline earlier we distinguished boldness and fear as opposites, and they do in a way lie in contrary quarters; so it is clear that those who are described in terms of these dispositions[2] will similarly lie in opposite quarters to each other, for example the cowardly person, for the description 'cowardly' relates to their fearing more than they should and having less confidence[3] than they should, and the bold one, because calling someone 'bold' tells us that they are such as to have less fear than they should and more confidence than they should. Hence the actual derivation of the description, i.e., its derivation from 'boldness'.[4] So that, since courage is the best disposition in relation to fears and when and when not to feel confidence, and one should neither do as the bold do, because they are defective in one respect and excessive in the other, nor as the cowardly do, because they do the same except not in relation to the same things but the opposite way round, being defective when it comes to confidence but excessive when it comes to fear, it is clear that the intermediate disposition between boldness and cowardice is courage, for this disposition is best.

1228b5 The courageous person is thought to be fearless for the most part while the cowardly one for the most part inclined to fear, fearing many things and few things[5] and big things and small ones, intensely and quickly, the

---

1 Aristotle puts it carefully: not all the excellences are intermediate, because the intellectual ones are not.
2 'Dispositions', *hexeis*, is used somewhat loosely here; if boldness is a disposition, fear is not; one has or does not have a disposition to fear.
3 I.e. being less bold; *tharrein*, the verb cognate with *thrasus*, 'bold', is to be properly confident, 'be of good heart' given the circumstances.
4 On the face of it this looks so obvious as not to need saying, but perhaps the point is that the description 'bold' brings with it just the connotation of confidence, without the qualifications (like the grounds for confidence or otherwise) that would be likely to surround the use of *thrasos*, 'boldness', or *tharrein* in a given context.
5 'Few' if they are big?

courageous the opposite, either not having fears at all or mild ones barely felt, on a few occasions and in relation to big things; and he puts up with things that are intensely fearful, his opposite not even with the mildly fearful.

b10 So what sort of things does the courageous put up with: first, is it things fearful to him or things fearful to someone else? If the latter, there would be nothing very interesting[6] about that, but if it is things fearful to himself, then big things would be fearful, and lots of them. Now fearful things are those that tend to create fear in the person to whom they are fearful, as for example if they are intensely fearful to him his fear is strong and if they are mildly so it is weak, in which case it turns out that **b24** the courageous person creates many great fears for himself.[7] But it seemed to us the opposite way round: courage seemed to put the person on the way to being fearless, and this seemed to lie in their fearing either nothing or few things, and then mildly and barely. But perhaps the fearful, like the pleasant and the good, is said in two ways. For some things are without qualification both good and pleasant, some for this or that particular person, not without qualification but rather the opposite, bad and not pleasant – all the things that benefit the bad, and that small children find pleasant just because of their age. **1228b23** Similarly, some fearful things are so without qualification, some for this or that person. Some of the things the cowardly person alone fears *qua* cowardly are fearful to no one, some mildly fearful. The things that are fearful to most people, and all those that are so to human nature – these are the things we say are fearful without qualification. The courageous person is fearless towards these, and puts up with such fearful things, which are in a way fearful to him but in a way not; insofar as he is a human being, they are fearful but insofar as he is courageous, they are either only mildly so or not at all. **1228b30** Nevertheless these things *are* fearful, for they are fearful to the majority of people. This is why the disposition, courage, is an object of praise, for the courageous person is like the strong and healthy one; it is not that the strong person is worn down by any sort of labour or the healthy person by any degree of excess, but rather that they are unqualifiedly unaffected or only mildly affected by the things that affect the many and the majority of people. The sickly, then, the weak, and the cowardly are affected somewhat by common afflictions, but more quickly and more severely than the many, but the healthy, the strong and the courageous are either wholly or mostly unaffected by the things that affect the many.

---

6 *Semnon*: 'grand'?
7 I.e., because he goes out to meet them. Walzer-Mingay's adoption of *phobeisthai*, 'fear' for *poieisthai*, 'make for oneself', is justified neither by the manuscripts nor by the argument.

1228b40 It is a puzzle whether there is actually nothing that is fearful to the courageous person, and whether **1229a1** they would actually feel fear. Or does nothing prevent it, in the way we have described? For courage is a following of reason. And reason commands that we choose the fine; which is why the person who puts up with fearful things without such reasons is either mad or rash, whereas the person who is fearless because of the fine alone is courageous. So the cowardly person fears the sorts of things he should not, the rash person is confident about the sorts of things he should not be confident about, while the courageous one does both things as they should be done, and in this way is intermediate, for whatever reason commands, these are the things he has confidence about or fears. And reason does not command one to put up with great, painful things that threaten our existence, unless that is the fine course of action. The rash person, then, has confidence even when reason does not command it, the cowardly even if it does, the courageous only when it does.

1229a12 There are five kinds of 'courage' so-called by way of similarity to it, for the people who display them put up with the same things, only not for the same reason. One is civic courage,[8] and this is the one that comes about from a sense of shame. **a14** Second is soldierly courage, born of experience and knowledge – not, as Socrates said, knowing what is properly to be feared,[9] but rather knowing by what means to help oneself out of such situations. Third is the 'courage' that comes about through inexperience and ignorance, and makes madmen put up with anything they come up against, and small children handle snakes. Another kind relates to expectation, which we find in people that have had many lucky escapes in the past – and in those under the influence of drink, for wine builds up one's expectations. Another kind arises through irrational passion, for example through love and temper.[10] For if someone is in love, they are rash rather than cowardly and will put up with many dangers, like the tyrannicide at Metapontum[11] and the one they tell stories about in Crete.

1229a25 And it is the same way with anger and temper/rage, for rage makes someone beside himself. This is why even wild boars are thought to be courageous, but they are not. For when they are beside themselves with rage, they are like this but when they are not they are as unpredictable as their rash human counterparts. Nevertheless, it is the 'courage' born of rage that is most natural to us, because rage is something indomitable. Hence the fact that young boys

---

8   I.e., citizen courage, that of the *politês*.
9   See Plato, *Laches* 684b.
10 I.e., *thumos*, now conventionally translated as 'spirit', but closely tied to anger and rage.
11 Antileon, killer of Archelaus of Heraclea, who had designs on his (Antileon's) beloved Hipparinus (the Cretan example following is presumably Theseus).

are best fighters. Civic 'courage', by contrast, is a product of law and custom. But in truth none of these five kinds is courage, although all are useful when it comes to exhortations in times of danger.

1229a34 So now we have spoken in general terms about what is fearful; but it is better to go into more detail. In general, then, it is the things that cause fear that are called fearful, and these are things that appear likely to cause life-threatening pain. People who are expecting some other pain will perhaps be affected by another pain, another affection but it will not be fear; for example if someone were to foresee that he was going to experience pain of the sort people suffer when they envy someone, or are jealous, or are humiliated; fear comes into the picture only in the face of pains that appear to be such that their nature is to be destructive of life. **1229b1** This is why certain people who are very soft are courageous about some things, while some who are hard and tough are also cowardly. Indeed it seems pretty much a special feature of courage to be in a certain way concerned with death and the pain surrounding death. Suppose that someone were such as to be reasonably tolerant of heat and cold when they posed no danger, but soft and fearful when it came to death for no other aspect of the process than the fact that it brings extinction, while another person was soft in relation to heat and cold but unaffected by the prospect of death: the former would be thought cowardly, the latter courageous. **1229b10** For we speak of danger only in the case of such sorts of things among things fearful, when what is likely to cause such extinction is close by; and it is when it appears close by that danger appears.

1229b14 So, as for the fearful things we say the courage of the courageous person properly has to do with, we have said that they are the ones that appear of the sort liable to be productive of life-destroying pain, when these appear close and not far off; they will be, or appear, on a scale that is proportionate to human beings; for necessarily there are some things that are fearful to each and every human being, and utterly disturb them For just as things can be so hot, or cold, or possess other such powers to affect us, on a scale that is beyond us and the dispositions of the human body, nothing prevents there from being things that are beyond the capacity of the affections relating to the soul.

1129b23 The cowardly and the rash, then, go wrong because of their dispositions, for to the cowardly what is not fearful seems fearful, and what is mildly fearful seems intensely so. but to the courageous person what seems is most of all what is true. This is why it is neither the case (a) that a person is courageous if they put up with fearful things through ignorance – for example if someone goes to meet a lightning storm because they are mad, nor (b) that they are courageous if they recognise how great the danger is but go on nevertheless, by reason of rage, as the Celts take up weapons and confront the waves of the sea. (And in general barbarian courage is accompanied by rage). And some put up with fearful things because of other pleasures – because rage, too, contains a certain element of pleasure, insofar as it goes along with an expectation of revenge. But all the same neither is it the case (c) that if because of this or some other pleasure someone puts up with the prospect of death, or indeed by way of avoiding other pains, any one of these would justly be called courageous. For if dying were a pleasant thing, the self-indulgent would be found dying in numbers out of lack of self-control, just as, even as things are, **1229b38** with dying itself not being pleasant, just some of the things that tend to cause it, lack of self-control does bring many to embrace it knowingly – of whom none would be thought courageous, even if they were wholly ready to die. Nor (d) if a person died in order to avoid suffering, which many do: **1230a1** no such person is courageous either, as Agathon agrees when he has his tragic character say 'It is the mean and low among mortal men that, /overcome with toil and suffering, / fall in love with death.' The poets tell the story of Chiron too, who prayed to die, despite being immortal, because of the agony from his wound.[12] Similarly with all those who put up with dangers because of their experience.[13] This is the manner in which practically the majority of military men put up with dangers. **a8** For it is the exact opposite of what Socrates used to think, namely that courage was knowledge. For the confidence of those who know how to climb safely up a ship's rigging comes not from knowing what is [truly] fearful but from knowing how to extricate themselves from the fearful situations involved. Nor is what makes people fight with greater confidence always courage, because if it were, then as the poet Theognis suggests, strength and wealth would be courage; 'Every man', he says, 'is in thrall to poverty'. Some that are plainly cowardly do sometimes put up with dangers in spite of it, because of experience, and this is because they do not think there is danger – they know how to help themselves away. And there is **1230a16** evidence of this, because when they do not think there is an escape-route and the fearful situation is upon them they do not stand and fight.

a18 But of all those motivated in these various different ways, it is those who stand firm out of a sense of shame that would most appear to be courageous. Think of Homer's description of Hector's stand against the peril of Achilles: 'But shame took hold of Hector: 'Polydamas will be the first to reproach me.'"[14]

---

12   This is Chiron the centaur, wounded by Heracles' arrows.
13   'Similarly with': i.e., they are not really courageous: an important point for Aristotle to drive home against (Plato's?) Socrates, which he duly does.
14   The second line is line 100 of Homer, *Iliad* Book XXII: it is the climax of what must surely rank as the greatest poem to survive from Greek antiquity. Interestingly, the other line

a23 And this is civic courage. But the true courage is neither this one nor any of the others; it is [*sc.* merely] similar to true courage, as is the 'courage' exhibited by wild animals, whose rage carries them forward to meet the strike [from the hunters]. For one must stay despite one's fear not because of the prospect of losing reputation, or because of anger, or because of not thinking one will die, because the resources available will be sufficiently capable of guarding against it, for this way one will not even suppose *anything* to be fearful. 1230a30 But since every excellence has to do with decision – and how we intend this, we have said before: it makes us choose everything *for the sake of* something, and this something is the that for the sake of which: the fine,[15] it is clear that courage, too, as an excellence, will cause its possessor to stand up to what is fearful in such a way that they will do so neither through ignorance, for it rather makes

---

Aristotle quotes is not in the texts of Homer available to us. But he is quoting from memory: As his general fondness for him (shown in part by the frequency with which he quotes him) attests, he knew his Homer as well as anyone.

[15] i.e., *to kalon*, 'the beautiful', which in the sphere of ethics translates into the fine and 'noble' ... Surely, but quite inconspicuously, Aristotle restates and reinforces two points that are utterly central to his ethics: that living the best life, which is the life of excellence, depends on our coming to understand what that best life is *for*, and remaining aware of that goal in everything we do. Some interpreters of Aristotle continue to suppose that the *Nicomachean Ethics* puts an intellectual, 'contemplative' life, perhaps what we would call a life of research, ahead of a truly ethical life (for a characteristically nuanced exploration of this type of view, see Broadie (unpublished). This is not intended as a teaser, nor do I think it is: I have found at least traces of the original paper, delivered first, I think, at Berkeley in 2014, on the worldwide web, and I somehow have the original full text, probably given to me by Sarah herself; I imagine others will have it too). But however we take the *NE*, and especially *NE* X, I can only say that there is absolutely no trace of such a view in the *EE* – with the single possible exception of the very last chapter, Book v, ch.3; but that chapter, along with v.1 and v.2, has in my view been radically misunderstood, at least partly because of the terrible state of the text in those three chapters. One of the chief contributions of my newly restored text will, I hope, have been to give new clarity to, and allow a full and proper appreciation of an aspect of Aristotelian thinking that has no parallel in, although it is closely connected with, other parts of the corpus. If v.3 ends with a plea that we recognise a 'theoretical' part of the human soul, this is not because the Eudemian Aristotle wants us to disappear into the library every day and concentrate on metaphysics or theology; rather, he is using another opportunity to drive home a message that he means to have come across from the very beginning of the work; namely that thinking, reflection, and in particular, philosophical reflection, on the nature of which he has so much to say in the opening Book of *EE*, is indispensable in our ordinary, daily lives. How will we live the best life – and who would want anything less than the best if we do not know what it is? Anyone with any sense will need to investigate; not research into metaphysics, then, or mathematics, or logic; nor even research into ethics; just good plain thinking about what it is all for. But first we, all of us, have to recognise it as a question we have to ask. – If all of this appears to undermine that apparently familiar Aristotelian distinction between the theoretical and the practical, no matter (I propose); that is a distinction that in any case speaks for itself if we need it.

them judge correctly, nor through pleasure, but because it is fine, since if it is not fine but rather insane they do not stand up to it, for that is something shameful.

1230a36 We have, then, said pretty well enough for our present approach about the kind of things in relation to which courage is an intermediate, and what it is intermediate between, and why, and what capacity fearful things possess.

EE Book III, Chapter 2

1230a38 Next it is moderation and self-indulgence or 'intemperance'[16] we must try to make distinctions about. People are said to be 'intemperate' in more ways than one, for there is both the person that has not yet been 'tempered' somehow, or cured, just as the person that has not been cut is uncut – [*sc.* which leaves it open whether he is just not yet cut or actually not cuttable]; and of these one will be capable of it, the other not.[17] For what is 'uncut' is either so because it is incapable of being cut or because while capable of being cut it has not been cut. **1230b3** It is the same way with the self-indulgent/not tempered, for that will include both what is not naturally ready to accept the process of tempering and what is so prepared by nature but has yet to go through the process in relation to the errors in the area in which the moderate person acts correctly, as in the case of children, for their 'intemperance' is of this sort.[18] **b7** In yet another way the hard to cure are 'uncured', and the altogether incurable through tempering.[19]

---

16 'Intemperance' would actually not be so bad a choice for *akolasia* in itself, given the historical associations of temperance in English – and that it includes the verb 'temper', with its connotations of treatment, thus bringing it somewhere close to the metaphor of 'curing' for punishment perhaps might seem a further advantage; but 'self-indulgence' captures the essence of the Greek term more simply: something that needs cutting back, certainly, (so, treatment: see n. 19 below), if not perhaps actual *kolasis*, 'punishment', insofar as other people, and society in general, are not obviously or necessarily affected by the disposition and actions of the types in question.

17 The Greek here is actually untranslatable into English: as other translators have seen, the point is better conveyed by changing the personal subject into a neuter but since they have taken that route, it is probably the more helpful option for a new translator to try to convey what Aristotle actually does with the Greek.

18 It cannot be said that this passage shows Aristotle at his best as a prose-writer, and the drawing out of the point is remarkably laborious, nonetheless it is made, by the end; the same cannot quite be said about the next part.

19 So how many types of *akolasia*, exactly, has Aristotle introduced? I take it, three, the main one being represented by, but not restricted to, children, the other two being those hard to 'cure' and those who turn out to be not just hard to 'cure' but actually beyond

b9 So now the point is made that self-indulgence is said in more ways than one, and it is clear both that all the self-indulgent types in question have to do with pleasures and pains, and that it is in their being disposed in a certain way towards these that they differ both from each other and from all other types of people. **1230b12** (We illustrated earlier in our sketch how we apply the term 'intemperance' metaphorically).[20]

1230b13 Those that are unmoved because of insensibility in relation to the same pleasures people call 'insensitive' or by some other such name, but this particular affective state is not so well recognised or **b16** widely shared, because everyone tends rather to go wrong in the other direction, and giving in to and being sensitive to pleasant things of the sort involved is something inborn in all of us. The sort of people we are talking about are most of all the rustic types comic playwrights put on the stage, who have no truck with enjoying pleasure even in ordinary and necessary things.

b21 But since the moderate person and moderation are all about pleasures, they are also necessarily all about a certain sort of appetites, and we must grasp which these are. For the moderate person is not moderate in relation to any and every appetite or in relation to any and every pleasant thing, but – or so people suppose, the objects of two of the senses, taste and touch; **b25** in truth, however, it is just one, namely touch. The moderate person is not moderate about the pleasure that comes from the sight of beautiful things, unless sexual activity is involved, or the pain of the sight of ugly ones, or the pleasures and pains of listening to harmonious music or cacophony, or again about those of smelling sweet or noisome odours; **1230b30** for neither is anyone said to be self-indulgent for being the sort to be affected or unaffected by them. At any rate if someone were gazing[21] at a beautiful statue, or a horse, or a beautiful human figure, or listening to a singer, without wanting to eat or drink or have sex but just to gaze at the beautiful and listen to the singers, they would

---

'curing' – that is, by punishment, *kolasis*, which the non-translation above has so far rendered with 'tempering', and Aristotle himself treats as a kind of medical treatment: thus making the self-indulgent/intemperate like inhabitants of an asylum for pleasure-addicts. The double metaphor hardly helps with the sense of the passage, but in the end does not irretrievably obscure it.

20   The aside is mysterious; no such metaphorical usage has been mentioned in the transmitted text, and from this it does rather look like an intrusion. Or is Aristotle referring to 1221a19–20, and slightly recasting 'Similarly, a self-indulgent person is the one who is characterised by appetite and goes to excess in every way possible'? That would perhaps be consistent with the immediate switch in the present context to a more precise account of the sphere of self-indulgence.

21   Here is one place where 'contemplating' might be appropriate for *theôrein*, there being nothing to the looking apart from the gazing itself, and, presumably, its prolongation.

not be thought self-indulgent any more than those charmed by the Sirens. Rather, moderation has to do with the two senses that alone have objects to which animals other than ourselves are sensitive and which give them pleasure or pain, namely taste and touch; in relation to the pleasures that come from the other senses practically all other animals **1231a1** are clearly equally insensitive, for example the pleasure of harmonious sound or visual beauty; for they are plainly unaffected to any extent worth noting by the looking itself, when they see beautiful things, or by the listening when they hear harmonious sounds, unless in some prodigious cases.[22] Nor are they affected by sweet or foul odours, despite the fact that all their senses, at least, are more acute than our own. When they do take pleasure in smells, the pleasures are coincidental, not enjoyed for themselves. By pleasures 'not enjoyed for themselves' I intend those that we enjoy through anticipation or through memory, for example of food or drink, for the pleasure in these cases comes from another source – not the smelling but the eating and the drinking. **1231a10** An example of pleasures that are 'enjoyed for themselves' will be those of flowers; Stratonicus[23] struck the right note when he said that some smells smell beautiful, some just delightful. But other animals are not excited by all the pleasures of taste, or of those sensed by the top of the tongue, but rather those sensed in the throat, and what happens to them seems to be a matter more of touch than of taste. This is why **1231a16** the glutton prays not for a long tongue but for the throat of a crane, as Philoxenus son of Eryxis[24] did. The outcome is that we should strictly speaking identify the sphere of self-indulgence with the objects of touch; and the self-indulgent person is similarly occupied by this sort of pleasures, all the parts or types into which the self-indulgent is divided, **a20** the drunkard, the gourmand, the glutton, the lecher and everything of that sort all being occupied with the pleasures we have specified; no one is labelled as self-indulgent if they go to excess in relation to the pleasures of sight or hearing or smell, and if we do criticise someone for errors in these respects we do so with no sense of reproach. This is our general approach to all those things in relation to which people are not called self-controlled; and the un-self-controlled are not self-indulgent any more than they are moderate.

1231a28 So the person that is of such a disposition as even to fall short in those things that everyone, if one speaks for the most part, must necessarily

---

22   The reference is to Orpheus, whose music – so the poets said – had the power to stir not only other animals but even Nature herself; the trees, the mountains and the rivers.
23   A fourth-century Athenian musician.
24   Eryxis, as a proper name (if it existed), would come out as 'Belch'; the Philoxenus in question may have been a real person, caricatured by one or more comic poets.

share in and enjoy is insensate, or whatever term one should use to describe them, while the one that goes to excess is self-indulgent. For everyone by nature both takes pleasure in the things in question and acquires appetites for them without being or being called self-indulgent, because they do not go to excess by enjoying them more than they should when they get them or by feeling more pain than they should when they fail to get them; but neither are they unaffected, because they are not defective when it comes to enjoyment or the feeling of pain, but rather tend to excess.

a36 But since there is excess and defect in these things, clearly there is also an intermediate, and this disposition is both best and opposite to both the other two. So if moderation is the best disposition in relation to which the self-indulgent person relates, the intermediate in relation to the pleasant things we have specified among the objects of the senses will be moderation, lying as an intermediate between self-indulgence and insensitivity; the excessive disposition will be self-indulgence, the defective either nameless or to be called by one of the names we have suggested. But we must make more precise distinctions about the kind of pleasures involved in the course of our later discussion of self-controlledness and un-self-controlledness.

EE Book III, Chapter 3

1231b5 In the same way we must inquire into mildness and bad-temperedness, for we see the mild person turning out to relate to the pain arising from rage, that is, by virtue of having a certain disposition towards this. We included him in our sketch, and over against the irascible, the bad-tempered and the savage,[25] for all such things belong to the same disposition, we located the slavish and the stupid, for **b10** these are pretty much the terms people use for those who are not moved to rage even where they should be, but are content to be treated insultingly and are submissive in the face of slights. For to the quick is opposed the barely, to the quietly the intensely, and to being subject to this painful affection we call rage for a long time, a capacity to get over it. **1231b15** And since there are excess and defect here, as we said there were in the other cases – for the bad-tempered is the sort that feels anger too quickly, too much, for too long a time, towards the sort of people they should not feel

---

25   The *agrios*; cf. the wild boar (1229a26), known for the intensity of its rage against the hunter; so more, used independently, than merely 'wild' (this will be important for a later context (v.3, 1249a1).

it, and towards many,[26] while the slavish individual is the opposite way round, **1231b20** it is clear that there is also someone intermediate to this unequal distribution between too much and too little. Since, then, both the dispositions in question are in error, it is plain that the disposition intermediate between them is fitting, for such a person is neither too quick nor too slow with their response, nor do they get angry with the people they should not or fail to get angry with those they should. So, since mildness too is the best disposition in relation to these affective states, **b25** mildness too will be an intermediate, and the moderate individual too, between the bad-tempered and the slavish.

EE Book III, Chapter 4

1231b27 And great-souledness and magnificence and open-handedness are intermediates too, and open-handedness in relation to the acquisition and expenditure of money. For the person that takes more pleasure than they should in every acquisition and feels more pain than they should at every expenditure is avaricious, the one that does both less than they should is wasteful, and the one that does both as they should is open-handed. When I say this 'as they should' in these cases and in all the rest, I intend 'in accordance with the correct reasoning'. Since the avaricious and the wasteful lie respectively in excess and defect, and where there are extremes there is also **1231b35** a middle, and this is best, and one thing alone in relation to each kind of thing, it follows necessarily that open-handedness is an intermediate between wastefulness and avariciousness in relation to the acquisition and expenditure of money. We speak of money in two different ways of money and money-making, one being use a possession for what it is, for example a shoe or a cloak, the other a coincidental use – not coincidental in the sense in which one might use the shoe as a weight but rather selling it or hiring it out, which is a use of it *as* a shoe. The money-lover is the person that has devoted himself to the very thing, money, itself,[27] and money in this case is a matter of possession instead of coincidental use, whereas the avaricious person can also be wasteful in relation to the coincidental way of money-making, because what he pursues is

---

26 The thought, perhaps, is that rage and anger are properly or typically directed towards individuals rather than towards a group, or perhaps society in general; in any case 'many' here = too many.
27 'Money' here is *nomisma*, the primary reference of which would be to actual coinage; 'money-lover' is literally 'lover of silver'.

increasing his wealth though money-making as it is by nature.[28] The wasteful person goes short even of necessities, while the open-handed one gives away his surplus. **1232a10** There are different kinds of these that are talked about, excessive or deficient in relation to different parts of the sphere in question: for example an avaricious person may be parsimonious and a skinflint and a sordid profiteer, parsimonious when it comes to not letting money go, a profiteer in not caring about the source of any addition to his wealth, a skinflint because he exercises himself greatly about small expenditures, and if the unjust person is avaricious he is a fraudster and a cheat. **1232a15** Similarly, among the wasteful we can distinguish the indulgent squanderer by his disorganised spending, and the non-reckoner who will not put up with the pain and trouble of keeping accounts.

EE Book III, Chapter 5

1232a19 When it comes to great-souledness,[29] we must define what is specific to it from the attributes ascribed to the great-souled individual. There are cases where dispositions are so close and similar to each other, up to a certain point, that things escape us as they go forward, and it happens with great-souledness as it happens in other cases. It is why sometimes opposites lay claim to the same thing, as for example the wasteful person claims to be open-handed, the self-centred to be dignified and venerable, and the rash to be courageous; **1232a25** for they relate to the same things and to a certain point are neighbours, just as the courageous person is the sort to put up with dangers, as is the rash one, except that one does it *this* way, that one *that* way, which differ to a very considerable degree. The great-souled person, according to the name we give them, we identify as having a certain greatness of soul and of capacity, so that they seem to resemble the dignified and venerable and the munificent.

---

28 I.e., perhaps, broadly speaking, money-making as, e.g., a farmer does by using his land and other natural resources (for what they are), rather than by using property/money to make money (cf. the somewhat more helpful discussion of the distinction between 'unnatural' and 'natural' money-making in *Politics* I.10).

29 Kenny 2011 helpfully suggests 'pride', i.e., proper pride, as it must be, since it is an excellence; as a translation, however, the negative of connotations of pride in English make it less useful than the admittedly unwieldy 'great-souledness', which has the particular advantage of reminding us that we are dealing with what Aristotle regards as a kind of super-excellence ('an adornment [*kosmos*], as it were, of the excellences, because it augments them, and does not occur without them', *NE* IV.3, 1124a1–3). The present Eudemian chapter comes not so far from according it a similar status in 1232b24–8.

a31 Again, great-souledness also appears to accompany all the excellences, for judging between great and small goods is something praiseworthy, and the ones that are thought great are the ones pursued by the person with the disposition that is supreme in such matters, which is great-souledness. But the excellence in each sphere judges too much and too little in that sphere correctly, following the prescriptions the wise person and their excellence would give, **1232a37** with the result that all the excellences go with this one, or else it goes with them all. Again, people think it belongs to the great-souled person to be disdainful, and each excellence makes its possessor disdainful of things treated as great in its sphere, **1232b1** for example courage in the case of dangers, for thinking something great, here, he treats as something disgraceful, not all things on a large scale being properly to be feared, and the moderate person similarly disdains great and numerous pleasures while the open-handed disdains wealth. This is thought to belong to the great-souled individual because there are few things that exercise him, and if they do exercise him, they are things of importance, to him and not what someone else thinks so. A great-souled man will be more concerned about what one good person thinks than what appears to a crowd of people who chance along, as Antiphon[30] after his condemnation said to Agathon for having praised his defence speech. And it is the **b10** disdain that seems the most specific trait characteristic of the great-souled. Again, about things like honour, about living, about wealth, the things humanity in general seems to occupy itself, the only one they are thought to pay attention to is honour: they would be pained by dishonour and by being ruled over by someone unworthy and get the most pleasure from receiving honour. **1232b15** Looked at in this way, the great-souled person would seem in contradiction with himself, for to be most of all about honour, and disdainful of the many and of what they think, seem not to go together. Here we must make some distinctions: honour, great or small, is of two different kinds, depending on whether it is bestowed by a large random group or by people worthy of note; and it also makes a difference what the honour is for, **b20** for the greatness of the honour is not measured by the number of those bestowing it or their quality alone but by its being itself honourable. In truth, public offices and the other goods are honourable and worth pursuing only when they are truly great, **b24** so that there is no excellence, either, without greatness[31] – which is why each of them seems to make its possessor great-souled in relation to those things that constitute its own particular sphere, as we said. But **b26** nevertheless, alongside all the other

---

30 An Athenian politician and orator, executed after the restoration of democracy for his part in the establishment of the oligarchy of the Four Hundred in 411 BCE.
31 That is, because the excellences themselves are goods?

excellences, there is a singular great-souledness, just as we must specifically identify the person who has this as great-souled. But since among goods some are honourable and some are not, and among honourable goods some are truly great and some truly small, and some people both are worthy of the truly great ones and think themselves worthy of them, it is among these that we should seek out the great-souled individual. **b32** There will necessarily be four different sorts of case here: where someone is worthy of great things and thinks himself worthy of them, where the things in question are small, and the person both is is worthy of things on that scale and thinks himself so, and either of these cases can be reversed, so that there will be someone so disposed as to think himself worthy of great goods from among the honourable ones when he is actually only worthy of small ones, while someone worthy of great things will think himself worthy of small ones. The person that is worthy of small things but thinks himself worthy of great ones is blameworthy, for it is stupid, not fine, to get things one is unworthy of; and blameworthy too is the person who is worthy of what he actually has but does not think himself worth his **1233a1** share in such things. There remains, here, the person that behaves in the opposite way to both of these: being worthy of great things he thinks himself worthy of them, and he is such as to think of himself so. This is the praiseworthy one, and he is in the middle between the other two. Thus since great-souledness is the best disposition in relation to choosing and using honour and the other honourable goods, and this is how we define great-souledness, and not in relation to what is useful, and at the same time this intermediate disposition is most praiseworthy, it is clear that great-souledness too will be an intermediate. **a8** Of the opposites, as in our sketch one is conceitedness, which tends towards thinking oneself worthy of great goods when one is not – the sort of people we call conceited are precisely those that think themselves worthy of great things when they are not, while the opposite that has to do with being worthy of great things but not thinking oneself so is little-souledness; if someone has the very things that would allow him justly to be thought worthy and yet thinks himself worthy of nothing great, that seems to belong to a little-souled person. **1323a14** Necessarily, then, great-souledness too is an intermediate, in between conceitedness and little-souledness. As for the fourth of the different cases we distinguished, he is neither entirely blameworthy nor is he great-souled, having no greatness about him at all – neither being worthy of great things nor thinking himself so. Hence, he is not an opposite type to the great-souled. One might suppose that being worthy of little things and thinking oneself worthy of them would be the opposite of being worthy of great things and thinking oneself worthy of *them*, but the type with this disposition is not opposed to the great-souled even by being deserving of blame, since he is as reason commands; indeed he is by nature identical to the great-souled, given that both of them think themselves worthy of the things they are actually worthy of – and he might even become great-souled, since he will think himself worthy of what he deserves, whereas the little-souled individual, who **a25** when he actually has great and honourable goods thinks himself unworthy of them – what would he say if he were only worthy of small ones? Either he would be conceited, thinking he deserved great things, or he would think he deserved even smaller ones. **1323a27** Hence, too, no one would call it little-souledness if a resident alien[32] does not think himself worthy of holding public office and gives way to others, but would do if it was someone from a good family who thought it a great thing to hold public office.

EE Book III, Chapter 6

1233a30 And the sphere of the magnificent person, too, is not any chance sort of action or decision but has specifically to do with outlay, unless perhaps we are talking metaphorically; unless outlay is involved it has nothing to do with magnificence. What is fitting[33] in this case has to do with adornment, and adornment is not a matter of any ordinary, day-to-day, expenditure but rather expenditure that exceeds **1233a35** what is strictly necessary. The person, then, that characteristically chooses the fitting scale and this sort of intermediate when great expenditure is involved, and desires this sort of pleasure, is magnificent. The type that goes too far and spends unsuitably has no name[34] but has a certain **1233b1** proximity to those we call tasteless and show-offs. **1233b1** But suppose that some rich person is paying for the wedding of his beloved and it seems to him fitting for someone like himself to make the same kind of provision as he would for hangers-on at a feast, such a person will be shabby, whereas if someone does it the other way round, entertaining hangers-on as if they were at a wedding resembles the show-off, unless he is doing it to enhance his reputation or by way of gaining public office; the magnificent type is the one who treats the occasion as it worthy to be treated, and as reason dictates.

---

32 Incidentally, Aristotle's own status in Athens.
33 Aristotle is doing more etymology: the 'fitting', *prepon*, is the *prep-* part of *megalo-prepeia*.
34 In Book II, this extreme did have a name, *dapanêria* ('obsession with spending', 'extravagance' (1221a10), perhaps coined there for the occasion (if the *dapanêros* 'has no name', i.e. in common use) and now abandoned.

For what is fitting is what is according to worth;[35] nothing that ignores the worth of a thing is fitting, and the expenditure should be fitting – for what is fitting is according to worth and what is according to worth is fitting – both fitting in relation to the occasion, as for example what befits the wedding of a household slave is different from what befits that of a beloved, and fitting for the agent himself, whether in quantity or quality – as for example people thought the spectacle Themistocles put on for the audience at the Olympic games **1233b13** was unfitting for him, because of his inherited meanness of status,[36] whereas it would have befitted a Cimon.[37] But then there is the person who is indifferent to questions of worth, which none of the above is; and similarly with open-handedness, for there is a certain type of person that is neither open-handed nor avaricious.[38]

EE Book III, Chapter 7

1233b15 Speaking in broad terms, with all the remaining praiseworthy and blameworthy aspects of character too, some fall into the category of excess, some into that of deficiency, while others are intermediate affective states: there is the envious person, for example, and the one characterised by *Schadenfreude*, for we recognise their dispositions, the one a matter of being distressed when people who deserve it do well, while the other's state as such has no specific name, but he is easily identified by the pleasure he takes at undeserved misfortunes. Intermediate between these is the righteously indignant, and what the ancients used to call **1233b25** Nemesis,[39] which is a matter of being distressed when things go badly or well for others if it is undeserved and being delighted

---

35   *Axia*, 'value', what a thing is (truly) worth.
36   The reference is apparently to his mother's side of the family, which was non-Athenian; that, it seems, would be enough to trump all his success as a general and naval commander.
37   Another distinguished Athenian military leader, but of noble, and wealthy, family on both sides.
38   I suppose this to refer to the 'wasteful' person (1221a5), whose behaviour exhibits a similar indifference to any proper criteria for expenditure.
39   I.e., personified and treated as a goddess (b27), a part, as it were, of the nature of things as it/she still is for Aristotle's contemporaries ('people think …'); the capitalisation, 'Nemesis', in b25 is supplied in the translation; there is no capitalisation of any kind in the transmitted text. Aristotle noticeably makes no commitment on the status of nemesis/Nemesis; he will have other, more interesting roles to introduce for 'god', and for divinity in general, in *EE* V.

if it is deserved. This is why people even think of Nemesis as a god.[40] Modesty is an intermediate between shamelessness and bashfulness: if someone does not care at all about what anyone thinks about them they are shameless, while caring equally about one's reputation with anybody and everybody is bashful; being modest is caring about one's standing with people that stand out as respectable. **1233b31** Friendliness is an intermediate between surliness[41] and sycophancy: if someone falls in readily with others' appetites when in company they are a sycophant, if they resist them all they are surly; what is friendly is neither to go along with nor to resist every pleasure proposed but to respond as seems best under the circumstances. **b35** Dignity is an intermediate between obsequiousness and self-centredness: someone that lives with no regard but only contempt for another is self-centred; someone that defers to another in everything or else submissive to everyone is obsequious; the person of dignity is the one that defers in some things, not in others, and when they do defer, defers to people worth deferring to. The truthful, uncomplicated sort people call 'blunt' is intermediate between the dissembler and the **1234a1** impostor: the dissembler knowingly belittles himself,[42] the impostor knowingly builds himself up, while the truthful sort is the sort that presents himself as he actually is – Homer's 'sound'[43] man, in general a lover of truth as opposed to the lover of falsehood. Conviviality[44] is an intermediate too, the witty person being intermediate between the humourless boor and the scurrilous buffoon. **a6** For just as the fastidious eater differs from the glutton, the one taking nothing or just a little, and not even enjoying that, the other taking everything as it comes and enjoying it all, so the boor is, too, in relation to the vulgar buffoon, taking a joke, if he takes it all, **a10** without any pleasure, while the buffoon takes in anything and everything and enjoys it equally; neither of which is as it should

---

40   I.e. because they suppose that there is, or should be, a natural match between desert and reward, and that we inhabit a world governed by gods?
41   *Echthra*, it was a cognate, *apechtheia*, back in Book II (1221a7).
42   The archetypal *eirôn* is Socrates, accused of *eirôneia*, for example, by Thrasymachus in Book I of Plato's *Republic*; but the accusation, so far as Plato is concerned, is false, and Aristotle, too, if he does have Socrates in mind in the present context, is doing no more than picking up Thrasymachus' caricature; otherwise he treats Socrates as a serious philosopher.
43   'Sound': *pepnumenos*, the epithet applied most commonly, e.g., to Telemachus, Odysseus' son, apparently marking his growth into adulthood; so 'sound', 'sensible', 'grown-up'.
44   I borrow this rendering from Kenny (2011: 162), who rightly insists, against the usual translation of *eutrapelia* as 'wittiness', that the excellence in question 'can be passive as well as active; the ability to take a joke no less than the ability to make one' [since Aristotle spells out the point at length in a14–21, 'wittiness' for *eutrapelia* here was always a bad choice, however appropriate it may be in non-Aristotelian contexts].

be, which is to accept some things as humorous and not others, according to reason, and the convivial person is the one that does this. **a12** The proof of it is the same: conviviality of this sort (and not the sort we call conviviality by extension)[45] is the most respectable[46] disposition, and it is the intermediate that is praiseworthy and the extremes that are blameworthy. – **a14** But there are two sorts of conviviality, one of which consists in enjoying a joke, perhaps a tease, if it is genuinely amusing, even when it is directed at oneself, while the other is the capacity to do the joking oneself. The two sorts are different from one another, but both are intermediates; for the person with the capacity for making jokes **1234a20** that will give pleasure to a person of good judgement, even when they are on him, will be intermediate between the vulgar and the humourless. This is a better way of defining the intermediate in this case than requiring that what is said should not cause distress to the butt of the joke, whatever his status; it should rather please someone who is himself in the middle, for he is the one with good judgement.

1234a25 All these intermediates are praiseworthy, but they are not excellences, and neither are there forms of badness in opposition to them, since none of them involves decision. All these things do nevertheless appear in divisions of the affective states, because each of them is a certain sort of affective state. Because of their being natural to us, they contribute towards the natural excellences. **1234a29** For, as will be said in what follows,[47] each excellence both occurs in us in a way naturally, and in another way when it is combined with wisdom. While envy contributes towards injustice, because the actions it engenders affect others, righteous indignation contributes towards justice. So too does modesty to moderation, which is why people actually do locate moderation in this kind; the lover of truth and the lover of falsehood count respectively as sensible and foolish.[48]

1234b1 The middle is more opposed to the extremes than the extremes are to each other, because it never occurs with either of them but they are often found with each other; for example, sometimes the same people combine

---

45 Perhaps just a general, undefined ability to shine in a social context?
46 The use of the superlative of *epieikês* here rather than a straightforward 'best' has the effect, I think, of reducing the status of conviviality, as a praiseworthy quality, by comparison with others; we need it because we are social beings, but it is not itself one of the excellences, and neither, as it turns out, are the other qualities being discussed here (1234a25–6).
47 'The later discussion is in v.13, 1141b1–17' (Kenny 2011: 162), i.e., in the fifth book of an eight-book *EE* with the 'common books' included; alternatively (since 'the problem of the 'CB'' is not resolved), it might have been a different discussion, now lost.
48 I.e., *emphrôn* and *aphrôn*: so, in effect, with and without *phronêsis* (a30–31)?

rashness with cowardice, and wasteful in some things but avaricious in others, and generally **b5** they tend to be inconsistent in a bad way; for when they are inconsistent in a good way they turn into the middle types, because in a way the extremes are contained in the middle. The oppositions between the two extremes and the middle do not seem both to be the same; sometimes it is greater on the side of excess, sometimes on that of defect. The causes are threefold: firstly the two we mentioned earlier, **b10** the rarity of one extreme, for example insensitivity to pleasant things, and the fact that if we are more prone to one extreme it makes it feel more opposed to the middle, the third being that what is more alike seems less contrary, as for example in the case of rashness in relation to confidence and wastefulness in relation to open-handedness.

1234b15 So now we have pretty well discussed the remaining excellences that belong among praiseworthy things.[49]

---

49 Not 'the other praiseworthy virtues' (Kenny, e.g.), since presumably there are no excellences that fail to be praiseworthy; the phrasing is in recognition of the fact that we have just been discussing praiseworthy things that are not excellences (1234a25–6). 'The remaining excellences': the big item that is missing, and an immediate discussion of which is now announced in some manuscripts, is of course justice; but I note (a) that Aristotle's main interest, in talking about the different excellences in the preceding chapters, has been in showing them to be intermediates; (b) that the intermediacy of the *dikaion*, the just, between 'profit' and 'loss', as originally introduced in 1221a4, is of a strikingly limited kind; and (c) that the full treatment of justice in *NE* V itself struggles to make it an intermediate between two opposing extremes. In short, I am inclined to wonder whether the omission of justice (and others?) – acknowledged by that 'pretty well', *schedon*, is actually of much significance for Aristotle's own argument.

EE Book IV

EE Book IV, Chapter 1

1234b18 We must investigate friendship[1] no less than any of the fine and desirable things relating to the affective states: what is friendship, and what are its attributes? What is a friend? Is 'friendship' used in a single sense only, or in many senses, and **b20** if in many senses, how many kinds of friendship are there? And further: how should one treat a friend? How does justice relate to friendship?[2] For it is thought to be a task above all for the statesman's art to create friendship,[3] and people say that excellence is useful for this reason, that it is impossible for people to be **1234b25** friends if they are being wronged by each other. Furthermore we all say that that the just and the unjust have to do most of all with our friends.[4] Again, it is the same man that is thought to be both good and a friend,[5] and love or friendship[6] to be a disposition of character, so that if one wants to ensure that someone does not wrong them, it will suffice to make them one's friend; for true friends do not wrong one another. But then neither will they if they are just; **1234b31** in which case justice is either the same thing as friendship or something close to it. Over and above all this, we take the friend to be one of the greatest goods, and friendlessness and solitude something particularly to be feared, because it is with friends that we pass our whole lives, and to friends that we volunteer our company; **1235a2** for we spend our days with those that belong to us, whether our relatives or our companions. Our private compacts with our friends are up to us alone, whereas our relationships with others are laid down in law and not up to us.

1235a5 There are many problems raised about friendship, for example by way of people's bringing in extraneous matter and extending 'friendship' beyond its natural limits. For some suppose that like is friend to like; hence Homer's line[7] 'To like god ever brings like', and the sayings 'Jackdaw to jackdaw

---

1 Or 'love', *philia* (thought of as an ethical disposition, 1234b28); 'friends' in this context may include family and 'loved ones' in general as well as friends in the usual sense, but the emphasis is overall on the social context, as an essential part of the good life.
2 'What are the claims of friendship?', Kenny 2011, helpfully.
3 So, for example, in Plato's dialogue *Statesman*.
4 'Friends' here are perhaps to be understood in the widest sense, including society at large.
5 I.e., if someone exhibits the excellences, we think of him as a friend/someone to be embraced as such?
6 Just *philia* in the Greek.
7 *Odyssey* XVII.218.

'and 'A thief knows a thief, a wolf a wolf'. The natural philosophers even order the whole cosmos taking it as a starting-point that like tends to like; compare **1235a12** Empedocles' explanation of why the dog always sleeps on the same tile ('because there is the most resemblance between them'). So some people talk of the friend[8] this way, but others claim that it is the opposite that is friend to opposite. **1235a15** For – so they say – it is what is loved and desired that is dear as friend, and the dry does not desire the dry but the wet: hence the line 'Earth sighs for rain', and 'Of all things change is sweet', change being to the opposite, whereas like is hateful to like, because 'Potter with potter is never at one', and animals that rely on the same food are natural enemies.[9] So far apart are these conceptions of friendship, the one claiming that like is friend, opposite enemy, 'For the less is always enemy of the greater, and begins the dawn of hatred',[10] and again, opposites/opponents are even located separately, while friendship is thought to bring things together; **1235a25** but for the others it is opposites that are friends, and Heraclitus rebukes the poet for the line 'Perish all strife from the world of gods and men',[11] for there would be no harmony if there were not both high and low notes, nor animals without the opposites male and female. These, then, are two views about friendship, on too general a level and so far apart from each other; **1235a30** but there are others that are closer to each other and akin to the appearances, for some people think it impossible for the bad to be friends, and only possible for the good, while others think it strange if mothers fail to love their children, and there is clearly such love even among wild animals, **a35** since they choose to die for their offspring. Others think it is only the useful that is loved, offering as evidence that it is the useful that everyone actually pursues, while throwing away anything of theirs that is useless, as the old Socrates used to say,[12] citing spittle, hair, and nails as example, **1235b1** and that we get rid of whole body-parts if they become useless, and finally the whole body when it does, since the corpse is useless, except that those who do have a use for it, like the Egyptians, preserve it. Now all these considerations seem at odds with one another, for the like is of no use to what it is like, and contrariety is at the furthest distance from likeness, an opposite being as useless as it could be to its opposite, as something that tends even to destroy it. Again, some people think acquiring a friend an easy matter,

---

8 Here neuter, *to philon*; the principle of friendship?
9 An interesting collection of folk wisdom, some sourced from poetry (Euripides, Hesiod).
10 Euripides, *Phoenissae* 539–40.
11 Homer, *Iliad* XVIII, 107.
12 Aristotle for once seems to be using Xenophon (*Memorabilia* I.2, 53–4) as his source for Socrates rather than Plato.

while others suppose that recognising one is a rare event, and does not happen unless one is in misfortune: everyone, after all, wants to be thought a friend to people that are doing well; and still others think one should not trust even someone that stands by them in misfortune, but rather treat them as deceitful, pretending to be friends and offering their company in adversity in order to claim friendship when good fortune returns.

EE Book IV, Chapter 2

1235b14 What we need is to discover an account of friendship that will simultaneously represent what people think about it and resolve the problems and the contradictions between the differing views,[13] and that will come about if these views can be shown to be reasonable, for then our account will be most in accord with the appearances. **1235b18** In the outcome, the contradictions will remain if what is being said is in one way true, in another way not.

b19 One particular problem is whether what is loved in a friend is the pleasant or the good.

For if we love what we have an appetite for, which is most of all the case with erotic love ('No lover he who e'er ceased to love'),[14] and appetite is for the pleasant, then this way what is loved is the pleasant, but if it is what we wish for, then it is the good, and the pleasant and the good are not the same thing.

1235b25 On these matters and the others related to them we must make some distinctions, taking the following as our starting-point: what is desired and wished for is either the good or the apparent good; this is why the pleasant too is something desirable, namely because it is something that appears good: some people think it is good, while to others it appears so even if they don't think it is;[15] for appearance and judgement are not in the same [*sc.* part] of the soul. But that both the good and the pleasant are loved is clear enough.

1235b31 With these distinctions clear, we must make another assumption. Of goods, some are good without qualification[16] and some are good for someone in particular but not without qualification; and the same things are good without qualification and pleasant without qualification. For we say that the things that are beneficial for a healthy body are good **1235b35** for the body without qualification, while those that are beneficial to a sick body, like medications

---

13 See I.6, 1216b27–36.
14 Euripides, *Troades* 1051.
15 As in the case of the un-self-controlled, the acratic.
16 *Haplôs*: 'in the abstract', Kenny 2011.

and surgery, are not, and similarly what is pleasant to a body without qualification is what is pleasant to a body that is healthy and complete, like looking at things in the light rather than the dark, when for someone with ophthalmia it is the other way round. The wine that is more pleasant is not the one that is more pleasant to the person whose palate has been ruined by habitual drunkenness, because he will even **1236a1** add vinegar to the wine, but rather the one that is more pleasant to the person with an uncorrupted sense of taste. And as it is in the case of the body, so it is with the soul: what is pleasant without qualification is not what is pleasant to small children or wild animals but what is so to mature adults; at any rate it is those pleasures that we prefer over the others when we compare them in memory. **a4** As a child or a wild animal is to a mature human being, so the bad and unwise individual is to the decent and wise one, and the things that are pleasant to the latter are those that accord with his dispositions, **a6** namely those things that are good and fine.

Since, then, good things are said to be good in more than one sense, for we call one thing good in virtue of the sort of thing it is and another thing good because it is helpful and useful, **a10** and since what is pleasant is either pleasant without qualification and good without qualification or pleasant for a particular person and only an apparent good, just as in the case of inanimate things we can choose something and love it for any of these reasons, so we can a human being: **1236a13** this person we will choose because of his being of such and such a sort, and because of excellence, that one because he is helpful and useful, and yet another because he is pleasant, and for the pleasure he affords. **a15** And someone becomes a friend when he is loved and loves in return, and both of the two are fully aware of the reciprocity between them.

1236a17 Necessarily, then, there are three kinds of friendship, and neither are they called so by virtue of a single feature, nor are they species of a single genus, nor yet are they all called friendships by pure equivocation.[17] They are rather called friendships in virtue of their relation to a single kind of friendship, which is primary; it is as with the term 'medical', which we apply to a soul, a body,[18] an instrument, and a procedure, but which properly belongs to what is primarily so called, that being the thing whose definition is implicit in that of all the other cases, as for example a medical instrument is one a doctor would use, and the definition of the instrument is not implicit in the

---

17 Not *pampan homônumôs*; they do not just happen to be called by the same name, but there is a reason for it, of which we can give an account, in terms of 'focal meaning' (see Appendix 2).
18 The medical 'soul' and 'body' presumably together constitute the practising doctor, who applies his mind and skill to physical patients.

definition of the doctor.[19] **1236a24** In every case, then, people seek after what is primary, but because the universal is primary they also suppose that the primary is universal, which is not true. The result is that they are unable to do justice to the appearances in the case of friendship either, because when they find that one account fails to fit in all cases, they conclude that the others are not friendships – which they are, only in a different way, but the assumption that the primary must be universal makes people claim, when the primary one does not fit, that the other sorts are not friendships at all.[20] **1236a31** But there are many kinds of friendship: that was one of the things we already said, as soon as we distinguished three ways in which we talk about it, one being on the basis of excellence, one resting on the useful, the third on the pleasant. Of these the one based on the useful is the commonest, **a35** because it is their usefulness to each other, and just this, [*sc.* they say], that brings friendship, as in the proverbial 'Glaucus, a fellow-fighter is a friend just so long as he fights beside me', and 'The Megarians are no longer anything to the Athenians'.[21] The friendship based on the pleasant is typical of the young, for that is where their sensitivity lies; as their characters change, with their transition to adulthood, so too does what gives them pleasure. But the best people's friendships are based on excellence.

1236b2 From what we have just said it is clear that the primary friendship is a matter of reciprocal friendship and choice between people of excellence, for a thing that is loved is an object of love to the one loving it, but the person loved is a friend when they love the other back. **b5** This kind of friendship exists only among human beings, because only a human being is aware of choosing;[22] but the other kinds exist among wild animals too. Indeed, an element of utility exists between tame animals and humans, and between tame animals themselves, as in Herodotus' account the Egyptian plover is useful to the crocodile,[23] and as evidenced by the gatherings and dispersals of birds reported by seers. **1236b10** Even the bad will be friends, both on the basis of the useful and on that of the pleasant, whereas our opponents deny that they are friends because theirs is not the primary kind of friendship. If a person is

---

19 Sc. in the way that the definition of the doctor is implied in that of the medical instrument.
20 There is an unusual repetitiveness here (for the EE), perhaps reflecting the importance of the point, for Aristotle, against his opponents (the Platonists, in the first instance).
21 The first 'proverb' looks as if it comes from epic poetry; the second reflects a frequently changing relationship between two neighbouring cities.
22 I.e., presumably, of making a deliberate choice of someone/something for a particular reason; if non-human animals only 'choose' in that they will select if presented with multiple options.
23 See *Histories*, II.68.

bad, they say, he will wrong his bad counterpart, and people that are wronged by one another do not love each other. In fact they do; theirs is just not the primary friendship, because nothing prevents there being the other kinds of friendship between them; **b15** the pleasure they get from their relationship makes them put up with any harm they may do to each other, for so long as they are un-self-controlled.

b17 When people look into things with precision, not even those loving each other on the basis of pleasure seem to turn out to be friends, their friendship not being the primary kind, either, for that is a secure relationship, while one based on pleasure is insecure; but it *is* friendship, as we have said – not that primary friendship itself, but derived from it. **b20** To restrict the title 'friendship' to the primary kind is to do violence to the appearances and make paradoxes inevitable, but it is impossible to give a single account of them all; so the only remaining option is the one we have proposed, namely that in one way only the primary kind of friendship is friendship, but in another way they all are, not by mere homonymy, **1236b25** that is, a chance relationship to each other,[24] nor by being species of a single genus, but rather as being related to some one thing.

b27 Now since, unless something prevents it, the same thing is simultaneously good without qualification and pleasant without qualification, and the true friend, the friend without qualification, is the first one,[25] and such a one is choiceworthy, himself for himself – he must be such, for just as a person [*sc.* in this sort of friendship] wishes good things for [*sc.* the friend] because of the person he [*sc.* the friend] is, so he must choose him to be [*sc.* good and pleasant without qualification][26] – the true friend is also pleasant.[27] **1236b32** This is why a friend of any sort whatsoever is thought to be someone that brings pleasure. But again we must make a further distinction here, for it is a matter of dispute whether **1236b33** what is loved is what is good for oneself

---

24 The chance, that is, of their happening to share the same name.
25 I.e., a friend in the first kind of friendship (the 'first friend' of the *Lysis*, *to prôton philon* (*passim*) (see Penner and Rowe 2005), is something quite different – the final object of all desire, the real good; part of the background, then, to the EE as a whole, insofar as the treatise is about the final end of human life).
26 Not 'choose him to continue in being' (Kenny 2011; similarly Inwood and Woolf 2013), which would surely not be relevant to the argument in hand.
27 I take it that this serves as the main clause of the labyrinthine sentence that started at b27; the (usually connective) *de* is 'apodotic', i.e., introducing a main clause, not necessarily indicating that Aristotle has momentarily forgotten where he had got to, though that would be understandable, since such a *de* will often add emphasis; the conclusion is in any case the one we need.

or what is good without qualification, (and whether the activity of loving is accompanied by pleasure, so that the loveable too is something [*sc.* inherently] pleasant, or not).[28] The answer is that the two things must be brought into one, for it is both the case that things that are not good without qualification, and are even bad, should it so turn out, are to be avoided, and that what is not good for a particular individual is of no concern to him. Just this is what is looked for – that the things that are good without qualification should be good for the individual. **1237a1** For the good without qualification is choiceworthy, but what is choiceworthy to the individual is what is good for him, and the two things must be in harmony. This is what excellence brings about, and this too is the aim of the art of statesmanship, to bring about the coincidence in those in whom it has not yet come about. A human being is fitted and on the way [*sc.* towards that end] just *qua* human, for by nature things good without qualification are good for him [and similarly with a man rather than a woman and someone endowed with a good nature rather than one without];[29] and the way forward runs through pleasure, because what is required is that *fine* things should be pleasant; until the fine and the pleasant are in harmony, a person is not yet perfectly good, because room is left for the loss of self-control; for lack of self-control just is disharmony among the affective states between the good and the pleasant.

1237a10 So since the primary friendship is based on excellence, the friends in this case will also themselves be good without qualification. This is not because they are useful but in a different way, for the difference between what is good for a particular individual and what is good without qualification is twofold,[30] and it is with the dispositions as it is with the beneficial; for what is beneficial without qualification is different from what is beneficial for a particular individual, as for example training differs from medication **a15** – so too, then, with the disposition that is human excellence: let us suppose a human being to be

---

28   It is hard not to treat a35–6 'and whether ... or not' as a parenthesis; an afterthought, perhaps, giving an alternative reason why all friendship should involve pleasure; we certainly go straight back to the first matter for dispute, and the second (*pace* Kenny 2011) is left hanging.
29   The square brackets here mark a clear intrusion into the text (even the syntax is odd).
30   Kenny 2011 and others suppose that Aristotle is simply repeating the by now familiar point that good without qualification is not the same as good for x, but (a) this is to under-translate the formula *dichôs* (*sc. legetai*), which signals a difference of sense, not just difference; and (b) what Aristotle will spell out is actually two senses in which good for x contrasts with good without qualification: (i) useful for x as against useful without qualification, and (ii), in the context of ethical excellence, good for x as something that x aims for but is yet to be achieved, as against excellence understood as the completion of human nature without reference to any particular individual.

something that is by nature good, for the excellence of what is by nature good is good without qualification, while that of what is not good [*sc.* as it should be][31] by nature is good for that thing. Similarly, too, with the pleasant.[32] **1237a18** For[33] we must pause here and investigate whether there is friendship without pleasure, what difference pleasure makes, and on which of the two, the good and the pleasant, a friendship is based: **a21** is a person loved even if they do not afford pleasure, or in any case not for his pleasantness? Given that there are two senses of loving,[34] is it because the other person is good that active loving appears always to be accompanied by pleasure? **1237a23** Clearly, recognising what is congenial and familiar[35] is, like fresh investigations and learning in the sciences, an experience particularly marked with pleasure, and the reason is the same in both cases.[36] By nature, at any rate, what is good without qualification is pleasant without qualification, and to those to whom a thing is good it is pleasant; **a28** and this is why things that are alike immediately take pleasure in each other, as for a human being most pleasant is another human being. **a29** Since this is true for someone as yet incomplete, clearly it will be true for them when completed, and the good person is complete. **1237a30** Now if active loving is a mutual choice, accompanied by pleasure, to keep each other's company[37] it is clear that the first kind of friendship is a mutual choice of things that are good and pleasant without qualification because they are good and pleasant. **1237a34** This friendship is the disposition from which such a choice is made, for what it produces is an activity, and this is not external but in the one loving; the activity of all of our capacities, by contrast, is external, for

---

31 The supplement is, I think, required in order to make any sense of Aristotle's argument here (see preceding note).

32 I.e., (I propose), 'pleasant without qualification' similarly contrasts with 'pleasant for x' in two ways, the second being where x has work to do in order to make the two coincide (so that the fine [certainly something good without qualification] becomes pleasant for x (1237a6–7)).

33 Susemihl 1884 prefers *ara*, 'then', to *gar* ('for'), but 'for' fits well enough: the pleasant seems always to go along with the good – or does it?

34 I.e., as it turns out, just feeling love for someone, and doing something about it, e.g. through shared activity.

35 'The congenial and familiar' are here *sunêtheis*, 'people that share our character traits'; 'recognition' is perhaps a nod to tragic drama, in which *anagnôrisis*, the hero's realisation of the true situation, is often a critical moment in the play.

36 Discovery in the sciences seems to be being treated as itself a kind of recognition: cf. *NE* VI.8 = 'CB'2, 1142a25 ff., on intelligence (*nous*), 'So wisdom is antithetical to intelligence, for intelligence has as its objects the definitions for which there is no account ...' (seeing these *as* starting-points).

37 Or 'get to know one another' (now *gnôrisis* instead of *anagnôrisis*, although the latter will still be involved, insofar as each recognises the other's excellence).

it is realised either in something other or in something *qua* other.[38] This is why the pleasure is in the loving and not in being loved, because loving is the activity belonging to friendship, and being loved is [*sc.* merely] the activation of a lovable object, whereas the activity of loving belongs to friendship too.[39] The one occurs only in living creatures, the other in inanimate objects too, for they too are loved. **1237a40** In fact, though, active **1237b1** loving is using the thing loved, *qua* loved;[40] and the friend is a loved thing *qua* friend, not *qua* musician or doctor; the pleasure of friendship, then, is the pleasure that derives from him, *qua* himself, because it is he himself that is loved, not for being something else. So, if someone does not take pleasure in his friend *qua* good, it will not be the first kind of friendship. **b5** Nor should any accidental feature be allowed to get in the way of the pleasure brought by the friend's goodness – if he smells badly, he is left alone; he enjoys good will, and that is enough; living with him is another thing.

1237b8 This, then, is the first friendship, which everyone agrees to be a friendship, and the others are both recognised and disputed because of it. Friendship is thought to be something stable, and only this friendship is stable. Stability belongs to what is judged, and it is when things do not happen quickly or easily that judgement is correct. **1237b12** A friendship is not stable without trust, and trust does not come without time; one must put people to the test. As Theognis says, 'To know the mind of man or woman, / First try them like an ox before the plough'. Without time there is no friend, only a wish for friendship, and that sort of disposition is most easily mistaken for friendship itself: when people are keen to be friends, because they are doing all the things that friends do for each other they think they are friends rather than merely wishing for friendship. **b20** But it is the same with friendship as with other things; wanting to be healthy does not make people healthy, and no more does wanting to be **1237b22** friends make a friendship. Evidence for this is that people in this situation, who have not put each other to the test, are easily put at variance; in matters where they have given each other the opportunity to test them they are not so easily set against each other, but where they have not, they will be persuaded by any evidence produced by those wanting to make them fall out. **1237b26** It is clear at the same time that this friendship does not occur among bad people, for they

---

38   As when the doctor heals himself (Kenny 2011).
39   Kenny objects, in correspondence, that 'an *energeia* is an activity, not an activation', but I think the 'too' at the end of the sentence (which Kenny 2011 omits) is enough to confirm that this is Aristotle's intention (and is not something lovable that is now actively loved now also loved 'in activity'?).
40   Sc. so that despite the fact that we have been saying that the activity of friendship is in the one loving, it does still have an external aspect.

are distrustful and malevolent towards everybody, measuring others by their own standards. Good people do the same, which makes them easier to deceive unless they have learned through trial and error to mistrust people. The bad choose the natural goods before a friend, and none prefers a human being over things, so that they are not friends, because that way the characteristic sharing between friends does not occur, the friend being a mere addition to the goods rather than the goods to the friend. **b34** The first kind of friendship is not a matter of a large circle of friends, because it is hard to put a large group to the test; one would have to try living with each of them. Nor should choosing a friend be like choosing a cloak: true, in everything it is good sense to choose the better of two things, but while one should choose a better cloak in place of a worse one that has been well-worn, one should not substitute a new friend for an old one before knowing he is a **1238a1** better one, and that needs testing; a friend is more than a matter of a single day – time is required; hence the proverbial status of 'the bushel of salt.'[41] But at the same time the friend should not be just good without qualification; he must also be good for *you*, if he is to be *your* friend. For he is good without qualification just by being good, but a friend by being good for the other person, **a5** and good without qualification and a friend when the two things are in harmony, so that the very thing that is good without qualification is good for another,[42] or alternatively, good without qualification for a good person, good for someone else because useful. The very nature of loving prevents one from being a friend to many people at the same time; active friendship towards many simultaneously is impossible.

1238a11 From what we have just said it is clear that it is correct to say that friendship is something stable, just as happiness is something self-sufficient.[43] Correct, too, is the saying 'Nature is stable, money is not',[44] but far finer to substitute 'excellence' for 'nature'. **1238a14** Two more things people say are that time demonstrates whether someone is [*sc.* truly] loved, and that misfortune does so more than good fortune, for it is then that it is revealed that 'what belongs to friends is common between them',[45] for only friends prefer a person over the presence and absence of the things by nature good and bad that constitute the sphere of good and bad fortune. Misfortune shows up those that

---

41   Or, as it might be, 'breaking bread together', with shared meals as emblematic of a shared life.
42   I.e. to judge by what Aristotle has said and will go on to say, by enabling his progress towards perfection, and/or joint activity of the best kind.
43   The linking of the two statements underlines the importance of friendship for the good life; friendship, and its stability, are part of what makes happiness self-sufficient.
44   Euripides, *Electra* 941.
45   *Koina ta philôn*, another well-worn saying about friendship.

are not really friends, and are only there because it happens to be useful to them; **a20** but it takes time to show up both types, for the friendship based on utility is not quick to reveal itself either; that is something that belongs more to the friendship based on pleasure, though not so much in the case of the pleasant without qualification, since people are like wines and food-dishes – their sweetness may be immediately apparent, but with more familiarity the sweetness turns into unpleasantness, and it is like that with people too. What is pleasant without qualification itself needs to be judged by where it ends and how it develops over time, and the many would agree with this, not on the basis of the consequences[46] alone, but in the way they talk about a wine as too sweet, for the perceived lack of pleasantness is not because of any consequence but because it deceived at first but its effect was not sustained.[47]

1238a31 The first friendship, then, and the one by virtue of which the others are called friendships is the one based on excellence and the pleasure that comes from excellence, as we said before. The others occur among children, too, and among wild animals, and among the bad; hence the sayings[48] 'Like in age delights like', and 'Pleasure it is that fuses the bad together'; and it is possible for the bad to give pleasure to each other, too, not *qua* bad or neither [*sc.* bad nor good],[49] but for example because both are musicians, or the one is a lover of music and the other is a musician, and insofar as everyone has good in them, and they fit together somehow this way. Or again they might be useful and helpful to each other, not without qualification but towards some project that has its origin in neither badness nor goodness.[50] **1238b1** It is possible too

---

46 Like Dirlmeier 1962, I detect a reference here to Plato, *Protagoras*, in which 'the many' are imagined as making their choices with full awareness of the future disadvantages as well as of present benefits.

47 The example makes sense in the context of a wine-culture that perhaps favoured sweetness over other qualities in wine (honey might even be added); a wine that at first taste seemed right might subsequently be found cloying.

48 Both, again, it seems, from Euripides.

49 Kenny 2011 has 'middling', Inwood and Woolf 2013 'morally neutral' for 'neither' (*mêdeteroi*), but each rendering raises more questions than it answers. My own view is that Aristotle is quietly introducing, for the purposes of his own argument, the third *genos* or kind that Socrates identifies at *Lysis* 216d6–7, alongside the good and the bad, in order to avoid the problems of both 'like loves like' and 'unlike loves unlike', in a context where the only object of love is the good. Does he (Aristotle) here see the need for a similar move on his own part, insofar as the bad, too, for him, desire the good (real or apparent)? In general, as I have urged before (n. 26 above), we should not underestimate the importance of the account of love and desire in the *Lysis* for understanding *EE* IV; the echoes are too clear and the connections too close, I think, to be accidental.

50 See preceding note.

for a good[51] person to be friends with a bad one, for one of them might be useful to the other for a particular purpose, the bad to the good for an already existing one, the good to the un-self-controlled similarly, and to the bad for a purpose that accords with nature; and he will wish for good things for him, the unqualified ones unqualifiedly and the things good for the friend as occasion arises, in the way that [sc. even] poverty or illness benefits a person [sc. in certain circumstances];[52] and he will wish for these for the sake of the unqualified goods, not for themselves, as in the case of **b8** drinking the medicine it is not the drinking itself that is wished for but what the drinking is for the sake of. Again, good can be friends with bad in any of the ways those who are not good may be; the bad might bring pleasure to the good not *qua* bad but because he shares some common attribute, for example musicality; or again a good person might sometimes seek the company of a bad one just insofar as there is something good[53] in everybody.

EE Book IV, Chapter 3

1238b14 So these are the three kinds of friendship, and in all three friendship is spoken of in a way in terms of equality; for those whose friendship rests on excellence, too, are friends with each other on the basis of a kind of equality of excellence. A variant of these three is when one side in the friendship is superior to the other, as it might be if one compared the excellence of god with human excellence, or generally the friendship between ruler and ruled, for this is another kind of friendship, in which the demands of justice, too, are different, **b20** 'equal' here being proportional and not arithmetical. To this kind belong the friendship between father and son and between benefactor and beneficiary; and there are differences here too, because the relationship of father to son is not the same as that that between husband and wife, the one being of ruler to ruled, the other of benefactor to beneficiary. **1238b25** In these cases there is either no loving in return by the superior, or it is on a lesser scale, for

---

51   Here *epieikês*, usually 'decent', 'reasonable', but here substituting for *agathos* or *spoudaios*, 'good'; the latter appears in its place in b3.
52   I.e., by preventing them from doing things that they would otherwise have done that would have had harmful consequences for them (a surprising example, perhaps, taken by itself, but not so surprising when we take into account the Socratic/Platonic background to the whole discussion; in this case, compare, e.g., Plato, *Protagoras* 352e–354e).
53   The same two possibilities as for friendships between the bad or the 'neither good nor bad' in 1238a36–8; but as Aristotle has just said, they are possible scenarios for any friendships between people not defined by goodness (b9–10).

it would be ridiculous if someone made it a complaint against god that he was not returning love to the same degree as he was loved, and similarly with ruled and ruler, **b28** for it belongs to the ruler to be loved, not to love, or else to love in a different way, and no less does the pleasure a self-sufficient person enjoys from a possession[54] or a child differ from that of an indigent person receiving bounty.[55] It is the same with those that are friends because of their utility or pleasure: sometimes they are on an equal footing, and sometimes they are related as superior to inferior. Hence those who think their friendship was on the former basis complain if the friend is not as useful to them and benefit them as much as they do the friend; **b34** and the same goes for pleasure, as is clear from love-affairs, where this is often the cause of partners' falling out with each other; the lover does not recognise that what lies behind the passion on the two sides is not the same. Hence Eunicus'[56] 'Such things you say! Are you the beloved or the lover?' But *they* think the rationale for both is the same.

EE Book IV, Chapter 4

1239a1 So as we have said, there being three kinds of friendship, based respectively on excellence, usefulness and pleasure, these are again divided into two, those between equals and those between unequals; both these latter kinds are friendships, but the friends are the ones in the equal relationships, for it would be strange for a grown man to be friends with a small child, **a5** and yet he loves and is loved. There are cases where there should be love for the superior partner,[57] but if he loves in return he is reproached for loving an unworthy object, **a7** the measure being the worth of the friends and the expectation of a certain sort of equality. Some cases deserve less love because of a difference of age, some because one side is superior in excellence or family or in some other such respect; in every case the **a11** superior deserves either to love less or not at all, whether the friendship is based in utility, in pleasure or in excellence.

Where the differences are small one can reasonably expect disputes, for sometimes a small difference counts for nothing, as when one is weighing timber as opposed to gold; **a15** but people are not good at judging what is small because what is good for them, being close to them, appears large to them

---

54   A human possession, presumably, and one suitably inferior, i.e., a slave.
55   I take it that the pleasure differs in being greater, i.e., that of an agent as opposed to that of a mere recipient.
56   A relatively unknown Athenian comic writer.
57   Presumably because he is good.

while someone else's good appears small because further away. When the difference is too great, not even the superior partner himself will insist either on being loved back or on being loved back in the same way: just suppose he was a god[58] – what then? It is evident, then, that people are friends when they are on an equal footing, and that it is possible for there to be loving back without their being friends. **1239a20** But it is also clear why people seek out friendships based in superiority more than those based in equality, for with the former they have the benefit of being loved as well as the superiority itself. This is why some people prefer someone ingratiating over a friend, because he makes both benefits appear to belong to him. Lovers of honour are particularly like this, because being admired goes along with superiority. People generally tend by nature either to aspire to friendship or to love honour; the first type is the one who takes more pleasure in loving than in being loved, whereas the one who takes more pleasure in being loved is more the honour-lover. What the one who takes pleasure in being admired and loved really loves is the superiority, while the lover of the pleasure in loving is the one that aspires to friendship, **1239a30** for pleasure is necessarily present in the active exercise of love,[59] whereas being loved is something accidental: one can fail to notice that one is being loved, but not that one is loving. Friendship is also itself more a matter of loving than of being loved, which is more dependent on the object loved, as is indicated by the fact that the one loving would prefer knowing the object of their love over being known by them, if both are not possible, as when women secretly give up their children for adoption, like Andromache in Antiphon's tragedy.[60] Wanting to be known seems to be for one's own sake, and for having something good happen to oneself rather than doing it, whereas **1239b1** wanting to know the other seems to be for the sake of doing something and for the sake of the one loved. This is why we also praise those who continue loving the dead, for they know them [*sc.* as their loved ones] without their being known themselves.

b4 We have said, then, that there are several modes of friendship, and how many there are, namely three, and that being loved and being loved back are

---

58   Not the Aristotelian god, nor any particular god; what is at issue here is no more than an assumed contrast between the unlimited powers of divinity and the strictly limited ones possessed by us.
59   'For ... in the active exercise of love' is borrowed from Kenny 2011, which precisely captures the essence of Aristotle's laconic phrasing here.
60   This Antiphon was a fourth-century tragedian from Syracuse, the play in question seems to have portrayed Andromache substituting her son – either Molossus, as in Euripides' *Andromache*, or perhaps Astyanax, for someone else's in order to prevent his being killed (as Astyanax is in the epic cycle known to us).

different, as are the friends in friendships based respectively in equality and in the superiority of one of the partners in the relationship.

EE Book IV, Chapter 5

1239b7 But since, as we said at the beginning, the term 'friend' is also used in a more general way by those who bring extraneous contexts into that of friendship proper, some saying that like is 'friend' to like, others that it is opposite to opposite, **b10** we must say how such considerations fare in relation to the friendships we have identified. Likeness comes into play with both the pleasant and the good, for the good is singular while the bad comes in many shapes, and the good person is always alike and does not change character, whereas what the bad and unwise is in the evening bears no resemblance to what he was in the morning. **b14** This is why **1239b15** unless they make contracts with each other the bad do not last as friends but fall out, and an unstable friendship is not a friendship. Hence, looked at in this way, it is the like that is friend to like, because the good is like, but there is a way in which the same is true of the pleasant, for those that are like one another find the same things pleasant, and everything there is, is by nature pleasant to itself, which is why the voices, the dispositions and the pastimes **1239b20** of members of the same family bring most pleasure to them, one to another, as happens too in the case of other animals; that way, too, even the bad can love each other [('Pleasure it is that fuses the bad together')].[61] **1239b22** Opposite, for its part, is 'friend' to opposite in the form of the useful, for what is like, by itself, is useless to itself.[62] Hence master needs slave and the slave a master, and wife and husband need each other. The opposite is pleasant and desirable as being what is useful, not, that is, as a constituent of the final end but as contributing towards it. When a thing has what it desires it has already reached its end and no longer desires its opposite; for example, the hot does not desire the cold [*sc.* when it is no longer too hot] nor the dry the wet [*sc.* when it is no longer too dry]. **1239b29** But in a way love of the opposite[63] is also love of the good, for opposites reach out to each other

---

61 Surely an intrusion, repeated as it is without introduction or apology ('as we said'?) from 1238a35.
62 'Itself', here, I take it, is shorthand for 'its pair', itself taken as just something like.
63 I.e., opposites' love for each other; we are after all considering the thesis that love is in general that of opposite for opposite; but the discussion is taking some strange turns; or, to put it another way, readers are left (not unusually, for the *EE*, as I have observed before) to do a lot of work – in this case, to relate what is being said to the actual human situations that the discussion is designed to illuminate.

through the middle, seeking each other like matching tallies because when they meet a single intermediate is formed from the two of them. Further,[64] it is only love of the opposite by coincidence; in itself it is love of the intermediate, for what the opposites are reaching out for is not each other but the middle: when people that are too cold are heated up they are brought 1239b35 into the middle, and so too when they are overheated and cooled down; and similarly in the other cases.[65] Otherwise they [*sc.* the extremes/those at the extremes] are permanently in a state of desire/appetite [*sc.* for the opposite] because they are not in the middle. But the person that is in the middle takes pleasure in the things that are by nature pleasant without appetite, whereas the others [*sc.* those at the extremes] do so in everything that takes them out of their natural disposition. This kind of 'friendship', then, exists even in the case of inanimate things, but it is actual loving 1240a1 only when we find it among animate ones – where it explains why sometimes people take pleasure in those unlike themselves, the dry and humourless in the convivial, for example, or the energetic in the slothful, for either brings the other into the middle. So, as we have said, by coincidence opposites are 'friends', and because of the good.

1240a5 We have now discussed, then, how many kinds of friendship there are, and in what different ways both those that love and those that are loved are said to be friends, both where the relationship is such as to constitute genuine friendship and where it is not.

EE Book IV, Chapter 6

1240a7 A question requiring much investigation is whether a person is or is not a friend to himself. For some people think that everyone is most of all a friend to himself, and use this as a standard by which to judge friendships with other people. From the point of view of theory, and the attributes thought to belong to friends, this friendship and friendship for others are in some respects opposed to each other but in others plainly alike. For friendship with oneself is friendship only by analogy, not friendship plain and simple, because both being loved and loving involve two distinct people, which is why a person is a friend to himself more in the way, in the case of the un-self-controlled and the self-controlled, we said that they were acting either voluntarily or countervoluntarily, by virtue of their having the parts of the soul in a particular sort

---

64   The argument, evidently, is trending away from 'opposite loves opposite'.
65   I.e., presumably, including the ones immediately relevant to ethics, to which we now turn.

of relationship to one another;[66] similarly, too, with all questions of this sort – whether one can be a friend or an enemy to oneself, whether it is possible to wrong oneself – insofar as all of them involve two **a20** distinct sides, and that condition holds in the case of the individual soul just insofar as it is in a way two, but insofar as the two in question are not truly distinct it does not hold.

1240a22 The remaining modes of loving according to which we[67] are accustomed to investigate the subject, when we discuss it themselves derive from our disposition towards ourselves. For we think of a friend as someone who wants good things or things he thinks good for someone else not because it will benefit himself but for the sake of the other; and we think of a friend in another way too, as someone for whom one wants existence for his sake rather than for one's own, even where one is not assigning goods, let alone existence itself;[68] indeed one might think of this as friendship to the highest degree. Another way we think of a friend is as someone with whom one chooses to live for the sake of their companionship and not for some other purpose, as for example fathers wish for their children's continued existence but actually prefer to live with others, not their children. **1240a30** All these notions tend to clash with one another, for some people think they are not loved unless their friend wants good things for them, others unless they want their existence for their own sake, others unless they want to live with them. Then again [*sc.* we think of a friend][69] as sharing the other's grief, not for some other purpose, as slaves share their masters' because grief makes them harsh and not because of those themselves that are grieving, in the way that mothers grieve with their children and birds share each other's pain;[70] **a36** for a friend wants more than anything not only to share the other's pain but to share the same pain, being thirsty with him if he is thirsty, were that to be possible, and if not something as close to it as possible. The same applies with shared pleasure: it is a mark of a friend to be pleased **1240b1** for no other reason than that the other is. And there are other

---

66 See II.8, 1224a33–8.
67 'We' here are perhaps, again, people generally; that is, Aristotle is still talking about *endoxa*, ideas commonly held; I see no reason to suppose, with Kenny 2011, that the reference is to discussions within the Lyceum.
68 'Let alone …' is presumably intended to exclude the relationships between parents and children, as a separate matter.
69 The two words in square brackets in the text (*agapan thêsomen*, 'we will put down as loving') I take to be someone else's supplement to the same effect (that they are not part of the original text seems assured by the unlikelihood of Aristotle's suddenly substituting a new word for 'loving' (*agapan* for *philein*).
70 Kenny 2011 cites Aristotle's description of the behaviour of pigeons at *Historia animalium* IX, 612b35.

things said about friendship, like 'equality is sodality.'[71] or 'true friends are but a single soul'. All of these can be referred back to the individual's relationship with himself, for this is the way he wants good things for himself; no individual *qua* individual does himself a good turn for some ulterior purpose or for the sake of favours [*sc.* being given or returned], or advertises the fact that he was doing a good turn, as people do when they want to be thought to be a friend rather than be one. The same goes for wanting the friend's existence above all, wanting to share his life, his pleasure and his pain, 'two friends but one soul', or 'we cannot even live without each other – better die together'. For that is how the individual is, and he is perhaps his own companion;[72] But these are all features of the good person's relationship to himself; for in the bad person, for example the un-self-controlled, they are in conflict, and it is because of this that it is thought to be possible for someone to be an enemy to himself, even while as one and undivided he is the object of his own desire. **1240b15** Such, at any rate, is the good person, and the friend on the basis of excellence, since the bad person is not one but many, and in the course of a single day unpredictably different. So one's love for oneself too traces its origins back to love for the good; for it is because he is in a way like himself, because one, and good, as himself, for himself, that he is an object of love and desirable to himself; and he is naturally such, **1240b20** whereas the bad person's disposition is contrary to nature. The good person does not reproach himself even while acting, like the un-self-controlled, nor does his later self reproach his former one like the remorseful or the former the later like the liar, and in general, if we really must bring the sophists in, with their two Coriscuses, Coriscus himself and the good one,[73] plainly the same amount of them is good, since when they do have something to accuse themselves of, they kill themselves.[74] **b26** But everyone thinks of himself as good, and the person that is good without qualification

---

71　An attempt to reproduce the play on words in the Greek (*isotês philotês*).
72　Or, just possibly, 'and he shares his own company on an equal basis' (but equality is already there in 1240b2 ('equality is sodality').
73　Sc. which is the only way in which we'll get two instead of one here?
74　So, again, behaving like two people instead of one; the language is that of the courts, with suicide figured as self-execution (a figure in principle complicated by the fact that one form of execution, as in Socrates' case, was self-administered hemlock, but that is hardly relevant here). Kenny 2011 and Inwood and Woolf 2013 both take the reference to suicide metaphorically ('when people reproach themselves, they assassinate their own characters'; 'when people criticise themselves, they are killing themselves'), but I see no reason to suppose that Aristotle would think suicide inappropriate for a good person who had done something sufficiently serious; indeed I think the point of the reference to the two Coriscuses is precisely that he would not: the good kill themselves just when they have given themselves reason not to love what they are.

seeks to be a friend to himself too, as we said, because he has two elements in him that are intended by nature to be in accord and cannot be torn apart. This is why in the case of human beings each individual seems[75] a friend to himself, but not in the case of the other animals: does a horse seem good to itself? If not, then he is no friend to himself either, nor are children, until they acquire the power of decision, because it is only then that the child speaks in a different voice from his appetite. Friendship towards oneself resembles that with one's kin insofar as it is not in our power to dissolve either of them, 1240b35 but even when there is a falling out kin are still kin and the individual is still a singular individual for so long as he lives.

1240b37 So, from what has been said, it is clear how many senses there are of 'being a friend', and that all kinds of friendship trace their origins back to the primary kind;

EE Book IV, Chapter 7

1241a1 but it belongs to our inquiry to reflect on[76] two further topics, like-mindedness and good will. Some people think they are the same thing, others that neither will be found without the other. Good will, for its part, is neither an entirely different thing from friendship nor the same thing, for with friendship divided into three modes, good will is not to be found either in friendship based in utility or in that based in pleasure. If – to take the first case – one wants what is good for one's friend because it is useful for oneself, one's motive will not be his interest but one's own, and good will, like friendship, seems to be focused on its object rather than on the subject exhibiting it; and – the second case – if good will were to be found in friendship based in pleasure, people would feel it even with inanimate objects. a10 So it is clear that good will has to do with friendship based in character. But good will expresses itself merely in the wishing of good, whereas friendship goes further and acts on the wish. For good will is a starting-point for friendship: every friend has good will, but not everyone who has good will is a friend; someone with good will and only good will resembles a beginner, and so it is that it is just a beginning of friendship, not friendship itself. 1241a15 For friends are thought to be like-minded,[77] and the like-minded to be friends, but it is not like-mindedness about anything

---

75   Sc. naturally?
76   Another instance of the verb *theôrein*.
77   In other words, like-mindedness (of a particular kind, to be specified) needs to be added too, if there is to be friendship; editors and translators suspect a lacuna here, in the text and in the argument, but all seems in order.

and everything that belongs to friendship, just like-mindedness about things that the friends can do together, and that contribute towards a shared life – like-mindedness, that is, not just in the friends' thinking, or just in their wanting, for it is possible for what moves us[78] to desire in opposite ways, as illustrated by the disharmony we find in the un-self-controlled person, 1241a20 nor, if there is like-mindedness about a decision is there [sc. always like-mindedness] when it comes to the desire to carry the decision through. But there is [sc. such] like-mindedness between good people; if people are bad, their deciding on and desiring the same things leads to their harming each other.[79] It seems that like-mindedness, too, like friendship, is something that is spoken of in more than one sense, and that the primary and natural kind is good, which is why the bad a25 cannot be like-minded, but that there is another kind according to which the bad are like-minded too, that is, when they decide on and desire the same things. But they must want the same things under conditions that allow both sides to get what they wanted, since if they want the sort of thing that cannot be shared, they will end up fighting with each other, and if a30 people are like-minded they will not fight. It is like-mindedness when[80] people make the same choice about who should rule and who should be ruled, not each choosing themselves but choosing the same person. Like-mindedness, in fact, is what friendship is in the civic context. Let that be our account of like-mindedness and good will.

EE Book IV, Chapter 8

1241a35 People puzzle about why benefactors love beneficiaries more than the beneficiaries love them, when it seems that justice would demand the opposite. One would suppose that the reasons for it have to do with utility and self-interest: one party is owed something and the other has to pay what he owes. But this is not the whole explanation; there is also something natural about it: activity is more worthy of choice than being its product, and in this case product and activity share the same account, the beneficiary being as it were a product of the benefactor. This is why animals show the concern they do for offspring, whether for the act of producing them or for looking after

---

78 There will be much more in Book v about the causes of movement in the soul that probably needs to be brought into connection with what is said here.
79 Which seems, from what immediately follows, to rule it out as true like-mindedness, the grounds presumably being that like-mindedness, like friendship and good will, is a positive rather than a negative feature of human life.
80 Aristotle introduces a central example of like-mindedness.

them **1241b4** while they being produced. Fathers do in fact love their children more[81] than they are loved by them, and these, again, love their children more than they do their own parents, because activity is the best thing; and mothers, too, love their children more than fathers do, because they think children more their own work, for people distinguish a product by the difficulty of producing it, and it is the mother that suffers more when a child is born.

EE Book IV, Chapter 9

1241b10 Let that be our way of distinguishing friendship with oneself from friendship involving more than one party. Justice is thought to be a sort of equality, and friendship, too, lies in equality, if 'equality is sodality' has any truth in it. All constitutions represent some kind of justice, for a constitution is a community, and everything involving sharing depends on justice, so that there are as many kinds of justice and of partnership as there are of friendship, though they all border on each other and the differences between them are small. **1241b16** But now there is a similar relationship between body and soul, craftsman and tool, and master and slave, and it is a relationship that means that there can be no partnership between the members of each pair; there are not two things in any of these cases, but rather a single entity to which the second belongs, nor is the good of the one separable from that of the other, but rather the good of both is that of the whole for the sake of which the other exists. **1241b21** For the body is a tool naturally attached to the soul, the slave is like a part and detachable tool of the master, and the tool like an inanimate slave. The remaining partnerships are part of those of the city, like phratries or religious or commercial associations. All the kinds of constitution can be found in the relationships between family-members, whether the correct or the corrupt kinds, for in this respect constitutions resemble musical modes:[82] monarchy in that between father and son, aristocracy between husband and wife, 'polity' between brothers; corruptions of these [*sc.* also found in family-relationships] are tyranny, oligarchy, and democracy. And there are the same number of kinds of justice.

---

81 '[and mothers than fathers]', adds the transmitted text, unhelpfully, borrowing what properly belongs in 1241b7 (*q.v.*).

82 'In this respect', i.e., in that both the more acceptable and the less acceptable are found together; Dorian and Phrygian modes, say, in music, monarchy/tyranny, aristocracy/oligarchy, 'polity' (more 'republic' than democracy?)/democracy in the case of constitutions (a classification Aristotle adopts directly from Plato).

b32 Since there are two kinds of equality, arithmetical and proportional, there will also be corresponding kinds of justice, friendship, and community. For the community represented by a polity is based in arithmetical equality, as is friendship between **1241b35** comrades, both being measured by the same standard. But the best aristocratic community and the community represented by kingship are based in proportionate equality, since what is just for superior and inferior is not the same but what is proportionate. And similarly with the friendship between father and son; in partnerships, too, it is the same way.

EE Book IV, Chapter 10

1242a1 We talk about friendships between kinsfolk, between comrades, and between partners, so-called 'civic' friendship.[83] Those between kin come in many kinds, one, for example, like that between brothers, another like that between father and son, for they may be based in proportionate equality like the latter, or in arithmetical equality like that between brothers. The latter is close to friendship between comrades, for comrades, like brothers, lay claim to privileges.[84] Civic friendship is based quite particularly in utility, because people seem to come together because of a lack of self-sufficiency, even though they would have done so for the sake of sharing their lives, too, and it is the civic community[85] alone, along with its corrupt form, that is not only a kind of friendship but **a10** also has members that share together as [*sc.* equal] friends; the others are based in the superiority of some over others. **a11** The justice found in friendship between people useful to each other is justice most of all, because this is civic justice.[86] A saw and the craft that uses it come together in a different way – not for the sake of a common purpose, because then tool and soul would constitute a single whole, but for the sake of the user. A tool does, of course, receive the attention it deserves in relation to its function, for it exists

---

83 Cf. 1241a32–3.
84 Brothers on the grounds of age, comrades similarly, or because comrades are typically also (like brothers) in competition with each other?
85 Or 'the community we call a 'polity'', *politeia*, because it is this, not 'the community of citizens' in the wider sense, that has a *parekbasis* or 'corrupt form/deviation'. There is a genuine ambiguity here, and one that is significant, because it appears to lead to an elision of the difference between polity and its 'corrupt' form, democracy: that difference is typically framed in terms of the quality of the citizens (see Rowe and Schofield 2000, esp. 371–86), but that is perhaps a point on which Aristotle could hardly insist in any case, in a context that depends heavily on *endoxa*, or what people are held generally to think.
86 I.e., what holds the city together, and the city is the unit on which everything else depends?

for the sake of what it does, and what it is to be an auger is twofold, but it is more properly identified with the activity of boring; body and slave follow the same pattern, as we said before.[87]

1242a19 To inquire, then, into how one should associate with a friend is to inquire into a kind of justice; for in fact, generally speaking, all justice is a matter of relationships with friends; for what is just is so for certain people, who are our partners, and a friend is a partner that shares in our family, or our life: a human being is an animal that lives not only in a city but in a household, and does not like other animals pair off with any chance partner, female or male, **a25** otherwise spending the rest of its life living in isolation; he is an animal that tends to enter into community with those with whom it has a natural kinship, so that there would be a community, and justice of some kind, even if there were no city, and a household is a kind of friendship. So the relationship of master and slave is the same as that of an expertise and its tools or of soul and body, and such relationships are neither kinds of **a30** friendship but something analogous, just as what is healthy is not just but analogous to it. The relationship between wife and husband is friendship, as something useful [*sc.* to both], and a community, while that of father and son is like that of god to human being, of benefactor to beneficiary, and generally of natural ruler to the naturally ruled; that of brothers towards each other is especially of the sort associated with comrades, on the basis of equality: 'Bastard brother never was I called; our father's name is shared by us both – Zeus, who rules me'[88] – this is the language of people **1242b1** looking for equal treatment. So it is that we find the beginnings and sources of friendship, of constitutional arrangements, and of justice in the household first.

1242b3 Since there are three kinds of friendship, based in excellence, in utility, and in pleasure, and two varieties of each of these, one involving the superiority of one side to the other, the other equality between them, and the justice appropriate to them is clear from the disputes people have, in the former kind any claim relates to what is proportionate, but in different ways, the one in the superior position claiming what is in inverse proportion, so behaving like a ruler towards a subject: what comes in from the lesser party, he says, should be to what he has to pay in as he himself stands in relation to the lesser party, or if not this, at least it should be an arithmetically equal amount. This is the way things happen in other partnerships, **1242b13** sometimes in accordance with

---

87   Indeed, so recently that one might wonder why the point (about the true nature of a community, with its members genuinely sharing a joint project), needed to be made again quite so soon (and yet again in a28–30).
88   A fragment, it seems, from a lost Sophoclean play.

arithmetical equality, sometimes with proportional; for if they contributed an arithmetically equal amount of money they also take out on the same basis, and if they did not what they take out is proportionate. Conversely[89] the inferior party inverts the proportion and joins the opposite points of one diagonal of the square [sc. a square with its four points representing the two parties and their respective contributions], but[90] if this happens the superior would seem to come off worse, and the friendship and the partnership more like a public service; in which case there has to be equalisation by other means in order to restore proportion, and this other means is **1242b20** honour, which belongs to a ruler and to god[91] in relation to the ruled. But the profit has to be equalised in relation to the honour.

Friendship on equal terms is civic friendship, and civic friendship exists on the basis of utility, and just as cities are friends with each other so are their citizens, as in 'The Megarians are no longer anything to the Athenians,'[92] so, similarly, when the citizens of a city are no longer useful to each other; it is a question of the balance between them at any moment; there is, here too a relationship between ruler and ruled, but it is not the natural or kingly one[93] **b28** but rather ruling and being ruled in turn, not for the purpose of benefaction, as it would be in the case of god,[94] but in order for there to be an equal distribution of benefit and of public service. **b30** Civic friendship aims to operate in terms of equality; but there are two kinds of utility-friendship, one regulated by law, the other dependent on character. Civic friendship looks to equality in whatever it is that is in play, in the way that sellers and buyers do: 'Pay a friend his due', as the poet[95] says. So when this civic friendship is by mutual agreement, **1242b35** it also comes within the scope of the law; but when people leave it to each other it tends towards the kind dependent on character, and friendship between comrades. This is why it is in this kind of friendship that recrimination most often occurs; the reason is that it is an unnatural kind; utility-friendship and friendship based in excellence are different, but

---

89 The contrast is with 1242b8 'the one in the superior position claiming what is in inverse proportion ...'
90 So proposing to equalise what the two parties get while ignoring their relative status.
91 The relationship between god and human being has become somewhat emblematic of that between ruler and ruled and benefactor and beneficiary (see esp. 1242a32–5).
92 Repeated from 1236a37–8, but here used differently: the Athenians' relationship with each other is apparently now compared with their relationship with the Megarians when the two cities are in alliance.
93 I.e., of superior over inferior.
94 God enters the picture again just as standard example of ruler/superior (see n. 92 above).
95 Hesiod, *Works and Days* 368.

the partners in this case want both things at the same time, getting together because it is 1243a1 useful to them but making it the friendship based in character that it would be if they were good people instead of a legal one, on the basis that they trust one another. In general it is in utility-friendships that recrimination occurs more than in the other two kinds, for excellence is not subject to recrimination, and pleasure-friends tend to part once both sides have given and received what they wanted; utility-friends, by contrast, a5 tend not to break things off immediately if they come together not on a legal basis and more as comrades do. But the legal kind of utility-friendship is free from recrimination, any obligations being measured in money and discharged accordingly, whereas the kind based in character is purely voluntary. Hence sometimes there is a law prohibiting those associating on such a basis from enforcing their voluntary contracts in court, 1243a10 and rightly so: it is not the nature of the good to require justice between them, and the people in question are entering into contracts as good and trustworthy people. In this kind of friendship recrimination on either side is of doubtful validity; what sort of complaint will either make if the other trusts in his character rather than the law? There is a puzzle, too, about how a15 to determine what is just, whether by looking at the scale of the service actually rendered, or rather what it meant to the recipient. It is possible for it to be as Theognis says: 'a trifle to you, goddess, but not to me [*sc.* as recipient]', or it may be the other way round, as in 'a mere game to you but death to me'.[96] a20 Hence the recriminations, as we have said, because one side expects returns for great services rendered, because he did it when the other needed it, or something of the sort, talking up the other's incapacity in relation to the benefit he received and not what it cost him, while the recipient conversely talks about how little it cost the donor and not about how much it meant to him. And sometimes there is also doubt [*sc.* and dispute] when they[97] are the recipients, because they insist on how little they got out of it, the donor on what it meant for him; for example, if one side put himself at risk for only a drachma's benefit to the other, he will talk about the size of the risk he took, the other about the paltry sum accruing to him, just as happens with the repayment of financial debts, for this is the focus of disputes in that sphere, if there has been no formal agreement, one party thinking they should work on the basis of how things were then, the other on

---

96 For human beings as playthings of the gods (if that is what Aristotle has in mind), see Plato, *Laws* 644d, 803c.

97 'They', I take it, being the people we might have expected to be the donors or benefactors.

the basis of how they are now.[98] **1243a30** So civic friendship looks at the contract and the facts of the matter, but friendship based on character rather looks to intentions, which makes this both more just and a justice more appropriate to friendship. A reason why people dispute in the way we have described is because character-friendship is finer, whereas utility-based friendship is more necessary. People begin as character-friends, friends on the basis of excellence, but when there is a clash of private interests it becomes clear that that was not what they were. For most people only pursue the fine when they are well enough off in other respects, and it is the same when it comes to the finer kind of friendship. **1243b1** So it is clear how we are to distinguish in these cases: If they are character-friends, we should look to see if their choices were made on the basis of equality, and if so neither should expect anything else from the other, but if they made their choices as civic friends, on the basis of their utility to each other, then the question is what would benefit them both; but if one party claims they did one thing and the other disputes it, merely making fine speeches will be no substitute for actually doing something fine in return, and similarly in the other case, but since they came to no formal agreement because they said they did not need one, someone will have to make a judgement and neither party must deceive the other with false pretences. **b9** So they will just have to put up with their luck. That character-friendship is based on intentions is made is clear from the fact that even if someone were to have benefited greatly from a friendship and could not pay the other back, from simple incapacity, all would be fine and good: god too is content to receive sacrifices according to what we can afford. But it will not be enough for a seller if someone tells him he cannot afford more, nor will it be for a lender.

Recrimination often occurs in relationships between people not on the same level, and to see what is just in these cases is not easy, **1243b15** for that means finding a single particular standard – one that is likely be inappropriate to measure one of the two sides – as happens in love-affairs; the one side pursues his pleasure-friend with a view to sharing his life, while the latter perhaps pursues *him* just as someone useful, and when the lover ceases to love, the beloved becomes something else and so does the lover, at which point they start to calculate the *quid pro quo*, as when Pytho and Pammenes were falling out[99]

---

98   Kenny 2011 takes this as a reference to fluctuations in the value of money (mentioned in 'CB' 1.5, 1133b11–140); similarly Inwood and Woolf 2013.

99   That the example is from Macedonian history, and evidently involved teacher and pupil, immediately makes one think of Aristotle's tutorship of the future Alexander the Great. I wonder whether this is deliberate – the point being [not about an unrevealed *grand passion*] but about the incommensurability of knowledge and money (it seems that anti-Macedonian sentiment led to Aristotle's leaving Athens after Alexander's death in

(and in general teacher and pupil, for knowledge and money are not measured by a single standard), or as Prodicus the doctor responded to the patient asking to pay a smaller fee; or there is the story of the cithara-player and the king, in which the king was there for pleasure, the musician because it was useful income, but when the time came for payment the king turned himself into a pleasure-friend, saying that just as the cithara-player had delighted him with his singing, so had he delighted the musician with his promise of payment.[100]

1243b27 It is nonetheless clear, here too, how we are to understand the matter: here too we must use a single measure, but a proportion rather than a single term, in the way a civic community is measured. **b30** For how will a cobbler be partner with a farmer, unless their products are equalised by proportion? Wherever exchange is not of like for like, proportion is key, for example if someone complains that he provided the other with some sort of intellectual accomplishment[101] while the other merely gave him money, the question is, first, how to measure such accomplishment against wealth, and then what **b35** each of the two parties has bestowed is to them, for if one gave half of the lesser thing and the other not even a fraction of the greater, clearly the latter is in the wrong. But here too there will be dispute from the beginning if one partner claims they came together as utility-friends and the other says they did not, and that their friendship is of some different kind.

EE Book IV, Chapter 11

1244a1 In relation to the good person, the one who is a friend on the basis of excellence, we should ask whether it is to him that we should render useful services and help, or rather the friend that is able to do us good in return. This is the same question as whether benefit is due more to a friend than to someone because he is a good person. If they are both, perhaps it is not too difficult unless one exaggerates one factor and minimises the other, treating him as very much a friend but as only a moderately good person; **a7** but if they are

---

323 BCE), and whether he is, in effect, saying to his opponents that it was all a financial transaction, however the terms were settled, and nothing more. The likely relative obscurity of the example, for an Athenian audience (the Pytho in question was from Byzantium, Pammenes from Thebes, though both became prominent figures in their own right) is perhaps enough to raise the question why Aristotle should have chosen it.

100 Another swipe at the Macedonians, if we took the king to be Alexander?
101 That is, *sophia*.

not both, many problems arise: for example if someone was [*sc.* a friend][102] once but will not be in the future, or will be but is not yet, or is now but once was not and will not be in the future. **a10** But the original question[103] is more troublesome; perhaps Euripides' lines are to the point: 'Words will be your just return for words,/ a deed for a deed [*sc.* so that we owe both our parents something in return for what they did for us], and not everything to our father, just some things, and others to our mother; and yet a father's excellence is superior. Neither does Zeus get all the sacrifices, or receive all **1244a15** the honours, only some. Perhaps, then, there are some things we should do for a useful friend, others we should do for the friend who is good. For example, if someone, gives you food and necessities, that is no reason for you to offer him your company too; nor, then, to the one to whom you are offering your company need you give the sorts of things it is not not he but the utility-friend that gives. People doing this – if, for example, they give everything to their beloved when they need not – are good-for-nothings.

a21 All the criteria of friendship mentioned in our discussions[104] are in a way criteria of friendship, just not of friendship of the same kind. Wanting for another the things that are good for the other belongs to the utility friend, and the benefactor, and indeed to any kind of friend whatever, for this way of defining friendship does not mark out any particular friendship, but wanting someone's **1244a25** existence is a marker of one kind of friend, wanting to share their life a marker of another, while sharing grief and pleasure belongs to the pleasure-friend; all these criteria refer to some kind of friendship, but none to one single pattern of friendship [*sc.* that will accommodate them all]. This is why there are many such criteria, each being thought to be of some singular friendship when it is not, as for example in the case of choosing that someone exist; for the friend on the basis of superiority and is a benefactor wants it for something **a30** that is his own product, and for the person that gave you your existence you should want their existence, too, in return, but share your life not with him but with the pleasure-friend.

---

102   But is, presumably, still a good person, the question being whether we owe him something just as such.
103   I.e., presumably, the one raised in a1–3, which is addressed at least in a way by the following Euripidean lines.
104   Kenny 2011 takes this as a reference to a written text, comparing II.2, 1220b11 (on which see my n. 38 to *EE* II), but all the 'criteria' (*horoi*) mentioned in any case belong to the general category of *endoxa*, 'things people think', and most if not all have appeared as such somewhere in Book IV itself, and my own view is that Aristotle is doing no more than to confirm, as he likes to do (see Book I.6, with IV.2), that his own outcomes are broadly in agreement with these, as well as summing up.

1244a32 Friends sometimes wrong each other because it is things they love more, not their owner, so that for them loving a friend is just like someone's choosing a wine because it is pleasant [*sc.* without a care about what wine it is];[105] in the case in question it was **a35** wealth they chose because it was of use to them – more useful than the owner [*sc.* considered apart from his wealth], who is then annoyed, as if having been chosen more in place of something of lesser value than himself [*sc.* than for himself],[106] while the other side complains, because now they want him as a friend on the basis of excellence, having looked before for the pleasant or useful one.

EE Book IV, Chapter 12

1244b1 We must also investigate the subject of self-sufficiency and friendship, and how their respective properties relate to each other. For one might raise the puzzle whether someone self-sufficient in every respect will have a friend at all, if we look for one when we are in need. Or not? **b4** If the good person is the most self-sufficient, and excellence brings happiness, what need would he have of a friend? Someone self-sufficient, being self-sufficient, needs neither people useful to him nor people to entertain him nor to live with anyone; his own is all the company he needs. This is most evident in the case of god; for clearly, being in need of nothing beyond himself he will not need a friend either, nor will he ever have **b10** what he was never lacking in the first place. It follows from this that the happiest human being, too, will have least need of a friend, except to the extent that it turns out to be impossible for him to be self-sufficient. **b12** Necessarily, then, the person living the best life will have the fewest friends, and their number will always be decreasing; he will not be eager to get them, instead disdaining not only useful friends but those desirable for their company. **b15**. But it is at this very point in the argument that it would seem evident that a friend is not for the sake of utility, or to provide help in time of need, the only [*sc.* true] friendship being the one based in excellence, for it is precisely when we are not in need of anything that people all look for those who will share the fruits of their prosperity, and beneficiaries rather than benefactors. **b20** Our judgement is better, too, when we are self-sufficient than when we are in need, and what we need most of all is people worthy of sharing our lives.

---

105   If this sounds anachronistic, no matter; the example works in any case.
106   'As if ... in place of ...': the friend, after all, does choose him, and does compare his value to that of his wealth, without actually recognising what his true value is.

1244b22 We must look at this puzzle to see if perhaps it is partly right but also partly misleading because of the comparison [*sc.* with god]. The matter is clear as soon as we grasp what life is, in activity and as final end. Well, evidently it is perceiving and knowing, so that sharing one's life is itself sharing perception and sharing knowledge with another. For each individual **b26** what is most choiceworthy is the activity of perceiving and the activity of knowing, themselves in themselves,[107] and it is because of this that the desire for living is inborn in all of us, for it should be one of our assumptions that living is a sort of knowing. **1244b29** So if one were then to cut out the reference to us and made living a matter of knowing, pure and simple, not of *our* knowing (something that the text just now left implicit, but is easy enough to supply if one thinks about what was being described),[108] it would be no different from someone else's knowing in our place, which would be like their living in our place; but it is reasonable to suppose that it will be more choiceworthy [*sc.* for us/the particular individual] to perceive ourselves and know [*sc.* ourselves], for[109] **b34** we must put together two points in our argument, namely that living [*sc.* understood as proposed] is choiceworthy and that so too is the good [*sc.* for us], and conclude from these that our having such a nature [*sc.* as to be able to perceive and know ourselves] is a good for us. **1245a1** So if, in such a listing of things [*sc.* choiceworthy and otherwise] one column always represents the former, that is where in general both the knowable and the perceptible belong by virtue of their sharing in the nature of the determinate; it follows that wanting to perceive oneself is wanting oneself to be of such and such a sort. **a5** So since it is not by ourselves that we are any of these things, but rather because we share in the capacities involved in perceiving and knowing – for it is when perceiving that one becomes an object of perception, in the very respect in which one is oneself perceiving beforehand, and according to how and what it was, and it is similarly when one knows that one becomes an object of knowledge;

---

107 I think this is the fundamental premiss we need (as supplied by Solomon's emendations, in b26–7) at this point; perceiving and knowing *oneself* (as per Kosman's emendations) comes in later, and its importance is argued for separately (i.e. just below, in two stages, the first starting in 1244b29, the second in 1244b32–3).

108 I here withdraw the suggestion made in Rowe 2023b *ad loc.* (following others) that b30–2 is a gloss; it is, I think, Aristotle himself that is doing both of the things I attributed to another hand, i.e., (1) referring back to 1244b22–3 ('partly right but also partly misleading'), and (2) anticipating the reference to 'what plainly happens in fact' at 1245a28–9; in other words, he is annotating his own text.

109 Aristotle sets out to establish the 'reasonableness' of the claim just made, and in the process explains both the importance of adding in the reference to the particular individual, as signalled by the thought-experiment in 1244b29–33 (it is not just an abstract truth that 'living is a sort of knowing', but *our* living) and the special sort of knowledge it is.

so it is because **a10** of this that one always wishes to live, too, namely because one always wishes to know, and one wishes for this because one wishes oneself to be the thing known. Choosing to live with others might seem in a way simple-minded, if one thinks about it, first of all from the point of view of what we have in common with other animals, like eating and drinking together: what difference does it make if we do it in proximity with each other or apart, if you take away any conversation; but then again sharing in casual chatter is itself a matter of indifference; consider also that between friends that are self-sufficient dispensing and acquiring new information will be impossible, since if he is learning he is not as he should be [*sc.* self-sufficient?] while if he is doing the teaching his friend is not, and similarity is what makes for friendship.[110] But surely the matter is quite evident, and **1245a20** we do all find it more pleasant to share good things with our friends, to the extent that these are available to each and the best of which each is capable, which in one case will be bodily pleasure, in another the study of music and poetry,[111] in another philosophy. And we need to be near our friends 'Far-off friends are a burden', goes the saying, implying that in such a case we should not have been separated from them. **a25** That is a way in which sexual love resembles friendship, because the lover desires the company of the beloved, only for sensual purposes and not for those he most should.

1245a28 That, then, is what the argument says, and creates a puzzle from it, but on the other side there is what plainly happens in fact, so that we are clearly being misled by whatever it is that is creating the puzzle. It is from the following that we should look for the truth: a friend, as the proverb says, is like another Heracles,[112] another self, but he is torn apart from us, and it is hard for the features of a single individual to be brought together, but still he is by nature what is most akin to us: one person may resemble us in body, others in soul, others in some or other part of either, but for all that **a36** it is the friend that is most like a separate self. Necessarily, then, perceiving one's friend is in a way perceiving oneself and in a way knowing oneself. It follows that it is reasonable for us to find it pleasant to share even the vulgar things, and to seek out another's company in life, **a40** for they will always be accompanied by perception of the other – but more pleasant to share the more divine **1245b1** pleasures, for the reason that it is always more pleasant to observe oneself enjoying a superior good, which will sometimes be an affective state, sometimes an action, sometimes something else, and if [*sc.* it is pleasant] for him

---

110 So they should not be friends, because they lack self-sufficiency in different ways?
111 *Theôria mousikê*: more, I think, than just 'listening to music' (Inwood and Woolf 2013).
112 Perhaps a reference to Heracles' relative, friend, and co-fighter Iolaus.

that he live well, and so too the friend, and that by living together they should be active together, their partnership will be most of all in the things that constitute the end of life. **b5** So we should reflect together as well as feast together, the latter for the sake of things other than food and necessities,[113] for if they are the purpose it is less a matter of getting together than of consumption. But each individual wants to share a life engaged in a goal he is capable of attaining; failing that, people choose most of all to do good to their friends **b9** and have their friends do good to them. So it is evident that we should share our lives, and that everyone wants this, and most of all the happiest and best of us; **b12** but that the argument did not make this apparent was also reasonable, since it contained truths. The solution lies in the way the comparison is put together, true though it is. Because god is not such as to need a friend, the argument supposed the same to be true of his human counterpart; yet on this account the good person will not even think; **1245b16** for the goodness of the divine state does not lie in this, but rather in the fact that he is too superior an entity to think of anything else except himself. The reason is that for us well-being involves something beyond ourselves, whereas god constitutes his own well-being by himself.

1245b20 It is correct to say both that we seek and pray for many friends for ourselves, and that we also say that the person with many friends has none; for if it were possible to live with and share the perceptions of many people at the same time, the more the better, but since it is a most difficult thing, our sharing of perceptions must necessarily be with a smaller number, so that it is not only difficult to acquire many friends, because of the need for testing, but difficult to enjoy them when we have them.

b27 Sometimes we want our loved one to do well away from us, sometimes to share the same fortune with ourselves, and to want to be together is characteristic of friendship. For if it is possible to be together and to do well, that is what everyone chooses; but if it is not possible, then they choose something else, as perhaps Heracles' mother would have chosen for him to be a god rather than be with her and serve as day-labourer to Eurystheus; or one might borrow the Spartan's joke when someone told him to call on the Dioscuri for help in a storm.[114] **1245b35** It is thought to belong to the loving friend to keep the loved one away if their circumstances are difficult, but of the loved one to want to share them, and both are reasonable expectations; for it should be the case that nothing is as painful to a friend as the [*sc.* seeing/being with] the friend is pleasant, and yet it seems one should not choose one's own interests

---

113   Religious occasions, for example?
114   As in 'I'm in enough trouble; why involve them too?'.

over theirs. This is why people prevent the friend from sharing; it is enough for them to suffer by themselves, in order for them not to appear **1246a1** to be looking to their own interests and choosing pleasure for themselves at the cost of the friend's pain, together with the relief that comes from not having to bear troubles on one's own. Since well-being and being together are both choiceworthy, it is clear that even being together with the accompaniment of a lesser good is in a way more choiceworthy than being apart with the accompaniment of a greater one. **a5** Since, then, it is unclear how much weight attaches to being together, people disagree, some thinking it a mark of friendship to share everything together, just as dining together makes eating the very same things pleasanter, whereas others refuse to accept this on the grounds that if one takes this to the extreme one will be agreeing that it is better to suffer great adversity together than to enjoy great good fortune apart. **a10** The case is similar with misfortunes: sometimes we want our friends not to be there, and not to cause them pain when they can do nothing to help us, whereas sometimes it is most pleasant to have such people there. But the contrariety is quite reasonable. It happens for the reasons we mentioned before: both because of the fact that we unqualifiedly try to avoid seeing our friend in pain or in a bad state, just as we do ourselves, and yet to see a friend is as pleasant as any of the most pleasant things we enjoy, for the reason we have given, and to see him not ill if we are not ill ourselves; whichever of these is the more pleasant **1246a20** makes the difference between our wanting our friend there or not. This happens in the case of inferior people, and for the same reason, for they feel the greatest pique that their loved ones should do well, or even exist, if they themselves cannot avoid misfortune, which is why suicides sometimes kill their beloveds along with themselves; for they think [*sc.* the continuing presence of their beloveds will make them] more aware of their own misfortune, in the same way as someone who remembers doing well before is more aware of present suffering than if he thought his life one of misfortune throughout.

EE Book V

EE Book V, Chapter 1

1246a27 One might raise the following problem, whether it is possible to use a given thing both for its natural purpose and in another way, and this either *qua* what it is, or alternatively by coincidence or accident. For example, if the thing is an eye, one can use it to see, or else use it otherwise to mis-see, by twisting it so that a single thing appears to be two things. These uses are both because it is an eye and what was in question was the use of an eye, but there would be another, incidental or accidental, way of using it, for example if it were a case of selling it or eating it. Similarly then with knowledge, for it is possible to use it correctly and to make a mistake, such as when someone involuntarily writes incorrectly and [*sc.* so] uses knowledge like ignorance, as if one were turning over one's hand and changing it for the other,[1] just as dancing girls sometimes use a foot as a hand and a hand as a foot. **a36** So if all the excellences are [*sc.* forms of] knowledge,[2] it would be possible even to use justice as injustice. A person will then be acting unjustly from justice when they do unjust things in the same way as [(*sc.* in our example)] they do ignorant things from knowledge. But if this is impossible, it is clear that the excellences will not be [*sc.* forms of] knowledge and neither, if it is not possible to be ignorant from knowledge but only to make mistakes and do the same things as one would from ignorance, will an agent act at all from injustice as they would from justice.

---

1   Is Aristotle again thinking, here, of writing – perhaps of his switching his stylus – or more likely, his slave's switching his – from one hand to the other? I note that dexterity comes up in the 'CB' (1 = *NE* V, 1134b33–5), with the claim that any of us could acquire it. That might make it a matter of note for Aristotle if he observed someone (in this case his scribe?) apparently acquiring it. Such a proposal would fit reasonably well with the parallel Aristotle immediately offers, and would be at least consistent with other uses of *metastrephô*, in Aristotle and elsewhere. We are commonly encouraged to think, and people have often supposed, that Aristotle lectured from notes; I think he read his own complex texts, any notes that were written being written by his students (that, I continue to think, is the most likely original starting-point for the *MM*. I think he read his full texts to his students in the Lyceum, mainly because of their extraordinary complex and highly articulated structures (the *EE* is a good example); it is hard to conceive of *notes* (and with *EE*, it is patently obvious that we are not dealing with any sort of notes), that would convey more than a fraction of what he was saying. My conclusion, and my proposal, is that the present context in *EE* may well take us back to the stage of actual composition, in private, with Aristotle thinking aloud to his scribe.
2   This is a somewhat surprising formulation, given that Socrates has just been told off for saying knowledge instead of wisdom.

1246b6 But further, if wisdom is knowledge and something true, it will do the same things as it does, for it [*sc.* knowledge] would be possible to act unwisely from wisdom and make the mistakes that the unwise person makes. But if the use of a given thing insofar as it is that thing is single, in such cases people would be acting wisely in so acting. Well, then, in the case of the other [*sc.* forms of] knowledge there is another controlling knowledge that brings about the turning; and what knowledge is in control of the one that controls them all? It cannot be a question of knowledge any longer. But neither will it be an [*sc.* ethical] excellence, because it [*sc.* that is, whatever it is, that is controlling in this case] is using excellence. For it is the excellence of the ruling [*sc.* element] that uses that of the element that is ruled over. What [*sc.* knowledge], then, is it?[3] Or is it just as self-indulgence is said to be a badness of the unreason[*sc.*-ing element] of the soul, and the unself-controlled person to be somehow self-indulgent while possessing intelligence? **1246b15** But in that case, if appetite is strong, it will turn the agent, and the outcomes of the agent's calculations will be the opposite [*sc.* of what they would have been]. Or is it clear that even if there is excellence in this [*sc.* the appetitive element], while there is also ignorance in the reason[*sc.*-ing element], they are made to change their functions to that of the other, [*sc.* so that what rules is ruled and what [*sc.* should be] ruled rules]? The result is that it will be possible both to use justice unjustly and badly and [*sc.* to use] wisdom unwisely. **b19** In which case the opposites [*sc.* will also be possible], for it would be strange if with the appropriate excellence present in the reason[*sc.*-ing element] the arrival of badness in the unreason[*sc.*-ing element] will turn it and produce ignorance, while excellence in the unreason[*sc.*-ing element] when ignorance is present will not turn this round and make the agent judge wisely and as they should. **1246b24** And once again [*sc.* it will be possible] for the wisdom in the calculative [*sc.* element] to make self-indulgence in the unreason[*sc.*-ing] act moderately; which is just what self-control appears to be. The result is that there will even be the [*sc.* using of wisdom] from ignorance, wisely.[4]

---

3 Reeve's (2021) and others' simple 'What?' for *tis* is a mistake. Aristotle is still working with the possibility, however remote, that what controls the knowledge that controls all knowledges ought to be a [*sc.* form of] knowledge. [Note: the reference to Reeve here and elsewhere in the notes is mainly an accident of the fact that the notes were revised in the context of a reading group that was starting partly from his translation. In general I confess to finding more substantial help from Kenny 2011 and Inwood and Woolf 2013; but it seemed useful to record differences with Reeve as these emerged (none of the translators of course had access to the new text)].

4 The translation here, which renders an implied noun as participial/a gerund, because of the concluding adverb, may well seem to be pushing against the limits of what is possible in

1246b28 But these things are strange, especially the matter of using ignorance wisely. For in the other cases we do not see anything of the sort, as for example self-indulgence overturns medical or grammatical knowledge but it will certainly not turn ignorance around, if it comes up against it, because [a] [*sc.* the relevant] superiority[5] is not in it, but [b] in general it is excellence that stands in this relation to badness. For the fact is that everything the unjust person can do the just person can do [*sc.* too], and in general a capacity includes the **1246b34** [*sc.* corresponding] incapacity. So that it is clear that people's being wise goes together with those dispositions of the unreason[*sc.* -ing element] being good, and the Socratic [saying] is correct, that nothing is stronger than wisdom; only he was incorrect in calling it 'knowledge' instead of 'wisdom'. For it is an excellence and not knowledge but [rather] a different form of cognition.

EE Book v, Chapter 2

1246b39 But since it is not only wisdom that brings about doing well, along with excellence [*sc.* of character], but we say that the fortunate also do well, on the basis that good fortune too **1247a1** brings about doing well, and [*sc.* does] the same things as knowledge, we must inquire whether it is by nature that one person is fortunate and another is unfortunate, or not, and how things are in relation to these things. For that some people *are* fortunate is something we see; for they succeed in many things in which fortune is controlling, and again, even in things in which there is expertise there is nevertheless a large [*sc.* element] of fortune, **a6** for example in generalship and steersmanship, even while they are lacking in wisdom. So then is it from some disposition that these fortunate people come to be fortunate, or is not by their being themselves of a certain sort that they are capable of doing the fortunate things they do? That is how people think it is, as things presently stand, on the basis that some people are fortunate by nature and that it is nature that makes people of a certain sort [*sc.* fortunate], and they differ from birth onwards, just as some are born with light-blue eyes and some with dark eyes, by virtue of the fact

---

Greek. My response is that this case is merely an example, if an extreme one, of Aristotle's frequently laconic, abbreviated style in *EE*. I claim that it is clear what he is saying; the problem is with the way he chooses to say it (as I have reconstructed that on the basis of the evidence of the MSS).

5 Reeve's 'excess' is odd, and I find his whole note here quite unhelpful. The point is straightforward: what is there in self-indulgence that would be powerful enough to change ignorance into knowledge?

that *this* particular thing [*sc.* the eye] is of *this* particular sort [*sc.* light-blue or dark]. It is in this way [they say] that people are divided into the fortunate and the unfortunate; for that they do not succeed by means of wisdom is clear, for wisdom is not unreason[*sc.*-ing], but is in possession of a reason why [*sc.* the agent whose wisdom it is] is acting in the way they are acting, and the type we are describing would be unable to say why they are succeeding. For [*sc.* if they were able] it would be by virtue of expertise; and what is more they are plainly lacking in wisdom – not only in relation to other things[6] – for there would be nothing strange about that (for example Hippocrates was an expert geometer but it seems he was stolid and unwise about everything else, for example losing a large quantity of money on a [*sc.* commercial] voyage to the customs officials in Byzantium, out of simple-mindedness, or so they say) – but in the things in which they are fortunate even while lacking wisdom. For in relation to steering a ship[7] it is not the most expert that are fortunate but it is as in the fall of the dice, where one person throws nothing while the next person makes the throw that [*sc.* according to the explanation just described][8] was in accordance with his fortunate nature; **1247a23** Or [*sc.* are the fortunate people in question fortunate] because they are loved by god, and because of some external factor that causes them to succeed, as for example a sailing-vessel that has been badly put together often sails better, not because of how it is itself but because it has a good steersman.[9] Yet it would be strange if a superior being like a god were to love such a person [*sc.* as our fortunate, unthinking type] rather than the best and the wisest. If, then, a person succeeds from one of three [*sc.* causes], [i] by nature, [ii] through intelligence, or [iii] by virtue of some kind of [*sc.* outside]

---

6 I.e., things in general?
7 *Nauklêria* can also refer to ship-owning, and Hippocrates evidently owned at least the cargo, but steersmanship is clearly meant here.
8 The supplement is justified by the 'philosophical' imperfect *ên* in 1247a22. With the text as printed [*kath' hê= kath'hên bolên*], Aristotle is saying two things at once with utter efficiency, and perhaps even a certain sly *humour*: (i) there are genuine cases of good fortune or luck [sc. despite what Socrates may claim in the *Euthydemus*, to be referred to shortly]; [ii] here is one example that rules out any connection with individual natures [do the dice know who is throwing them?]. Quite apart from the manuscript evidence (Jackson's *hex*, for example, is a plain guess), alternative reconstructions to my own offer an altogether flatter, quite pedestrian sense. I know which Aristotle I prefer.
9 I note that Reeve supplies a sentence of his own here; one that I think is seriously misleading: Aristotle's point is merely about whether or not an external factor is involved, not about what that factor might be; he makes no suggestion, as Reeve suggests he does, that it might be an actual outside agent (like a god). Something like that will surface eventually, as this highly dialectical argument goes on its course, but it is unhelpful to give the reader the impression that it is prefigured here.

superintendence, and [ii] and [iii] are not in play, our fortunate type will be so by nature. But this must be wrong, because nature is precisely cause either of what is always as it is or of what is for the most part, and it is the opposite with chance/fortune. Again, if someone hits or fails to hit the mark because they are of *this* sort, in the way that the sight of the light-blue-eyed person is not sharp, nature and not chance/fortune is cause. In that case [*sc.* our type] is not fortunate but as it were well-natured – which will leave us having to conclude this much, that the people we say are fortunate are not so through fortune/chance. In which case they are not fortunate. **1247b1** For the fortunate are those of whose goods fortune/chance is cause.

But if so, will there not be such a thing as fortune/chance altogether? Or will there be such a thing without its being a cause? But there *must* be, and it must be a cause. In which case it will also be cause for some people of good things or bad ones. **b4** But if we should in general remove it [*sc.* from the list of causes] and say that nothing [*sc.* at all] occurs from fortune/chance, but we say it is a cause, when there is another one, because we do not see [*sc.* that other cause] – this being why when in fact people are defining fortune/chance they posit it as a cause that it is beyond the range of human calculation to reason out, on the assumption that there is some such real thing – **1247b8** well, this would be another question to be resolved. But since we [*sc.* actually] see particular people experiencing good fortune on a single occasion, what is the reason that they will not also succeed again because of the same thing and again? For the same thing will have the same cause. In which case this [*sc.* repeated success] will not belong to fortune/chance. But when there is the same outcome from an unlimited and undefined set [*sc.* of factors], there will be what is good and what is bad, but there will not be knowledge of it, i.e., the knowledge that comes from experience, since if there were people would learn how to be fortunate, or else all [*sc.* forms of] knowledge would actually be forms of good fortune, just as Socrates said.[10] So what is it that prevents such things [*sc.* repeated successes] happening to a particular person many times

---

10   The reference is undoubtedly to Plato's *Euthydemus*, the *locus classicus* for this claim (see esp. 279d); Aristotle's close knowledge of Socrates' argument in the dialogue is evident from repeated echoes of it in the present discussion. 'Fitzgerald's canon' holds that references in Aristotle to Plato's Socrates always use the definite article ('that Socrates); the plain 'Socrates said' here at *EE* 1247b16 (prefacing what is in part direct citation), is enough to show the falsity of the claim; meanwhile Aristotle also does refer to 'old man Socrates' for the idea of virtue as knowledge (*EE* 1216b3), which – given that the key evidence for attributing the equation to Socrates is in the dialogues – may suggest that he was somewhat less interested in distinguishing between the fictional and the historical Socrates than Fitzgerald was in Dublin in 1853.

over in succession not because they are *this* particular sort of person but in whatever way it might be that someone would always make the 'lucky' throw?

1247b19 What, then, should we consider next? Are there not impulses present in the soul, some arising from calculation, others from unreasoning desire, and are the latter not prior? **b20** For if the desire for [the] pleasant because of appetite is also by nature, by *nature* everything would make for the good.[11] If, then, there are particular individuals that are 'well-natured' in the way that capable singers that do not know how to sing[12] are well endowed by nature in the relevant respect, and if even without reason[sc.-ing] they are impelled in the way in which their nature is constituted, and their appetite is both for *this* and *at that moment* and in the way that it should be, where the 'this' and the when are also as they should be,[13] these people will succeed even if they are without wisdom and an account to give of [sc. what they are doing], just as [sc. our singers] will sing well while being incapable of teaching anyone else how to do it. **1247b27** But it is just this sort of people that [sc. we are calling] fortunate, namely those who succeed for the most part without reason[sc.-ing]. In which case it is by nature that the fortunate are so. Or: is 'good fortune' being spoken of in more than one way? For some things are done from the impulse [sc. of desire] and by the [sc. reasoned] decision of the agent, while others are not, but rather the opposite,[14] both in those cases in which people seem to have calculated badly but nevertheless succeed, and we say they have experienced good fortune, and again, if in these things what they were wishing for was something else, or something less than the good they actually took away. It is possible, then, [sc. for us to say] that the agents in the former cases are being fortunate through nature, for the impulse and desire set them straight by being for what it should, **b35** while their calculations were simple-minded; and in this sort of case, when with [sc. any] calculation [sc. of theirs] appearing

---

11 'For ... the good': after all, we are trying to explain how it is that some people get what is good contrary to expectations.
12 I.e., I suppose, because they have never learned, and couldn't say how they do it.
13 My rendering here is a little loose, perhaps, but the Greek construction is quite difficult to track, and once again the general sense is pretty clear: we are talking about a type of person who apparently mimics the wise without having the wisdom, getting every aspect of the decision right. Aristotle's phrasing here itself mimics his description of the wise person's decision-making (*passim*). Most importantly, we are not talking about, e.g., the acquisition of external goods, as in the parallel discussion in the *MM*.
14 I.e., clearly, without the element of decision; by implication, an action driven by impulse in the absence of reasoning is the opposite of one originating in a combination of both; that seems reasonable enough, if the latter is the standard type of human action. The only question, which is about to be resolved in some sort of way, is whether *any* human action can in fact be driven by desire only.

not to be correct [*sc.* the] cause of it [*sc.* their unexpected success] turns out to be appetite, it is this [*sc.* appetite] that saved them by being correct. But sometimes because of appetite [*sc.* the agent] calculated again in the same way and came to misfortune. But then in the other cases how will good fortune correspond with well-naturedness of desire and appetite?

1248a1 Here is what we must say:[15] either the good fortune here and that/the other one[16] are the same, or else there are more sorts of good fortune than one, and fortune/chance has a double aspect. And since we see particular individuals enjoying good fortune alongside all the [*sc.* forms of] knowledge and the correct calculations [*sc.* in different spheres], it is clear that something else will be cause of their good fortune. But *is* that good fortune? Or is it not? If [*sc.* the agent] in that moment[17] had the appetite for the things they should and when they should, **1248a6** calculation of a human sort certainly will not be [*sc.* the] cause of this,[18] for [*sc.* if there is something, as in this case,] desire for which is natural, it is not something wholly uncalculated, but [*sc.* the agent/their calculation/reason [*sc.*-ing]] is corrupted by some factor or other. So they appear to be enjoying good fortune because fortune/chance is a cause of things that happen contrary to reasonable expectation, and the phenomenon we are discussing is just that, **1248a10** for it is contrary to knowledge and the general rule, but as it seems, its explanation does not lie in fortune/chance, but it [*sc.* merely] appears like this for the reason just stated. We may conclude[19] that this argument of ours does not demonstrate that enjoying good fortune occurs by nature[20] but rather that not all those that seem to be fortunate [*sc.* in the sort of case we have been discussing] succeed because of fortune/chance, but [*sc.* some of them] rather because of [*sc.* their] nature. Nor does it [*sc.* our argument] demonstrate that fortune/chance is cause of nothing [*sc.* else] either, just not of all the things it appears to be cause of.

---

15 An unusual rendering of *alla mên*, but I think it conveys the tone of the turn in the argument well enough.
16 I.e. good fortune as we ordinarily think about it, apart from that of the special type of 'fortunate' people whose fortune Aristotle is currently interested in understanding.
17 'in that moment' is intended to mark the (I think important) use of the aorist tense here.
18 I.e., the phenomenon we are endeavouring to explain. I propose that the claim in this sentence will go through if we supply at least two unstated premisses, both of which are apparently under threat in the present context but which Aristotle will jointly defend as the chapter continues: (i) rationality/reason[?ing?] is an essential part of human nature; (ii) the agents currently in question (the 'fortunate' ones we are talking about) are fully human agents.
19 'So that' in the Greek.
20 I.e. some natural disposition.

1248a17 Yet one might raise the following problem. Is fortune/chance cause of this very thing – that [*sc.* the agent] should have the appetite in that moment[21] for what they should and when they should? Or, if we take it *that* way, will it [*sc.* fortune/chance] be cause of everything?[22] For it will also be cause of our beginning to think and deliberate at some particular moment,[23] for one surely does not begin deliberating having [already] deliberated, that deliberation leading to a new one, but there is somehow a starting-point; nor does one start thinking having thought before thinking, and so on *ad infinitum*. In that case thought[24] is not cause of one's beginning to think, nor is deliberation of one's beginning to deliberate. What else then is there [to be cause] except fortune/chance? So then it will all start from fortune/chance. Or is there some starting-point with no other starting-point outside it, **1248a25** and is this capable of doing the sort of thing it does because of its being the sort of thing it is?[25]

1248a25 What we are looking for is the following: what is the starting-point of movement in the soul? Clearly, just as god moves everything in the universe, so he does there [*sc.* in the soul];[26] for in a way the divine in us[27] moves everything, and the starting-point of reason is not reason but something

---

21 The aorist again is important: we are talking about the very point at which the agent does whatever it is that constitutes or leads to their unexpected success.
22 Sc. [as the sequel shows] which would not make it an obviously attractive route to go down.
23 Two more aorists!
24 'Thought' here is *nous*, which in the special Aristotelian use signifies a kind of insight (Broadie and Rowe favours 'intelligence', which looks less helpful out of the context in question). Here, like its related verb, it is clearly used to refer to thinking in general.
25 Sc. and so being predictable in its effects, as fortune/chance is not.
26 The significance of this new move can hardly be overstated. It is the first step in an account for which there is no parallel elsewhere in Aristotle's ethical writings (if we set aside the *MM*); recognition of its full novelty has, I think, been hampered by the condition of the received text, which has made coherent discussion of a complex argument nigh on impossible. The step in question is in itself remarkable: somehow or other divinity is working within us in a way comparable to that of the working of the prime mover in the cosmos. But it is not, I think, that mover itself; it is an inner presence whose resemblance to the prime mover is restricted to that role, in us, and divinity itself. So we are not talking about a god or a δαίμων acting on the agent from outside, as at e.g. 1247a26–7. On the other hand, the 'god' now being introduced does, I propose, retrospectively throw light on the wording in those two lines, for as I and others have proposed, *EE* VIII/V.3 includes an allusion to Socrates' personal δαίμων; in my view the 'god' of ch. 2 will turn out to bear more than a little resemblance to that.
27 'Namely the understanding' (i.e., *nous*), Reeve, n. 695, and I agree in the end that Aristotle must have his (special) *nous*, *pace* Reeve, in the same note, the 'starting-point' that *nous* has is not obviously an *archê* in the sense of VIII/V.2, i.e. not a (moving) cause.

superior. So what could ever be superior to knowledge except god?[28] For [sc. ethical] excellence [sc. if it were to put its candidacy forward] is an instrument of thought[, so it cannot be that]. And it is because of this [sc. whatever it is],[29] as I was saying some way back, that people that are impelled to do [what they do] and succeed when not reasoning, are called fortunate. And **1248a32** it does not benefit them to deliberate, because they have such a starting-point, which is superior to [sc. their] thinking and deliberation, whereas others have reason[ing], and this they do not have, and they are inspired,[30] but this [i.e. reasoning] they are incapable of. [There is no benefit, then, in their trying to reason], for [even] without having the reasoning they match even the speediness of divination achieved by the wise and knowledgeable, so that one could almost take it for that [divination] from reason[ing]. But some of them [achieve it, i.e. their speedy 'divination'] through experience, others through familiarity, instead of using inquiry, and these [processes work] by virtue of the god;[31] this[32] also sees well both what is to come and what is now,[33] even in those whose reason is disconnected in this way. **1248a40** This is why those of a melancholic disposition also tend to have clear dreams.[34] **1248b1** For [this thing we are calling] the starting-point appears to gather strength when reason is disengaged, and it as with the blind, who remember better when disengaged

---

28 Reeve's n. 696 is mistaken, if 'the god' is *nous*; his/its mode of operation is actually being *compared* with/illustrated by the way seers operate, not contrasted with it. The problem seems to start with Reeve's complete misconstrual of 1248a37–9, for which see his n. 700, with or without the text he chooses to translate.

29 'God' is hardly yet a sufficient description!

30 I.e., like seers, *manteis*, they 'see' things they would not be expected to see [in the absence of reasoning].

31 I.e. the one we've just introduced; the definite article with *theos* can make it refer to gods generally, but it plainly is not doing that here.

32 The neuter *touto* seems to refer us back to the alternative description of 'the god' and 'the divine in us' at 1248a28.

33 'Also' the future and the present, i.e., as well as the past as implied by the introduction of experience and habituation. Cf. the description of Calchas the seer at Homer, *Iliad* 1.70–2 (Aristotle knows his Homer, as a glance at Bekker's *Index Aristotelicus* shows).

34 On 'clear dreaming' (as opposed to dreams that merely happen to be or turn out to be true), cf. *De div. in somno* 463a23ff.: 'as ... when we are about to act, or are engaged in any course of action, or have already performed certain actions, we often find ourselves concerned with these actions, or performing them in a vivid dream; and the cause of this is that the dream-movement has had a way paved for from the original movements set up in the daytime; exactly so, but conversely, it must often happen that the movements set up first in sleep should turn out to be starting-points of actions to be performed in daytime, since the recurrence by day of the thought of these actions also has had its way paved for it in the images before the mind at night ...' (*The Oxford Translation of Aristotle*, ed. Barnes).

from the situation where the remembering [element] is confronting things actually being seen.

It is clear, then, that there are two kinds of good fortune, and one of them is divine, which is why one sort of fortunate person actually does seem to be fortunate because of god; and this is the person who tends to succeed in accordance with his impulse, whereas the other does so contrary to his impulse.[35] Reasoning is not [behind the success] in either case; the one sort of good fortune tends more to be continuous, whereas the other is not continuous.

EE Book v, Chapter 3

1248b10 So then we have earlier discussed each [ethical][36] excellence, as a part of the whole; and since we separated off what each is a capacity for, one by one, [now] we must also articulate precisely the excellence [composed] from these, which we shall now immediately call[37] 'nobility/fine-and-goodness'. That the person who is going to be truly described in this way will necessarily possess all the individual excellences, is plain. For it cannot be otherwise, whichever other case one considers: no one is healthy in body as a whole if none of the parts of their body is healthy; necessarily, either all or most of the most influential parts must be in the same condition as the whole. Now being good and being fine-and-good/noble [differ] not just because they have the names they have but by having the difference in themselves. For among goods taken as a

---

35 'Contrary to his impulse', I take it, because the impulse was actually in the direction of something other than what the agent actually succeeded in getting or doing (plain good fortune, one might say).

36 Reeve (n. 703) proposes, without giving any grounds, that the excellences 'of thought' are also included, but I see no reason to suppose that 'nobility' is for the moment being said to require a capacity for *theôria*, understood as philosophical inquiry in general – even though, later in the chapter, *theôria* will enter the picture.

37 The imperfect tense (plus *êdê*) in the MSS, and as printed in the new text, is problematic, given that Aristotle has not mentioned such an excellence before in the *EE* (But see my footnote 40 to Appendix 1.). Given how much has gone before, and that Aristotle believes in an excellence he calls 'nobility'/'good-and-fineness', we could just suppose that he is misremembering. But for what will be so central a topic this looks unlikely. The alternative (and I now [February 2025] think this the right solution, incorporating it into the text and translation) is to accept Jackson's *kaloumen*, reading it as future rather than present; we *shall now immediately call it ...*'. I hazard that it was the *êdê*, read as 'already', that first induced the error (imperfect for future; the translator of BF was as slow as modern translators (including Jackson, as reported by Rackham 1935, and myself) to recognise *kaloumen* as a quite regular contracted future, consistent with *vocabimus* as much as *vocamus*.

whole, there are ends that are themselves desirable for their own sake, and of these the fine ones that while all being [desirable] for their own sake are also praiseworthy. For these are the source of praiseworthy actions as well as being praiseworthy themselves – justice itself too[, for example,] because the actions deriving from it [are so], as are moderate actions, for moderation too [is praiseworthy]. **1248b24** But health is not something praiseworthy, for neither is the work it does, nor is [doing something] with strength, because strength is not praiseworthy either. They *are* good, just not praiseworthy. It is similarly clear by induction, in all other cases. So a person is *good* if the natural goods are good for them. For the [goods] that people fight for and appear greatest, honour, wealth, bodily excellences, strokes of good fortune and positions of power, all these are good by nature, but it is possible for them to be harmful for particular individuals because of the dispositions they have. For neither an unwise person nor an unjust nor a self-indulgent person will benefit from using them, any more than a sick person will benefit from using the diet of a healthy one, or a weak and lame one the trappings of a healthy person in perfect condition. A fine and good person, by contrast, is so by virtue of the fact that those goods that are fine belong to him for their own sake and that he is a doer of fine actions, and for their own sake. And fine things are the excellences and the things that are done from excellence.

But there is a certain civic disposition, of the sort that the Spartans have, or others of a similar sort might have. This is a disposition of the following sort: people think one should possess excellence, but for the sake of the natural goods. **1249a1** In which case they are good[38] men, for the natural goods are

---

38   The manuscript tradition gives us 'savage', *agrios*, not just 'wild', as suggested e.g. by Simpson 2013 at 186 [see my note 25 to Book III], but closer to 'full of rage', like a cornered wild boar, and there is nothing in Aristotle, even in the long treatment of the Spartan character in *Politics* II.7, that begins to support the idea that he could have described the Spartans, quite so casually, as 'savage': yes, they surely were, or could be, brutal, but even their brutality was, as Aristotle well knew, systematically organised; *agrios* is, then, already a suspect reading, even if it is what 'the MSS have' (Simpson, *ibid.*: never a good argument, let alone a decisive one, for a text all of whose surviving exemplars are descended from a single archetype); but quite apart from this, wildness or savagery or its absence is not relevant to the argument in the way that goodness, being *agathos*, is, as, I venture, Simpson's attempt at a translation, with *agrioi* in place, amply demonstrates ('Hence they are wild men, for while they have the natural goods' [what argument, I wonder, is being attributed to Aristotle here?], see now also Bobonich 2023). But in any case there is a mis-translation here: Aristotle is not saying, and has no grounds or reason for saying, that the Spartans 'have the natural goods', but rather 'while the natural goods [are good] for them' [the supplement is justified, indeed required, by the context: someone is good if and only if

good for them, but nobility/fine-and-goodness they do not have, for their fine things do not belong to them for their own sake, and those to whom they do so belong also choose them because they are noble/fine-and-good, and not only that, but **a5** also the things that are not fine by nature but good by nature are fine for *them*. For they are fine when the that for the sake of which they do and choose them is fine, which is why to the fine-and-good/noble person the natural goods are fine. **a8** For the just is fine, and this [sc. the just] is what is according to worth; and this person is worthy of these things, And the fitting is fine, and these are fitting for this person – wealth, good birth, [political] power. So that for the fine-and-good/noble person what is advantageous, too, is also fine. But for the many there is discord here, for those goods that are so without qualification[39] are not good for *them*, whereas they are good for the good person; for he does many fine actions because of them. **1249a14** the person who thinks one should possess the excellences for the sake of external goods, by contrast, does fine things [merely] incidentally. Nobility/fine-and-goodness, then, is excellence in its complete form.

    the natural goods are good for them, i.e., their nature has not been corrupted or distorted, so that what is naturally good for someone becomes harmful to them, amplifying the effect of the corruption or distortion instead of bringing benefit]. This is one case where manuscript 'authority', which is always in principle limited, since manuscripts (especially those of the EE) are typically full of mistakes, is trumped by the requirements of the argument. *agathos* in the MSS in question is also orthographically not far from *agrios* (a point I have verified by autopsy), and scribes typically write mechanically, without attention to the argument. *Autrement dit*, this would have been an easy mistake to make. Of course, the idea that the flawed, 'Spartan', disposition in question would be compatible with goodness is striking; but Aristotle is not denying that the Spartans or anyone like them possess the individual excellences (and few would have dared say they were not courageous!), merely saying that they prize them for the wrong reasons. In short: not only do I see no reason to regret preferring *agathoi* over *agrioi*, but I can see no reason at all to accept *agrioi*, which is in my view a simple scribal error, properly corrected in the Aldine. (Neither does it count against the correction that it was not made until then (as implied by comments like 'a reading that does not appear until the medieval period'), for if that were the case, we would be doomed just to make the best of the flawed text we have, with any emendation ruled out in advance ('No support for it in the MSS': but again, 'the manuscripts', while being the best and only evidence we have, often just get it plain wrong – as I think they plainly do here, with *agrioi* for *agathoi.*).

39 'in the abstract', Kenny 2011; i.e., presumably, without reference to the disposition of their possessor.

About pleasure, too, we have said what sort of thing it is and how it is good,[40] and that the unqualifiedly pleasant is also fine and the unqualifiedly good pleasant.[41] And pleasure does not come about except in action.[42] The consequence is that the truly happy person will also live most pleasantly, and this is not an idle thought on the part of those that think it.[43]

a23 Since the doctor too has a standard to which he refers when judging a body to be healthy or not and to what extent each activity should be done, and if [sc. the activity is done well] healthy is what [the body] will be, but no longer if [the activity] is done less or more [than the amount prescribed], so too for the good[44] person in relation to actions and choices of goods that are by nature good but not praiseworthy there must be a standard for the possession and choice or avoidance of wealth or paucity of money and [other] things bestowed by good fortune.[45] Well, earlier on in our discussion we said that it was 'as reason [prescribes']', which is as if in matters relating to food someone said 'as prescribed by the medical art and the account it gives of the matter', which is true but not clear.

Well then: one must as in everything live with reference to the ruling [element], and the disposition and activity of the ruling [element], as a slave does to their master and each and every person to the appropriate starting-point/[form of rule in question].[46] **1249b10** And since a human being too is by nature composed of what rules and what is ruled, each person should live with reference to his own starting-point. But there are two sorts of starting-point here, for [to go back to our parallel] the medical art is a starting-point in one way, health in another, and the former is for the sake of the latter. That is how it is with the

---

40   For this turn in the discussion, see 1.1, where Aristotle started the whole work by posing the question about the relationship between the good, the fine and the pleasant.
41   This is presumably what lies behind the claim at 1.1, 1214a6–7, that 'happiness, being finest and best of all things is the most pleasant'; we probably do not need to look for a previous exposition of the details, and if we do we shall not find one.
42   The text says 'does not come about not in action'; not quite the same thing, but near enough.
43   I.e., as a consequence of what we have said.
44   Here *spoudaios*, typically interchangeable with *agathos*.
45   This sentence by itself seems enough to rule out the line taken in *MM* that the whole discussion in v.2 was about external goods, though might the apparent equation here of external goods and fruits of good fortune also even be a source of the author's misunderstanding?
46   'Starting-point' is *archê* again, but *archê* is also rule or office; Aristotle is here exploiting the ambiguity, but we need 'starting-point' in order to maintain the connection with what went before.

reflective[47] faculty [in us]. For the god[48] is not a prescriptive ruler, but that for the sake of which wisdom prescribes, since *god* is in need of nothing – that for the sake of which has two senses, and they have been defined in other places.[49] So whichever choice and possession of goods that are good by nature will most bring about the reflection of the god[50] – whether bodily goods or money or friends or the other [sc. natural] goods, this is the best, and this is the finest standard; whatever choice and possession of such goods, by reason either of paucity or of excess prevents us from servicing the god[51] and [sc. so]

---

47   The word is *theôrêtikon*, which is commonly translated 'contemplative', and typically refers to, e.g., metaphysical investigation; but we should remember that Aristotle has earlier described the 'deliberative' element in the soul as a certain sort of cause (1226b27), which seems to invite us at least not to draw too firm a distinction between 'theoretical' and practical; both spheres involve reflection, and Aristotle gives no indication that the 'element' responsible is not the same in both. 'Reflective' is, then, my own preferred translation of *theôrêtikon*, as in Broadie-Rowe: Sarah Broadie's chief and for me decisive argument was that 'contemplative' suggests a primarily passive, receptive gaze rather active, discursive thinking. To achieve the appropriate contrast with 'practical', as in 'merely theoretical', one must of course bracket in the outcomes of the reflection with the activity; the reflection is not for the sake of the thinking, a kind of mental exercise. – Reeve's n. 717, on this part of the argument, depends on supposing that EE is to be understood from the NE. That is not, I think, a helpful approach; if Aristotle always thought and wrote the same things, one might ask why he went to the trouble of writing two versions of what would be essentially the same thing, and '*EE* after all more or less = *NE*' will continue to inhibit us from looking for, finding, and seeing the significance of the differences that stand out, in the new text, from the very page – including in the very passage on which Reeve writes his note.

48   I.e., the one we have introduced as starting-point of motion in the soul.

49   I.e., doing something for the sake of x is not always a matter of x's needing something; the next few lines will indicate what the 'for the sake of' relation in the present case is.

50   If god is to be like health and wisdom like medicine in the parallel case, it seems that god must be what is doing the reflecting, not what is being reflected on. Many, including myself in the past, have insisted on the opposite, but the logic of the context is against it, and as I have said, the terms *theôrein* and *theôrêtikos* are by no means restricted to theoretical subjects like higher causes (actually, whether in EE or in Aristotle more generally), which means, importantly, that 'the god' here can be fully what he was in the last chapter, and fully involved, however precisely it may be, in the practical successes of the special sort of fortunate people we were discussing. It is something else in the *theôrêtikon* [element], namely wisdom, that does the thinking, according to the implication of 1249b15–16, and god himself is the starting-point of any reflection, not in this context a thinker himself; the 'reflection of the god' will then mean 'the reflection started off by the god'.

51   It is more than tempting to take this as an echo of Plato's Socrates' portrayal of his philosophical questioning as 'service to the god (*Apology* 30a–b); 'god is in need of nothing' also has its counterpart in the *Euthyphro* (14a–15a); but the parallels are far from decisive, and the context is different.

reflecting, this is a bad choice and possession of them. And the soul does have this,[52] and this is the best standard – if one sees the rest of the other part of the soul, *qua* other.[53]

Let that then stand as our account of nobility/fine-and-goodness, and of the point[54] of things good unqualifiedly.

---

52   I.e., I take it, the complex 'element' that allows us to reflect.
53   I.e., *qua* non-reflective or actively interfering in reflection?
54   I.e., *skopos*, used in ordinary life of a target.

APPENDIX 1

Phronêsis and *sophia* in the *Eudemian* and *Nicomachean Ethics*

> By *phronesis* the *Eudemian Ethics* understands, like Plato and the *Protrepticus*, the philosophical faculty that beholds the highest real value, God, in transcendental contemplation, and makes this contemplation the standard of will and action; it is still both theoretical knowledge of supersensible being and practical moral insight.[1,2]

Jaeger's claim about *phronêsis* in the EE provided the core of his wider thesis of a development in Aristotle's thinking about ethics, from a 'reformed Platonism' in EE to the 'late Aristotelianism' of NE. The claim was widely, and rightly, disputed, ultimately receiving the *coup de grâce* in Kenny 1978. As Kenny pointed out

> The contrast which Jaeger drew between *phronêsis* in the EE and in the NE was in reality a contrast between *phronêsis* in the EE and in the [disputed books EE IV–VI '=' NE V–VII (hereafter 'C(ommon)B(ooks) 1–3')[3]]: his account of the nature of *phronêsis* in the NE rested almost entirely on the description of that virtue in the disputed book ['CB2']. The theory of a development, so far as concerns the [issue about] *phronêsis*, rests heavily on the assumption that the disputed books are Nicomachean: an assumption which Jaeger himself did almost nothing to defend, mentioning it only in an inadequate afterthought footnote. Given that we have shown that there are strong stylistic reasons for regarding the disputed books, as they stand, as belonging with the *Eudemian Ethics*, it would be possible to argue with as much justification as Jaeger that this *Ethics*, containing as it does the developed theory of *phronêsis*, must be the work of the later, mature Aristotle.[4]

---

1 Delivered as a paper in its original version in a series on the EE organised by the Centre Léon Robin, Paris 2016, then at the 'B' Club, Cambridge in 2017.
2 Jaeger 1923, tr. Robinson: 231. Jaeger's position here relies heavily on Kapp 1912.
3 That they are shared somehow between EE and NE is not controversial, even if there is dispute about exactly how 'common' they are to the two works: see e.g. n. 7 below.
4 Kenny 1978: 161.

I myself, in 1971, had argued that despite the overwhelmingly negative reception of Jaeger's thesis about *phronêsis* in EE and NE, in the terms in which it was stated, nevertheless 'in principle, [his] view of Aristotle's development was right'.

> There is ... no sharp distinction between ethics and the theoretical sciences in EE. In itself, this might not be of any great significance; much of [NE], too, is undeniably theoretical, if 'theoretical' means simply 'aiming at knowledge for its own sake'. But ... what is important is that Aristotle says nothing [in EE] about the peculiar nature of the objects with which ethics is ultimately concerned; and if, as I suggest, he is blind to this crucial point, or at least to its full implications, then it becomes possible that he not only regards ethics as theoretical, but regards it as *scientific*. ... I do not wish to suggest that it was ever a conscious tenet of Aristotle's that every particular moral issue could be resolved by the application of general scientific method. [Or, in other words (added in footnote), that argument about general principles could tell us how to act in each particular case. There is still plenty of room here for a process of deliberation; though again, Aristotle does not see this process as being different in *type* from the other (in fact, at 1247a13 ff., he describes it in exactly the same terms, as providing a *dia ti*, a rationale of action) ...] But if we take EE as being comparatively early, as I think we can, then it is surely plausible at least to suppose that, at this stage, he was not yet completely clear about the kind of science ethics represents; and that it was only in [NE] that he came to state his position clearly and explicitly ... In conclusion: in EE ... the practical and the theoretical tend to merge into one another ... But in [NE], the distinction between the two spheres is complete. Ethics [at the practical level] and the theoretical sciences no longer have anything in common, since their subject-matters are now established as being totally different in kind. Correspondingly, the rational faculty is now divided into two; the *phronêsis* of EE becomes the *aretê* of one half, and *sophia* is appropriated for that of the other.[5]

Like Jaeger, and indeed under his spell, I assumed in 1971 that the 'CB' originally belonged to NE, but with the difference that I proposed that two of them, i.e., what we habitually call NE V and VII, could be shown to be reworkings of original Eudemian material, as could other parts of NE that overlapped with EE;[6] and I duly set out to try

---

5 Rowe 1971a: 70–72.
6 By now a familiar idea: thus, e.g., Hendrik Lorenz (Lorenz 2013) says 'On stylistic grounds many scholars think that the common books were originally written to form part of the *Eudemian Ethics*, and so the recent trend to include them in translations of that work has something to be said for it. However, it is entirely possible, and in fact probable, that Aristotle

to show it. '*NE* VI', by contrast, including as it does the distinction between practical and theoretical reason, and so prominently, had on this account to be a new addition. This thesis about *NE* VI, of course, as I presented it, would fall with Kenny's demonstration that all three books are more at home in *EE*, even as they stand. (I shall come back to my thesis about reworking later on; and this will involve further reflection on that qualification 'even as they stand'.) Once '*NE* VI' becomes *EE* V, the Eudemian account of *phronêsis* becomes identical with what I, following Jaeger, had presupposed to be exclusively Nicomachean; and actually the '*NE* VI' account fits in some cases as well, in other cases better, according to Kenny, with the undisputed books of *EE* than it does with the undisputed books of *NE*. This he shows under four heads. *Phronêsis* is

> (1) an intellectual virtue concerned with the truth about mutable matters and the whole good of man. (2) ... the virtue of a particular part of the rational soul, and is distinguished from other intellectual virtues by being deliberative rather than intuitive and practical rather than theoretical. (3) ... indissolubly wedded to moral virtue ... (4) The union of *phronêsis* and moral virtue is dependent on the pre-existence of certain natural qualities, intellectual and affective.[7]

Some parts of Kenny's argument here seem to me to be stronger than others, but the net outcome is indisputable: so far as *phronêsis* is concerned, there is no incompatibility between the undisputed books of the *EE* and the second of the 'common' books.

Kenny has also succeeded over a larger front. We no longer have good enough reasons for calling the 'common books' exactly 'common', because they apparently belong more to *EE* than they do to *NE*.[8] Quite apart from Kenny's stylistic arguments,[9] there always remains the important question wh, in planning the *NE* as Jaeger, I, and many

---

himself revised and updated his discussions of such important topics as the nature of justice, the intellectual virtues, and lack of self-control for, and perhaps also after, inclusion in the *Nicomachean Ethics*. Furthermore, there are fairly strong historical reasons for thinking that these three books were included in a ten-book edition of the *Nicomachean Ethics*, long before someone decided to fill the large and rather conspicuous gap [caused by the removal of three books for modification and reuse in *NE*?] in the middle of an earlier five-book edition of the *Eudemian Ethics* by inserting the corresponding *Nicomachean* books, thus creating the appearance of a complete version of the *Eudemian Ethics* and at the same time presenting those three books as common to the two treatises.' Lorenz adds in a footnote 'The reasons [for so presenting them] are presented with clarity and force in [Primavesi 2007]'. I shall return to these issues later.

7   Kenny 1978: 163.
8   I still leave open the possibility that they belong to the *NE* more closely than simply through being borrowed wholesale from *EE*; that is, I remain interested in the possibility that they were to a greater or smaller extent reworked to fit their new context. See further below.
9   See the refined version of the arguments in Kenny 1978 in Kenny 1991, Appendix 1.

others have supposed him to have planned it, Aristotle would have wanted to include two separate discussions of pleasure, in Book VII and in Book X – discussions which not only present quite different treatments of their subject but fail to acknowledge the fact, containing as they do not a trace of a cross-reference between them. But then why not hand over one of those discussions to *EE*, which is crying out for it? And if there is no reason against that, why not similarly hand over the rest of *NE* VII, too?

And so on. In short, there appear to be grounds enough for editors and translators to print the three 'common' books as part of *EE*, and – if both works are included in the same volume, and *EE* comes first – no particular reason to print them again, as part of *NE*. (If on the other hand *NE* is being printed separately, it will appear oddly depleted and lacunose if a gap is left between Books IV and VIII, as it presumably did to whoever it was that first had the idea of importing three books of the *EE* into *NE*.) But this is far from the end of the story. The three books in question may in some important respects fit better in between *EE* III and VII than they do between *NE* IV and VIII, but that is not to say that the snugness of the fit is quite complete. One may wonder, for example, about the exact relationship between the first part of CB2.1 (i.e., *EE* V/*NE* VI) and *EE* V.3.[10] This particular case can perhaps be reduced to a mere matter of untidiness, in the way that – in effect – Kenny suggests,[11] and as such should worry us no more than the kinds of minor unevennesses, gaps, repetitions or part-repetitions that we expect to find, and do find, in the Aristotelian treatises in general. These are not, mostly, intended or written as finished, literary works, and Aristotle's style of argument is often one of starting and stopping, turning back on himself, beginning again, and so on. What we are used to treating as single treatises are in any case often assemblages of smaller, originally separate treatises, as notoriously in the case of the *Metaphysics* – and as in effect the *NE* will already be by virtue of its borrowing books from the *EE*; re-editing and revision, too (what I earlier called 'reworking') may also leave its mark.[12]

So let us suppose that the *EE*, with its missing books back in place, is more or less of one piece. I say 'more or less': if the manuscripts can be trusted, often a problem with the *EE*, what I call Book V looks and is fragmentary: it is unusually short, breaks off unexpectedly, is structurally somewhat loose, an, and as we have seen, in some manuscripts forms an extension of the preceding book. For its part, Book IV, on friendship, is or could be self-standing,[13] like its counterpart in *NE*, (i.e., *NE* VIII + IX). Still, *EE* with CB 1–3 feels reasonably complete, at any rate up to a point, and as Aristotelian

---

10   See Rowe 1971a: 109–13.
11   Kenny 1978: 181–2; cf. 1991: 100.
12   Cf. e.g. Burnyeat 2004: 179 'The surviving treatises, unlike the "exoteric" works he sent to the bookseller, remained with him, always available for additions, subtractions, and other forms of revision'.
13   Cf. Kenny 1978: 42.

treatises go; as complete, certainly, as *NE* used to be, and indeed continues to be if it is allowed to keep its borrowed material. But there is at least one peculiar consequence of the restoration of *EE* to its eight-book[14] status that somewhat disturbs or at least complicates this (relatively) neat picture. I propose to spend most of the rest of this paper discussing this peculiarity. It is not enough in itself to shake my own conviction about the general rightness of Kenny's attribution of the 'common' or 'disputed' books to *EE*. Nevertheless if it is true, as I hope to show, that in one central respect one of the disputed ('common') books is actually better adapted to the undisputed books of *NE* than it is to those of *EE* – or more precisely, that the undisputed books of *NE* are better adapted to one of CB 1–3 than are the undisputed books of *EE*, then at the very least that will make the attribution of CB 1–3 to *EE* a less straightforward matter than the growing consensus around the issue might seem to suggest.

The 'peculiarity' in question relates to the treatment of *sophia* respectively in the *EE* and in the *NE*. While granting that, by and large, *phronêsis* is handled in the same way in *EE* (with or without CB 1–3) and in *NE* (ditto), I notice that the same is not obviously true of *sophia*. This becomes clear if we use the same sort of test[15] as Kenny applied in the case of *phronêsis*, i.e., looking at the 'doctrine ... concerning' it first in the relevant 'common' book, then in *NE* without that book, then similarly in *EE* without it.

The first part is easy enough. *Sophia* as described in CB 2 (i.e., *EE* V/*NE* VI) is (1) reserved for a general accomplishment or mastery, rather than the accomplishment of experts in particular skills (*EE*/*NE* 1141a9–16). (2) *Sophia* is the most precise of the kinds of knowledge, involving knowledge both of what follows from first principles and of first principles themselves; thus a combination of intelligence (*nous*) and systematic knowledge (*epistêmê*), of the highest things[16] (1141a16–20). (3) *Sophia* is distinct from *politikê* and *phronêsis* in not being concerned with things human and things one can deliberate about, or about bringing things into being (1141a20–b22). (4) *Sophia* and *phronêsis* are the excellences of two separate parts of *to logon echon* in us (1139a5–15, 1144a2). (5) *Sophia* produces happiness by being a part of it, as do ethical excellence and wisdom combined (1141a1–9). (6) *Sophia* is not prescribed to by *phronêsis*, but rather *phronêsis* prescribes on its behalf, seeing to it that it comes into existence.

When we look at the undisputed books of *NE*, we find nothing incompatible with any of these six features, and plenty that is either compatible with them or better than compatible. In Book I, *sophia tis* appears as one of the things people have identified with *eudaimonia*, alongside *aretê* and *phronêsis* (and pleasure): 'For some people think it is excellence (*aretê*), others that it is wisdom (*phronêsis*), others a kind of intellectual

---

14 Or seven-book, depending on whether we treat 'Book V' as separate or not.
15 But, in the event, in a rather shorter version.
16 '... intelligence and systematic knowledge – systematic knowledge, as it were with its head in place, of the highest objects', 1141a19–20.

accomplishment (*sophia tis*)'[17] (1098b23–4). *Sophia* without qualification is used as an example of an intellectual excellence, the other examples used being *sunesis* and *phronêsis* (1103a5–6); the justification for distinguishing intellectual from ethical excellences is then framed with *sophia* and *sunesis* alone, without *phronêsis*.[18] Then in Book X, *sophia* is what is achieved by, the goal of, *philosophia*, the love of it (*sophia*); it is the highest *aretê*, the *aretê* of the highest part of us, activity in accordance with which is *eudaimonia* (1177a12–27). This passage can then be connected directly with the parenthesis at 1.7, 1098a16–18 '… if all this is so, the human good turns out to be activity of soul in accordance with excellence (and if there are more excellences than one, in accordance with the best and the most complete)'. In 1177a29 and 33, the *sophos* is the person who lives the reflective or theoretical life successfully (and the more *sophos* he is, the more capable he will be of carrying on his reflections even on his own: a32–4); similarly at 1179a30 and 32.

In all these instances, with the possible exception of the second, *sophia/sophos* appears to be used in a way that conforms precisely with the treatment of *sophia* in CB 2. All the six features of *sophia* listed above as deriving from that treatment are either actively or implicitly in play, especially in *NE* X but also, by virtue of the forward reference at 1098a16–18, in *NE* I too. Indeed, *sophia* as defined in CB 2 comes to play *the* starring role in the discussion of the best life that (all but) rounds off *NE* as a whole: see 1177a24, 29, 32, 33, 1179a30, 32. This is a special, Aristotelian *sophia*, as Book X confirms (i.e., in 1177a12–27). *Sophia* as used in ordinary speech – from which the specialized Aristotelian variety is distinguished at (CB 2) 1141a9–16 – is also in evidence here and there: see I.4, 1095a21; IV.7, 1127b20; IX.2, 1165a26; X.8, 1179a17. Maybe it is to distinguish Aristotelian *sophia* from this ordinary, common-or-garden *sophia/sophos*,[19] which is probably hardly distinguishable from ordinary, common-or-garden uses of *phronêsis/phronimos*, implying a quite unspecific – sometimes supposed, sometimes real – intellectual superiority, that Aristotle adds the *tis* in 1098b23–4: 'For some people think it is excellence, others that it is wisdom (*phronêsis*), others *a kind of* intellectual accomplishment (*sophia tis*)'. What he is hinting at here is, perhaps, already the technical sense of *sophia* introduced in CB3 (i.e., *NE* VII/*EE* VI); it is hard to think of anyone else who identifies *eudaimonia* with *sophia* as opposed to *phronêsis* – which has already

---

17   *NE* is cited in the version to be found in Sarah Broadie and Rowe 2002.
18   1103a7–8 'For when we talk about character, we do not say that someone is accomplished in a subject (*sophos*), or has a good sense of things (is *sunetos*), but rather that he is mild or moderate; but we do also praise someone accomplished in something for his disposition, and the dispositions we praise are the ones we call "excellences".' ('In a subject' and 'in something' are essentially fillers, which may need to be omitted: see further below.)
19   A model for the Nicomachean *sophos* might be the Thales of Plato's *Theaetetus*, representing the 'leaders of the [philosophical] chorus': *Theaetetus* 173c–174c.

done duty on its own, a couple of Stephanus pages before, as a representative of intellect in a listing of goods (1.6, 1096b23–5).[20]

When we turn to the undisputed Eudemian books, by contrast, whether preceding or following CB2, there appears to be no certain trace of the special kind of *sophia* introduced in that book; the only *sophia* that is certainly in evidence is that of ordinary speech. *Sophia* and *sophos* appear in total only six times: (1) 1215a23, (2) 1220a6, (3) 1220a12, (4) 1243b33, (5) 1243b34, and (6) 1248a35.[21] Of these occurrences, none clearly instantiates *sophia/sophos* as defined in CB2. (1) refers to what we term the 'older and wiser' (*kathaper tines ôiêthêsan tôn sophôn kai presbuterôn*). (2) is the Eudemian counterpart of *NE* I, 1103a5–6, giving examples of intellectual *aretai*; while the Nicomachean version gives us *sophia*, *sunesis* and *phronêsis*, the Eudemian version has just *sunesis* and *sophia* (*epainoumen gar ou monon tous dikaious alla kai tous sunetous kai tous sophous*). In (3), *sophia* is again an example of an intellectual *aretê*, along with *deinotês* (*ou gar legomen poios tis to êthos, hoti sophos ê deinos, all'hoti praos ê thrasus*). In all of (1)–(3), *sophia* is used in a wholly untechnical and not the technical Aristotelian sense (the 'we' in the last two cases surely refers to people in general). (4) and (5) are interesting insofar as they recall a familiar problem, about how to weigh wisdom/expertise (*sophia*) against wealth ('if one person complains that he has given wisdom, the other that he has given wealth ...'),[22] but the context is a discussion of justice in exchange, and *sophia* here need not be any particular kind of wisdom (or expertise). (6) is at least *prima facie* more interesting, as the only place in the undisputed books of *EE* where *phronêsis* and *sophia* – actually, *phronimos* and *sophos* – appear together: *kai toutôn phronimôn kai sophôn tacheian einai tên mantikên*, our text reads. But in the end even this instance seems to me to have no necessary connection with *sophia* as defined in CB2.

Michael Woods translates the context as follows:

---

20   Kenny, in correspondence, says he thinks the uses of *sophia* in *NE* I are untechnical; '*sophia tis* means "some kind or other of intellectual accomplishment" rather than "the special [*sophia*] that is exercised in contemplation'.
21   Thomas Case (Case 1910) claimed that the distinction between *phronêsis* and *sophia* familiar to us from CB2 was not well 'prepared for' in *EE* I–III, but was present in *EE* V (he concludes on this basis that 'probably therefore this part [of *EE*] was a separate discourse'), and cites '1246b4 seq, 1248a35, 1249b14'. (*EE* as a whole Case thought was a preliminary sketch for *NE*; the treatment of *phronêsis* in I–III he calls 'a chaos' [Case in Wians 1995: 31]) The first and third of these passages do not mention *sophia*, and it must therefore be a moot point whether they contain a reference to the distinction in question.
22   Cf. Protagoras' practice, of saying to his students 'pay me what you think my teaching is worth'?

they are called fortunate who succeed in what they initiate though they lack reason. And it is of no use for them to deliberate; for they possess such a starting-point as is superior to intelligence (*nous*) and deliberation (others have reason but do not have this nor do they have divine inspiration), but cannot do this; for, though unreasoning, they succeed ... [lacuna] that the power of prophecy of those who are wise (*phronimoi*) and clever (*sophoi*) is swift, and one must almost suppose that it results from reasoning.[23]

'Those who are wise and clever' is an odd way of rendering *toutôn phronimôn kai sophôn*; better '(the power of prophecy of) these wise and clever people', where 'wise and clever' should presumably be in quotation marks – they are people who because of their power are *supposed* to be, or have the appearance of being, wise and clever, but actually are not.[24] Kenny, for his part, thinks the text unsound, translating the last part 'For, though lacking reason, they succeed, and more than that of wise men and philosophers, their divination is speedy'.[25] Kenny does not try to reconstruct the text that would be needed to give this sense, but it is hard not to suspect that there is something wrong with the transmitted text. It is certainly possible to interpret the reference to *phronimoi* and *sophoi* as irony; indeed if the text is sound – and both families of manuscripts evidently have the same reading – it is the only show on the road. But one adjective, either *phronimôn*, or better *sophôn*,[26] would have been enough to achieve the ironic effect, if such it is; two are unnecessary. The sudden turn to indirect speech (accusative and infinitive), without an introductory verb is also unusual for Aristotle, if not unknown in the Attic orators.[27] But the question still arises, even with Kenny's reconstruction, why Aristotle would need to refer to the 'divinatory' powers of *sophoi* as well as of *phronimoi*, i.e., people who think things through. One attractive solution would be to see Aristotle as referring covertly to the thesis with which Socrates shocks the young Clinias in Plato's *Euthydemus*, that *eutuchia is* actually *sophia*.[28] But if so, *sophia* here is not the *sophia* of 'CB2' (and neither is it on any other interpretation).[29]

I conclude that *sophia* and *sophos* are not used in the technical Aristotelian sense, as set up in 'CB 2', anywhere in the undisputed Eudemian books. Does this matter, that

---

23   1248a30–36 Woods 1979.
24   Walzer and Mingay 1991 writes in the apparatus '35 *phronimôn kai sophôn* ironice'.
25   Adding in a note 'The text of this sentence is uncertain' Barnes and Kenny 2014; in Kenny 2011 we read 'And they attain to a power of divination that is swifter than the reasoning of the wise men and philosophers' ('the wise and learned' in Kenny 1991: 3).
26   *Sophos* is perhaps more often used ironically, at any rate in Plato.
27   But usually when preceded by direct reported speech, which is hardly the case here (even if we retain *ho palai elegon* in 1248a30).
28   *Euthydemus* 279d6. See further below.
29   *Pace* Case (see n. 21 above).

is, in relation to the question about the provenance of the disputed books? Possibly not, for the following reasons. Firstly, there is nothing in *EE* I–III or in *EE* IV–V that precludes the same sharp distinction that is conveyed in CB 2 through the opposition between *phronêsis* and *sophia*; *phronêsis*, it seems, is used according to the definition of it there, and given (a) that the intellectual excellences are said in *EE* II to have two functions, discovering 'truth, either about how things are (*pôs echei*) or about how things come into being (*peri geneseôs*)';[30] (b) that the second of these functions is clearly assigned, in the undisputed Eudemian books in general, to *phronêsis*; and (c) that *sophia* is said in 'CB 2' 'not to be of any coming into being' (*oudemias ... geneseôs*),[31] it is hardly much of a stretch to suppose that the only reason why *sophia* does not figure is that, as it happens, there was no occasion to introduce it.

Here we should recall the obvious point that the key passages in which *sophia* in its technical Aristotelian sense appears in *NE* I–IV, VIII–X relate to a question, about the best life, that the Aristotle of the undisputed Eudemian books fails to answer, at least fully and directly. He raises the question early on, in Books I–II, but does not come back directly to it, and while we may think we can work out what his final answer to it would be, there is nothing – here in the undisputed Eudemian books – to correspond to *NE* X.6–8 (which at least set out to give a precise answer, however difficult we may find it to decipher). *EE* V.3, though occupying a (roughly) corresponding position, is on a different subject, even if it turns out to be a quite closely related one.

Here I propose to look briefly at the structure and content of *EE* V.3, which I think needs to be read in close connection with the two preceding chapters. Aristotle does not go out of his way to link V.1–3 together, and indeed on the face of it the three chapters are on distinct topics: the difference between *phronêsis* and *epistêmê* (chapter 1); good fortune, *eutuchia* (chapter 2); the *horos* of *kalokagathia* (chapter 3). All three, however, can be seen as concerned – in effect, if not by design – with one over-riding question, about the role of *epistêmê* (and perhaps of *sophia*, even though the term barely surfaces, if at all,[32] in the context) in a successful life of practical activity, the question being approached by way of opposition to Socrates: that is, to Socrates in Plato, as the form of the references makes clear.[33] V.1 finds Aristotle returning (without

---

30   1221b30.
31   1143b20.
32   See above (text to nn.23–29).
33   According to W. Fitzgerald, *Sôcratês* preceded by the definite article refers to the Socrates of the Platonic dialogues, *Sôcratês* without the article to the historical Socrates (see Fitzgerald's *Selections from the Nicomachean Ethics of Aristotle*, Dublin 1853; 'Fitzgerald's canon' is enshrined, but unattributed, in the 9th edition of Liddell-Scott-Jones's *Greek Lexicon*, s.v. *ho, hê, to*). That does not hold for the *EE*. One is tempted to explain this by supposing that Bishop Fitzgerald thought the *EE* spurious; but then the rule probably does not hold consistently for the *NE* either. – Ronna Burger, *Aristotle's Dialogue with*

acknowledgement of the fact) to the Socratic identification of the *aretai* as *epistêmai* with which he began the discussion of *aretê* and *phronêsis* in Book I.[34] He concludes that the Socratic saying 'nothing is stronger than *phronêsis*' is correct, only he shouldn't have said that it (*phronêsis*) was *epistêmê*,[35] and the argument for that conclusion is a sort of commentary on Socrates' claim[36] in the *Hippias Minor* that the person who goes wrong voluntarily is preferable to the person who does so involuntarily. v.2's discussion of good fortune starts from the premiss that doing well (*eu prattein*) comes from good fortune as well as from (the combination of) *phronêsis* and *aretê*. This is a premiss that Socrates denies, in the *Euthydemus*, by identifying *eutuchia* with *sophia*; Aristotle adverts to the fact at 1247b14–15.[37] His question is: if there is such a thing as good fortune, and people really do get things right without apparently being intellectually equipped to do so, and regularly get them right, even continuously, not just every now and then, how does this come about? There then follows that notorious and extraordinary passage in which, if we accept the text handed down by the manuscript tradition,[38] the cause is said to be god, even a god that is somehow within us: an intellect, perhaps, that is indistinguishable – except by location – from the reason that operates in the universe at large, and that can function even unbeknownst to us. Even though Aristotle starts in this chapter from an anti-Socratic position, his answer (after a winding, dialectical argument) to the initial question, about the cause of good fortune, seems to me to belong to the same general type as Socrates' own evocation of a personal *daimonion*, an inner voice that tells him not to do things he was intending to do, and by implication is right to tell him not to do them.

v.3 has something of the same structure, to the extent that it begins with a set of ideas that contrast with Socrates' (though in this case there is no explicit reference to Socrates, and probably no implicit reference either),[39] but circles round and ends up using language, and apparently taking up a position, that is distinctly Socratic. The

---

Socrates: On the Nicomachean Ethics, Chicago 2008, is inclined to see the NE as a whole as a conversation with Plato's Socrates. A work on ethics written not so long after Plato's death could not avoid being in some sense a dialogue with the Platonic Socrates; here in EE V, at least in the first two chapters, Socrates is more immediately the moving cause.

34 I, 1216b2 ff.
35 v.1, 1246b34–6. The outcome of the chapter is a somewhat less expansive version of CB2.13, 1144b17–30.
36 Or takes off from it; in any case the connection between v.1 and the *HMi* seems to me to be close and undeniable.
37 The reference here to *Euthydemus* 279d6 is generally recognized.
38 I refer here to 1248a35, where the manuscripts have *tôi theôi*, which Spengel changed to *tôi theiôi*. This is probably right, given the neuter *touto* that follows (picking up *tôi theiôi/theôi*). But a26–7 already comes close to making *to en hêmin* god ('as in the whole, so in that [i.e., soul (? why neuter?)], *for* in a way the divine in us moves everything', sc. as god moves everything in the universe).
39 So no 'dialogue with Socrates' in this part (see n. 33 above).

chapter makes what looks like a new start, on the subject of 'what we shall immediately call *kalokagathia*',[40] i.e., the ethical virtues taken together, explaining the relationship first between the two elements of the term, *kalon* and *agathon*, and then, more briefly, in 1249a17–21, between them and the pleasant. Aristotle thus explains the thesis that he announced at the very beginning of the EE, about the convergence in *eudaimonia* of the fine, the good and the pleasant, and by doing so ties the end of the work to its grand opening, justifying with a splendid clarity his disagreement there with the inscription from Delos.

But now, having made the good man the measure, as he has, in action and in the choice of *haplôs agatha*, a.k.a. goods 'in the abstract',[41] Aristotle needs to say just how the good man will do the measuring; it's not sufficient to say 'as reason dictates', 'as we said earlier'.[42] He proceeds to give his answer: the *horos* is whatever 'choice and possession (? acquisition: *ktêsis*) of natural goods' will most produce (?) *theôria*, contemplation of/reflection on, god; any such choice that 'either through deficiency or through excess prevents service to (*therapeuein*) and contemplation of/ reflection on god' will be bad.[43] *Theôrein* 'the god' is usually taken as doing Aristotelian metaphysics, and this may be right, but we should probably consider taking 'the god' here more closely with what has been said about god and the divine in the preceding chapter,[44] that is, as something more like 'god/reason as operating in the universe (and us)'. The addition of *therapeuein* to *theôrein* seems to me to point in the same direction. I have argued elsewhere[45] that the expression *therapeuein ton theon* would have been recognizable to Aristotle's audience as referring to Socrates, and that 'Aristotle is here treating Socrates as a philosopher and theoretician like himself'.[46] On this interpretation, the addition of *therapeuein* will perhaps be for the purpose of clarifying *theôrein*: what Aristotle has in mind, more than anything, is *doing philosophy*, in a world that is supremely adapted as a subject for philosophy by the fact of its control by god/reason.

This gesture to Socrates, however, if such it is, is two-edged, insofar as it places Socratic philosophizing outside the very sphere to which he, Socrates, thought he was devoting himself: that is, the sphere of practical activity. A Socrates, like an Aristotle,

---

40 Cf. CB 2, 1124a4, where the term is introduced without explanation, and see my footnote 37 to Book V.
41 Kenny's translation of the phrase, the reference being to things that are good if one 'abstracts' them from the sort of person who possesses them (the 'natural' goods): they will be good only if possessed by the good person, while in the wrong hands they can be positively bad.
42 1249b3–4; see CB 1, which says about the formula *kata ton orthon logon* almost exactly what EE V says about *hôs ho logos* here: *alêthes men, outhen de saphes*.
43 1249b16–21.
44 Cf. Kenny 1978: 175.
45 See Rowe 2013.
46 *Op.cit.*: 322. See also, in this context, Broadie 2003.

may theorize about ethics, but the *kalokagathos* will apparently not require such theorizing in order to act in accordance with his *kalokagathia*. Socrates proposed that philosophy was itself the key to the good and happy life; not so, says Aristotle – the happy life one lived according to the ethical *aretai*, accompanied by *phronêsis*, or according to *kalokagathia*, which unites all these into one. EE v.1 establishes that the ethical virtues are not matters of *epistêmê*; EE v.2 allows in a sort of divine rationality into practical life, but only – paradoxically – via the reinstatement of *eutuchia* as a factor in human life; EE v.3 then finishes off the Socratic position by apparently emptying *kalokagathia* itself, and *a fortiori* activity in accordance with it, of *theôria* altogether.[47] As its concluding sentence confirms, this last chapter has been about *kalokagathia*, and *theôria* has only entered the picture as providing the *horos* for it, and the *skopos* of natural goods/goods 'in the abstract': 'So as to the standard/limit of *kalokagathia*, and the aim/purpose of [our choice and possession/acquisition of] goods in the abstract, let this stand as our account'.[48]

So where does this leave us, on the subject of *eudaimonia*, and of *sophia*, in EE v.3? *Kalokagathia* has just been identified as complete *aretê*, *aretê teleios*;[49] and happiness, *eudaimonia*, was said in Book II to be the 'activity of a complete life in accordance with *aretê teleia*'.[50] But given how Aristotle defines the *horos* of *kalokagathia*, i.e. in terms of serving and reflecting on (*theôrein*) god, this 'activity ... in accordance with *aretê teleia*' must presumably also include reflective (*theôrêtikê*) activity, and it is hard to see how, if one kind of activity is defined, as it were, by its capacity to produce the conditions for another, and the first activity is essential to human *eudaimonia*, the second activity would not also be part of that *eudaimonia*. (True, someone could say, perfectly reasonably, 'Playing football makes me happy, just so long as it doesn't impinge on my ability to do my work – which, incidentally, I hate', but then of course we would have to ask why they have to work, to which the answer will be 'So that I can live – and play football.') But then it would be odd to suppose that our first activity was meant to be defined by its capacity to produce the conditions for doing the second activity *badly*. So, if *eudaimonia* is activity in accordance with complete *aretê*, then that complete *aretê* will include the *aretê* relating to 'service to and *theôria* of god' as well as the *aretai* that go to make up *kalokagathia*, and *kalokagathia* will be *aretê teleios* at 1249a16 strictly by comparison with doing fine (*kala*) things merely *kata sumbebêkos* (1249a14–16).[51] If the *aretê* corresponding to theoretical activity is to be given a name, it might as well be *sophia*.

---

47 In which case *kalokagathia*, and by implication *eudaimonia* too, will be intended to be taken as excluding the *aretê* the exercise of which is *therapeia* and *theôria* of god (which would be a striking difference from *NE*).
48 1249b23–5.
49 EE v.3, 1249a16.
50 1219a38–9. (The adjective *teleios* appears as indiscriminately two- and three-termination in both treatises.)
51 And so will not refer back to Book II after all.

By this reckoning, even if the *EE* lacks an equivalent to *NE* x.6–8, and an explicit, final answer to the question about the content of *eudaimonia*, we can supply the one he perhaps would have given, had he got round to it (*EE* III is, after all, a fragment – ending with the sort of sentence,[52] introduced by *men oun*, that usually leads on to a new topic): namely that *eudaimonia* includes philosophical reflection as well as good practical activity, and that the first is a more important ingredient than the second.[53]

We should remember, all the same, that this is only one way of reading the last paragraph of what Kenny[54] calls the 'cryptogram' that is *EE* v, and I myself have at least half a suspicion that it is an overinterpretation, in one respect at least. A point that is often overlooked is that Aristotle sums up his discussion of the *horos*, i.e., as announced at 1249a21–b3, by saying 'And this holds (?*echei*) for the soul, and this is the best *horos* of the [healthy?] soul, namely when it is least aware (has the least perception of) the irrational part of the soul as such' (1249b22–3). This, so far as I can presently see, ought somehow to be the counterpart of what has just been said about the promotion of *theôria/therapeia* as the criterion for choosing and possessing natural goods (we don't need *another* criterion on top of that). If so, then the emphasis in the preceding context should be something to the effect of '... and this the best *horos* of the healthy soul, namely when it is most aware of the rational part of the soul as such'. That will be when it is philosophizing – serving and reflecting on god – as well as issuing the orders that will keep the irrational part down. Now we should certainly expect Aristotle here to distinguish two rational parts of the soul, one concerned with reflection, the other with issuing orders, though I note that he does not do so very clearly: 'so it is in respect of *to theôrêtikon*', he says in 1249b13, referring back to '... and this [our *archê*] is twofold, for medicine is an *archê* in one way and health in another, and the former for the sake of the latter' (b11–13); and he will certainly mean to distinguish two rational parts if CB 2 has preceded. But he fails actually to distinguish them; indeed on the most natural reading *phronêsis* as well as *theôrein* ought to belong to *to theôrêtikon* in 1249b13.[55] Perhaps that is just because it does not matter that much to him here. He is not here comparing or contrasting different aspects of human rationality, or talking about the choice between the practical and the philosophical life; he is not talking about kinds of life at all. We would expect him to raise that question at some point, given that he

---

52 A sentence that Donald Allan proposed to excise, for no reason that has appeared in print.
53 Cf. W.J. Verdenius 1971: 297.
54 Kenny 1978: 178.
55 Kenny renders *to theôrêtikon* here as 'the intellectual faculty' (Kenny 1978: 174). By contrast Dirlmeier 1962 has 'die seelische Schaukraft', apparently treating this as corresponding to the art of medicine in the analogy offered in the previous line, with *phronêsis* subordinate to it (and taking *theos* in b17 and 20 as subject rather than object); Inwood and Woolf 2013 goes for an ambiguous 'the contemplative'. Note the treatment of the *bouleutikon tês psuchês* as *to theôrêtikon aitias tinos* at *EE* II.10, 1226b25–6.

raised it at some length in Book I,[56] but he is not raising it here. Perhaps he answered it in some other part of Book V, now lost.[57]

But also perhaps not. The evidence of V.3 suggests that if faced with the choice between philosophy, *aretê* and pleasure, he would have plumped for the first two ingredients, mixed together (with the third in the mix too, as arising from these). Aristotle could still have gone one to ask, separately, whether a political or a philosophical life contributed more to *eudaimonia*,[58] providing that the philosophical included the political.[59] But from the perspective of V.3 even that begins even to look as if it might be a badly formed question. After all, from that perspective, just as the philosophical cannot in the ideal case be separated from the political, so, if the philosophical provides the *horos* for the political, neither can the political be separated from the philosophical (which is of course different from saying that living a successful 'political' life, in accordance with the requirements of *kalokagathia*, means actually being a philosopher).[60]

Nevertheless – to return to my main argument – there is still nothing in any of this to prevent us from supposing that the Aristotle of the undisputed books of EE would have endorsed the sharp distinction we find in CB 2 between *phronêsis* and *sophia*. – On the other hand (and here I come to the central point of this paper), it is the undisputed books of NE, not of EE, that prepare for it and then put it to use. As we have seen, *sophia* as such barely figures in the undisputed EE books at all. The most striking contrasts are between EE I–II and NE I: *sophia tis* appears alongside *aretê*, *phronêsis* and pleasure in NE I as one of the things people have identified with *eudaimonia* (1098b23–4), whereas a parallel context in EE I (1214a32–3) lists only *phronêsis*, *aretê* and pleasure; then NE I cites *sophia*, *sunesis* and *phronêsis* as examples of intellectual *aretai* (1103a5–6), while EE II cites only the first two (1220a6). In both cases, it looks as if NE is going out of its way to integrate the *phronêsis*/*sophia* distinction into its argument. Similarly in the case of the rider to the definition of *eudaimonia* in I.7. 'The human good', says Aristotle, 'turns out to be activity of soul in accordance with excellence (and if there are more excellences than one, in accordance with the best and the most complete)',[61] which he then picks up at the beginning of X.7 with 'But

---

56   '... there are three lives that everyone chooses to live who has the choice, the political life, the philosophical, the life of enjoyment', 1215a35–b1; picked up again at 1216a27–9.
57   I refer to the fragmentary state of our EE V.
58   The case for enjoyment/pleasure unmixed was never going to get off the ground: see e.g. I, 1216a29–37.
59   Or at least the life lived according to ethical *aretê*, if it is not the same thing.
60   I thus seem to leave myself sitting on the fence as to whether *kalokagathia* is or is not supposed to include the *aretê* that NE X identifies as *sophia*. My tentative conclusion is that the general trend of the argument of EE, minus CB, itself leaves the question open, and that it is only in its last gasp, in V.3, that the inclusion of a *sophia*-type *aretê* in *kalokagathia* and *eudaimonia* is confirmed (for the best/ideal case).
61   1098a16–18.

if happiness is activity in accordance with excellence, it is reasonable that it should be activity in accordance with the highest kind',[62] i.e., *sophia*. Earlier on, I accepted that 'complete *aretê*' in *EE* II.1, 1219a38–9, 'eudaimonia will be activity of a complete life in accordance with complete *aretê*', could in principle refer to a combination of the ethical virtues (plus *phronêsis*) and *sophia* (the latter as the *aretê* corresponding to *theôria*). But this came at the cost of our having to explain away v.3, 1249a16 'so *kalokagathia* is complete *aretê*', and perhaps the cost is too high. In either case, the references to *sophia*, or to whatever we are to call the *aretê* of the *theôrêtikon* part of the soul, have to be manufactured rather than being found lying in full view as they do in *NE* I.

So, while it still remains true that the lack of reference to *sophia* in the undisputed books of *EE* may be put down simply to the lack of any occasion for it,[63] it is undeniable that with regard to *sophia* CB 2 meshes more closely with the undisputed Nicomachean books than with the undisputed Eudemian ones. How to explain this state of affairs, if (as I still accept) the disputed books belonged originally to *EE*? I have no clear answer to this question. I am, though, particularly struck by the nature of the three references to *sophia* in *NE* I (i.e., in Aristotle's technical use), which when we compare the text of *EE* I–II look like additions specifically designed to look forward both to CB 2 and to *NE* X, binding them into a whole that is rather more unified than the corresponding whole represented by the sequence *EE* I–II – CB 2 – V. I also note that all three references can be removed without any damage to the syntax of the sentences to which they belong. I speculate, firstly, that they were the work of whoever was mainly responsible for organizing, or beginning to organize, what we know as the ten-book *NE*. Secondly, I speculate that what became *NE* VI in this process, having started life as part of *EE*, had already been to some degree re-worked, whether by the same person or by someone else. A third speculation is that the person who re-worked this book was Aristotle himself, and that he re-worked it at about the same time that he wrote *NE* X. But fourthly, as I have said, it cannot have been Aristotle who included CB 3 in what became our *NE*, if he had already written *NE* X, containing another treatment of pleasure. So, fifthly, the organizer-in-chief of the *NE*, who introduced those three references to *sophia* in *NE* I, need not have been Aristotle, although it was surely Aristotle who was responsible for developing the coordinated ideas, linking CB 2 and X, that motivate them, whether at the same time or at different times. My own provisional hypothesis, for what it is worth, is that Aristotle put together an *EE*, and then went on to revise various bits of it, which someone else[64] built into an *NE* (ours) on the analogy of the original *EE*. But who knows?

---

62   1178a12–13.
63   See above.
64   My favoured candidate for this role is Nicomachus. In a lecture in Paris 1 in May 2017, Kenny had Nicomachus transferring the common books to *NE*, and challenged anyone to show the presence in CB (the common books) of significant signs of changes that might

The truth, it seems to me, is that both our ten-book *NE* and our eight-book *EE* fall, and probably always fell, considerably short of the kind of unity suggested by labelling them treatises. For Aristotelian 'treatises', that is par for the course: what we know as big Aristotelian works are typically assemblages of smaller ones. The two ethical treatises look different, insofar as both have beginnings that link them to their ends and vice versa. But in between, in both, are parts that sometimes sit well with these beginnings and endings, and with each other, and sometimes fit less well, thus raising the possibility, even the likelihood, that they too are, or were originally, assemblages like the *Politics*, *Physics* and – the extreme case – the *Metaphysics*. Aristotle is a specialist in highly focused discussions of particular topics. For sure, these individual discussions are driven by the same general philosophical outlook and methods, but by and large it was evidently not his habit to set out the big picture, systematically, in any given area. He may have made an exception for ethics, but even here the results often betray Aristotle's preference for dealing with one sub-topic at a time (friendship; *akrasia*; pleasure …). Maybe there was once a fully worked and fully organized *EE*, just as someone tried – and failed – to construct a fully coherent *NE*. But I wouldn't bet on it myself. My own guess is that any original *EE* might have been hardly less uneven than the version we presently have. I also hazard, on the basis both of the retention of the treatment of pleasure in what became *NE* VII, and of the proven stylistic affinities to *EE* of all three 'common' books, that the degree to which CB1–3 were re-worked to fit them into their new home in *NE* was relatively small.[65]

have been made by Aristotle himself to fit them (CB) into *NE*. I mean to sidestep any such challenge by proposing that Aristotle may have revised parts of CB independently of any plan for the construction of an *NE*, in the same way that he certainly rethought and rewrote his treatment of pleasure (to which he attached a discussion of the best kind of life – perhaps sparked off by further thinking about the relationship between *phronêsis* and *theôria* as discussed both in *EE* v.3 and in the final chapter of CB 2).

[65] Hendrik Lorenz is thus in my view wrong to complain about Inwood and Woolf, as he does in Lorenz 2013, for merely noting in their introduction that 'the common books may have been somewhat revised for reuse in the *NE*', and not alerting the reader 'to the very real possibility that the proper home of what are presented as Books 4–6 of the [*EE*] is in fact the *NE*'. There would be rather greater justification, as matters presently stand, for complaining about translators and editors of the *NE* for not alerting readers to the likelihood that the proper home of what are presented as Books v–vii of the *NE* is in fact the *EE*. Primavesi's finding in relation to the *EE* (see n. 6), namely that our eight-book *EE* – i.e., *EE* as we know it – is of later provenance than our ten-book *NE*, is of less importance for the question of the original home of the common books than it is for giving us an explanation as to how these books could have acquired Nicomachean content. The story of the cellar in Skepsis, from which this explanation starts, has its own value in helping us to understand why *EE* is in so much worse a state than *NE*: not, paradoxically, as Primavesi retells the story, because it was eaten by worms and consumed by damp, but because it was not in the cellar, or in Skepsis, in the first place, as *NE* (presumably) was.

APPENDIX 2

On *EE* and the *Peri Ideôn*

The following is a lightly modified version of a paper that was originally delivered to the 'B' Club in Cambridge in the early 1960s – as it happened, with G.E.L. Owen, the inventor of the term 'focal meaning', in the chair; it was then heavily rewritten and published as Rowe 1979. Discussion has of course moved on since, but not, I think, sufficiently to take away significantly from the usefulness of reproducing the paper in the present volume.

Its chief purpose is to give substance to the proposal that Aristotle's idea of 'focal meaning' (see n. 35 to Book I above) will have arisen, if it may not have appeared as such, in the context of his *On the* [Platonic/Platonist] *Forms,(Peri Ideôn)*, which is lost to us as a document but was known to and commented on by, and is in in parts recoverable from the Platonic tradition itself. It seems to have been written relatively early on in Aristotle's career. He evidently spent some years listening to (and no doubt questioning) Plato in the Academy, but broke away and founded his own rival school – we are told by a late source that Plato nicknamed him 'the foal' (Aelian, *Historical Miscellany* 4.9); it is a reasonable hypothesis that the work question was a part of that break with Plato, written as a reasoned account of his disagreements.

Summary

In this appendix, I consider three attempts to reconstruct the Platonist argument *ek tòn pros ti* ('*from relatives*') preserved for us by Alexander from Aristotle's *Peri Ideôn*: Owen 1957, Leszl 1975, and Barford 1976.[1] Of these three, Owen and Leszl are broadly in agreement about the general strategy of the argument, but Barford's account is quite different. I suggest a compromise between these three accounts, although the interpretation I shall offer will be closer to Owen's and Leszl's than to Barford's.

1   The Argument

The argument runs like this (I mostly reproduce Owen's translation of the text as printed in Ross 1955, along with his (Owen's) tabulation of the argument [from I–V]:

  The argument (*logos*) which produces ideas of relations too (*ideas kai tôn pros ti*) is like this (*toioutos*).

---

[1] Barford's article was written without knowledge of Leszl's book, and centres on criticisms of Owen and of H. Cherniss' account of the argument in Cherniss 1962.

I. When the same predicate is asserted of several things not homonymously (*mê homônumôs*) but so as to indicate a single nature,[2] it is true of them *either* (*a*) because they are strictly (*kuriôs*) what the predicate signifies, e.g. when we call both Socrates and Plato 'a man'; *or* (*b*) because they are likenesses of things that are really so, e.g. when we predicate 'man' of men in pictures (for what we are indicating in them is the likenesses of men, and so we signify an identical nature[3] in each); *or* (*c*) because one of them is the model and the rest are likenesses, e.g. if we were to call both Socrates and the likenesses of him 'men'.

II. Now when we predicate 'absolutely equal' (*to ison auto*) of things in this world, we use the predicate homonymously. For (*a*) the same definition (*logos*) fit them all; (*b*) nor are we referring to things which are really equal, since the dimensions of sensible things are fluctuating and changes continuously and indeterminate. (*c*) Nor yet does the definition of 'equal' apply without qualification (*akribôs*) to anything in this world.

III. But neither (can such things be called equal) in the sense that one of them is model and another likeness, for none of them has more claim than another to be either model, or likeness.

IV. And even if we allow that the likeness is not homonymous with the model, the conclusion is always the same – that the equal things in this world are equal *qua* likenesses of what is really and strictly (*kuriôs kai alêthôs*) equal.

V. If this is so, there is something absolutely and strictly equal (*esti ti autoison kai kuriôs*) by relation to which things in this world, as being likenesses of it, become and are called equal. And this is an idea, a paradigm and likeness (*paradeigma kai eikôn*) for the things that come to be with relation to it.

(*Alexandri Aphrodisiensis in Aristotelis Metaphysica commentaria* 82.11–83.21 Hayduck)

2 *The General Strategy of the Argument*

Owen's interpretation, in its broadest outline, is as follows. I gives us an exhaustive account of the ways in which a predicate can be used without ambiguity.[4] II rules out the possibility that I(*a*) predication applies in the case of sensible things; III rules out I(*c*); hence there remains only I(*b*); hence 'equal' is predicated of sensible things solely as likenesses; and that entails the existence of a model over and above them (which is an Idea). Leszl agrees with this general interpretation; he differs from Owen mainly in the detailed interpretation of II and IV, and in refusing to draw

---

2 Owen translates *phusis* as 'character'; 'nature', or just 'thing', 'item', is better (and incidentally more in accordance with Platonic usage).

3 *Phusis* again.

4 Not, as Barford strangely attributes to him (p. 206), an account 'of the ways in which a thing can be predicated of something'.

certain implications from the argument that are drawn by Owen.[5] Barford, by contrast, believes that II–IV (treated as a single section in his analysis) rule out I(*b*) predication in the case of sensible equals as well as I(*a*) and I(*c*): according to his view, the argument is designed to show precisely that 'equal' is predicated *homonymously* of sensible things; and the existence of the equal itself follows as a necessary condition of the type of homonymous predication involved (apparently where there is *some* connection between the various uses of a term, but still not enough to justify calling them synonymous rather than homonymous).

It must, I believe, be clear that Barford's interpretation is on this general level much less plausible than Owen's and Leszl's. In particular it seems to require us to import too much into the text as provided by Alexander. Firstly, according to Barford we are initially told (I) that where things stand in the relation of model and likeness, synonymy exists (or can exist); whereas it turns out that in the crucial case, that of Forms and particulars, model and likeness are actually homonymous – though we are never explicitly told this in Alexander's version. Secondly, it must count against Barford that the argument says nothing explicitly about any special type of homonymy, or about how or why the existence of the Form is a necessary condition of it. Barford's account of the relation between Ideas/Forms and particulars which he thinks is suggested by the argument is also obscure in itself: perhaps some kind of *pros ti* relation – but in that case why should it be labelled a *homonymous* relation?[6] Owen, by contrast, has to import relatively little into the argument, and makes what is to my mind rather better sense. All that he assumes is the basic (and plausible) premise that 'equal' is predicated of sensible things non-homonymously; the argument then works out how this can be so, and discovers that it entails the existence of the Idea.

3   The Interpretation of 83.6–7

There is, however, one glaring weakness in the detail of Owen's account to which Barford points, and for which he also seems to me to suggest a remedy. The weakness in question lies in Owen's handling of the sentence at (83.6–7). He translates this sentence 'Now when we predicate "absolutely equal" of things in this world [note 4: 'We': not of course the Platonists, who make no such error, but generally the unwary or unconverted to whom the argument is addressed], we use the predicate homonymously'.[7]

---

5   On these, see the concluding section of the present paper. Leszl's views on II and IV will be mentioned in the course of the main argument.
6   Things of which a *pros hen* account can be given certainly would not belong to Aristotle's class of *ta apo tuchês homônuma* (*NE* 1096 b 23 ff.), 'things homonymous by chance'; Owen, indeed, goes so far as to call the *pros hen* relation a type of synonymy. On the other hand, Leszl suggests that Aristotle regards 'both focal meaning and analogy (including metaphor) as sorts of non-chance, but genuine, homonymy' (Leszl 1970: 448).
7   Owen 1957: 103.

Barford criticises this translation on the grounds that it reverses main clause and participial clause, thus suppressing the definite statement that 'we predicate "equal" in the strict sense of sensibles *homonymously*';[8] he also criticises the interpretation of 'we'. These two criticisms go together. If the argument had run 'when (or if) we predicate "absolutely equal"', then it might be plausible (or at least more plausible) to take 'we' as referring to anyone who happens (erroneously) to take the course in question; and that, of course, on Owen's interpretation, would exclude the Platonists, who as Platonists would never refer to sensible equals as if they were *kuriôs*, non-derivatively, equal. But as the sentence stands, Owen's is a far from natural way of taking 'we'; it does look, as Barford suggests, much more like a plain statement of fact – that 'we' regularly predicate *to ison auto* of things in this world (and that when we do, we do so homonymously). And in that case 'we' presumably means either 'we Platonists', or, much more likely, 'people in general'. (If Barford perhaps seems to imply that he takes the first alternative, this is probably only because he is occupied with rejecting Owen's view that the Platonists are actually excluded; and as I read his argument, the second alternative fits perfectly well. In any case, though 'we' in *Aristotle* can and does refer to the Platonists, it is not likely to do so, and does not normally do so, in Alexander).

If this is right, then it has consequences too for the interpretation of the expression *to ison auto*. Owen says that 'what is maintained in II would be predicated homonymously of things in this world; and *to ison auto* is expanded in v into *auto to ison kai kuriôs*. Thus the question broached by II is just whether *ison* can be used *kuriôs* of things in this world, i.e. as a case of the non-derivative predication illustrated in I(*a*); and the answer is that, except by a sheer ambiguity, it cannot be so used'.[9] This seems to say that *to ison auto* is the equivalent of *to ison kuriôs* and means something like 'non-derivatively equal'. But if, as I have argued, the sentence at 83.6–7 is actually an appeal to ordinary linguistic usage, to what people generally do as a matter of linguistic habit, this interpretation looks dubious; for surely only Platonists are likely to be interested in the strange predicate 'strictly equal'.[10]

---

8   Barford 197: 210.
9   Owen 1957: 105.
10 *The Hippias Major*, to which Owen refers, shows Hippias manifestly failing to understand what Socrates means by *auto to kalon; kuriôs ison* might perhaps be more meaningful to a non-Platonist, but it is not obvious what meaning he could attach even to this – perhaps 'really equal', i.e. a genuine as opposed to a merely apparent case of equality? But that cannot be what *to ison auto* means in II; if it were, II (b) at least, and II (c) as I would prefer to interpret it (see below), would be arguments not for saying that *to ison auto* was predicated homonymously of sensible things, but rather for saying that it was predicated falsely of them.

Barford's own interpretation of *to ison auto* avoids this objection (although I shall argue against his development of it).[11] 'The *auto* in the expression *to ison auto*', he says, '... is intended simply to rule out any qualification in the application of the predicate "equal". In that unqualified sense "equal" is predicated of participants homonymously'.[12] This is what 83.6–7 tells us: we regularly call 'the things here' simply 'equal' (that is, without adding specifications about *how* they are equal); but when we do, then we do so *homônumôs*. (I should add that I am in fact at this point already beginning to diverge from Barford, who paraphrases the sentence under discussion simply as stating 'the basic Platonist position: equality is predicated of things in this world homonymously (or ambiguously)',[13] where he appears to imply that '"equal" used without qualification of sensible things is homonymous' entails '"equal" used of sensible things is homonymous'; a point I shall dispute shortly.) In this sense, *to ison auto* obviously *is* a predicate which even non-Platonists apply to things. It also fits well into the structure of the argument. If *ison* were applicable to sensible things *kuriôs*, then it would be applicable to them by itself, without qualification or addition. But, as 11 tells us, when 'equal' is applied to sensible things by itself, it involves homonymy; therefore, since the *kuriôs* application of a predicate is non-homonymous, 'equal' cannot apply to sensible things *kuriôs*. Other arguments in favour of the proposed interpretation of *to ison auto*: (i) it enables us to make good sense of the normal Platonic use of the formula *auto to x*, and in general it is, to my mind, a *natural* reading of the expression. (ii) As Owen points out,[14] it is this aspect of the Form, in which it is 'just equal', equal without addition this may mean, against which Aristotle's critique in the *Peri Ideôn* is directed. (iii) The proposed interpretation leaves the argument saying something which is actually true:[15] for to say that two things are equal, without saying (e.g.) in what respect they are equal, may indeed involve ambiguity; even worse, if we say that *a* thing is equal,[16] without even saying what it is equal to.

Three objections. A) If 'equal' is used homonymously (is ambiguous) when applied by itself to sensible things, on the grounds that different *logoi* will be applicable in

---

11   Leszl's interpretation is different again: according to him, 'la qualifica *auto* attira l'attenzione sul fatto che *ora* si parla di *to ison* e non piu *anthrôpos*' (Leszl 1975: n. 15). This hardly seems a natural reading of the Greek; and in general the only consideration I can see in its favour is that it is compatible with the remainder of Leszl's interpretation.
12   Barford 1976: 213, n. 18.
13   Barford 1976: 200.
14   Owen 1957: 110.
15   A point of some importance, if the argument is to deserve the title of *akribesteros*, 'more accurate', accorded to it by Aristotle in *Met.* 990 b 15–16 – always assuming that Alexander is right in thinking that this argument is one of those said to 'produce ideas of relatives', which there is no reason to doubt.
16   Not something, obviously, that is possible in English, but perfectly possible in Greek, as the celebrated example of *NE* 11 6 (on the doctrine of the mean) clearly shows.

different cases, will not the same apply *pari passu* to 'man' in the case raised in I, where 'man' is predicated both of Socrates and a portrait of Socrates? Yet this is said explicitly to be a case of non-homonymy. B) According to Barford, saying that 'equal' when used by itself of sensible things is used homonymously entails that 'equal' is never used of sensible things except homonymously;[17] if so, then Owen's general interpretation (which I propose to accept) falls. C) In I, 'man' is in fact applied 'by itself' not only in the illustration of type (a) predication, but also in that of type (b) and (c) predication; thus if we take *to ison auto* in II to mean 'the predicate "equal" just by itself', it will not be clear to which type of predication II refers.

These objections can be met. First C, which is the simplest. The reference of II is clear and unambiguous, because it is only in type (a) predication that the predicate is always strictly applicable just by itself. In the case of the portrait, we may point to it and say 'this is a man'; but 'man' is not strictly applicable to it without addition. This is what is meant by the distinction between Socrates as *kuriôs* bearer of the predicate 'man', and his portrait as non-*kuriôs* bearer of it: what is non-*kuriôs* F is F to a qualified degree (the qualification being given by the 'addition').[18] Passing on to B: I believe that Barford is simply wrong to suppose that if 'equal by itself' is said to be used homonymously of things, so must 'equal'. According to II, ambiguity arises with respect to 'equal' used by itself of sensible things for three reasons: i) because they are equal to different things, and in different respects;[19] ii) because sensible things change in respect of quantity (so that 'equal' will mean different things at different times);[20]

---

17   Barford does not state this in so many words; but unless this is what he means, I can see no way of squaring his explicit interpretation of *to ison auto* (see above) with the statement e.g. on p. 200 that II tells us that 'equality is predicated of things in this world homonymously'.
18   The addition in the case of the portrait being '*painted* man' (or '*likeness* of a man').
19   Owen apparently wishes to restrict II (a) to the first of these two points, i.e. that equal things are always equal to something else, which is different in different cases; while Barford favours the second ('in this world we are confronted with *many* and *different kinds* of equals (e.g. equal measures, equal weights, equal intelligence, equal rights, etc.); hence, the same definition does not apply to all ...'). But on the interpretation adopted there is no reason for excluding any difference that might emerge in the unpacking of different applications of 'equal' (used by itself); whatever difference there was would entail that 'equal' was not 'indicating the same nature' (the definition of homonymy given in I). Leszl makes an interesting connection between II (a) and the argument of *Phaedo* 101a–b (p. 218). For him, II and III are concerned with showing how no rational account can be given of equality if we restrict ourselves to the level of the sensible world; and II (a) is concerned with the specific problem of how things can have the same predicate 'in virtù di cose (caratteristiche od altro) del tutto diverse'. I shall be commenting on this general line of interpretation at a later stage.
20   See Owen 1957: 108–9.

iii) because none of them is ever precisely equal (but this is what we imply of them, if we call them just 'equal').[21] But we can readily circumvent this ambiguity: all we must do is to provide the necessary specifications or qualifications – 'equal to that log', 'equal in length', 'equal now', 'imperfectly equal'.[22] If we do this, then arguments II (a)–(c) will no longer apply; and it will be open to us to assent to the intuitively obvious fact that there is something in common between the uses of 'equal' in the sensible world. Thus 'equal' applied to sensible things by itself is applied homonymously; 'equal' applied to them with the appropriate 'additions' is not.[23]

Finally, objection A, which is potentially the most serious. It is perfectly true that according to the canon of II, interpreted in the way I have suggested, 'man' when employed by itself of both Socrates and his portrait will be ambiguous (whereas it is said to be employed non-homonymously). But this is so *obviously* true, whatever the interpretation we place on II, that it ceases to be an objection; rather, we must look for an interpretation of I that does not require it to say something false. What I says, I believe, is that *to the extent that 'man' is applicable to the portrait of Socrates*, it is employed in the same sense as it is when employed of Socrates himself. I lists types of non-honomymy, or, perhaps better, cases in which predicates are used non-homonymously; and, in so far as Socrates and his portrait are both men (even if the portrait is only a *painted* man), the claim is that this is one such case.[24] If so, then the *logos* of 'man' must be the same when applied to Socrates and when applied to his portrait (or, as I puts it, 'man' must 'indicate the same nature'); from which it follows that I cannot be directly interested in the predicate 'man' as used by itself, which by II would involve different *logoi* in the case of Socrates and in the case of his portrait. The case being envisaged is not simply one where we might say 'that is a man' both of Socrates and of his portrait; rather, I think, it is understood that 'man' is used differently in the two cases (though the difference does not affect its sense) – in the one, *kuriôs*, and

---

21 Owen take *akribôs* itself in II (c) to mean 'without further specification', i.e. 'without addition'. But the means by which he seeks to establish this (e.g. *An. Post.* 87a34–7) are not adequate: see Leszl 1975: 215.

22 That Plato, at least, was willing to talk about 'degrees of equality' is established by *Phaedo* 74 d ff. (Leszl 1975: 216).

23 The various additions are parts of the *logos* of 'equal' as applied by itself for the obvious reason that they are included in its meaning. But where they are spelled out, they are evidently not regarded as affecting the sense of 'equal' (for if 'equal' is applied non-homonymously in such cases, it must according to I 'indicate the same nature'). On this point, see section 6 below. (There is of course no implication that one must specify when talking about equality in the case of sensible things. The argument is wholly specialized; 'equal' applies to the 'model' non-homonymously; but when it is applied by itself to sensible things, it is applied homonymously, because it hides different specifications.)

24 On this interpretation, see further in section 6 below.

in the other, non-*kuriôs*. This is, after all, the distinction on which the whole of I is based. Thus of Socrates, we are envisaged as saying 'that is a man'; of the portrait, 'that is (non-*kuriôs*) a man'; and in this situation the question of ambiguity does not arise. (But it *does* then arise in II, where we begin specifically talking of the application of predicates by themselves: leave out any applicable qualifications to the predicate, and ambiguity follows.)

4 The Interpretation of 83.12–14

One other weakness of Owen's account is his treatment of IV. As far as I understand him (his analysis seems to me at this point rather opaquely expressed), he would paraphrase IV as follows: 'Even if someone were to say "but even if *to ison auto* cannot be applied non-homonymously to physical things, *ison* can, in so far as likenesses are "non-homonymous with their model", it still follows that sensible equals are equal *qua* likenesses of what is strictly equal'.[25] The difficulty with this, if it is what Owen means, is that what is put into the mouth of the imagined objector actually seems to follow from II and III, and is the justification for saying that the conclusion follows 'in any case' (*aei*) (*ison* does not apply to sensible equals *kuriôs*, so it must apply to them as likenesses; but 'copies entail models', etc.). On this occasion, however, I do not find Barford illuminating; for his interpretation of IV is, among other things, tied to his apparently unacceptable view that the relation between Form and particular equals is homonymous. And though Leszl points out the weakness in Owen's interpretation,[26] his own account of IV seems less than satisfactory. On his view, II–IV show that none of the three types of non-homonymous predication listed in I fits sensible equals when *considered by themselves*. Thus II considers type (a), III type (c); while in IV, in answer to the objection that type (b) still remains to be considered, the answer is given that it has in fact been considered, and rejected, 'con riferimento alle cose di "quaggiù" soltanto', in III. 'Percio si puo ben concedere che questo è un tipo di predicazione sinonima, ma per far valere che esso deve collegare tali cose ad un'entita ad esse trascendente, in confronto con la quale esse vanno dette "uguali" in modo subordinato (appunto come delle copie).' Ingenious though this is, it falls foul of two objections. Firstly, *mê homônumon einai ton eikona tôi paradeigmati* ('that the model is not homonymous with the paradigm') is a strange way of referring to type (*b*) predication, and looks much more like a reference to type (*c*) (since after all it is non-homonymy *between likenesses* which is in question in type (*b*), not the non-homonymy between likeness and model). Secondly, one looks in vain for any mention in the argument of Leszl's crucial qualification 'cose di quaggiù '*soltanto*': certainly II and III do as a matter of fact consider sensible equals by themselves, but if, as Leszl supposes, the main

---

25 Leszl 1975: 300.
26 Leszl 1975: 198; IV has, from the point of view of Owen's interpretation, 'un carattere ... stranamente concessivo'.

bulk of the argument in II–IV rests on this qualification, one would rather expect it to appear in the text.

I believe, however, that a different interpretation of IV is possible. I begin from the point mentioned above, that the concessive clause in IV seems to refer to type (*c*) predication: 'even if one were to bring type (*c*) predication into play, it still follows that sensible equals are equal *qua* likenesses of *to kuriôs ison*'. The point is that type (*c*) has apparently just been ruled out as a way of accounting for the non-homonymy of sensible equals, insofar as it cannot be employed with respect to sensible equals alone; thus apparently leaving the field to type (*b*). But in fact type (*c*) can be re-introduced: if sensible equals are all equal *qua* likenesses, then there must be a model for them to be likenesses of; but if this is so, then sensible equals can after all be considered as members of a group including both likenesses and model – in which case their non-homonymy can now be accounted for under type (*c*). Even so, the argument says, it still follows that they are equal *qua* likenesses of *to kuriôs ison*. 'It still follows' implies that the conclusion follows from II and III alone, and so it does: sensible equals are not all *kuriôs* equal (II), nor is any one of them *kuriôs* equal (III); therefore (if they are non-homonymous, and I gives an exhaustive account of all possible types of non-homonymy) they must be equal *qua* likenesses of some model, which will be what is *to kuriôs ison*.

5   *A Reconstruction of the Argument*

I would now paraphrase the whole argument as follows.

I.   There are three types of non-homonymous predication: *a*) where things are strictly F; *b*) where the things to which the predicate F is applied are likenesses of the things that are strictly F; and *c*) where the group of things to which F is applied includes both things that are strictly F and things that are likenesses of these. 'Equal' is applied non-homonymously to sensible things; therefore it must be applied according to one of these three types.

II. 'Equal' by itself (i.e. without the addition which would mark it off as a likeness) is applied to sensible things homonymously (and therefore cannot be applied to them 'strictly', because this entails non-homonymy); because a) the *logos* to be given of 'equal' will differ in each case; b) sensible things fluctuate in quantity; and c) none of them is exactly equal.

III. Neither do we call sensible things equal non-homonymously on the basis that they are a group containing both model(s) and likenesses, since (from II(a)–(c), which show that 'equal' as applied to them always involves an addition) none of them is any more model or likeness than any other. Therefore they must be equal *qua* likenesses of *to kuriôs ison*.

IV. This still follows, even if one were to give a different account of their non-homonymy, i.e. not in terms of the non-homonymy of likenesses, but in terms of the non-homonymy of likeness and model.

v. But if this is the case, there exists something to which the predicate 'equal' *does* belong by itself and which is *kuriôs* equal, with respect to which sensible equals are called equal; and this is an Idea.[27]

6   *Forms and Particulars, and the Third Man*

According to this argument, 'equal' is applied non-homonymously to Form and sensible equals;[28] and I tells us that this means that 'equal' 'indicates the same nature' in the two cases. As Leszl argues,[29] this definition appears to make 'non-homonymy' indistinguishable from synonymy; if so, it is natural to assume that the term 'synonymy' was not yet available, since if it were, why should anyone choose to write 'non-homonymously' if he meant 'synonymously'?

I also agree with Leszl in his rejection of Owen's suggestion that the argument 'contains an obvious parallel to Aristotle's admission of a class of *pros hen kai mian phusin legomena* ['things said by reference to one and the same nature'] which are in a sense synonymous';[30] although my grounds are different from Leszl's. Owen argues that 'the wording of I (b) suggests that in its derivative use the predicate *is* to be paraphrased otherwise than in its primary use (i.e. in terms of "likeness"), though this difference of paraphrase does not constitute an ambiguity. Similarly we shall find ... that the argument of II can be construed as allowing, with one proviso, that a predicate can be used unambiguously of several things even when the *logos* of that predicate differs in the different cases; the proviso is that that different *logos* shall have a common factor. (In the cases distinguished in I this factor is the primary definition of 'man', and in II it is the definition of *to ison auto*'.[31] But I have argued that according to the argument difference of paraphrase does constitute ambiguity; and indeed that this is the explicit doctrine of II. If so, then the argument can envisage nothing analogous to a *pros ti* account. My own view is that non-homonymy is to be understood throughout in terms of plain synonymy. In I, we are told that to the extent that 'man' is applicable to the painted figure of Socrates (e.g. in that it is a man, not an elephant or a kangaroo), it is applied to it in the same sense as it is applied to Socrates himself – it 'indicates the same nature'. But 'man' is applicable to it only to a limited extent; it is not strictly a man, only a likeness of a man, a painted man. Similarly, 'equal' is applicable to sensible

---

27 Whatever one may think of the conception of the Form of equal as being 'just equal' (and one may clearly have serious doubts about its meaningfulness), this is what is inescapably proposed by the argument. Owen describes it as 'the extreme case of Greek mistreatment of "relative" terms in the attempt to assimilate them to simple adjectives' (Owen 1957: 110).

28 Again, this does not contradict II, which says only that 'equal' is applied to sensible things homonymously if shorn of the appropriate qualifying additions.

29 Leszl 1975: 188.

30 Owen 1957: 105.

31 *Ibid.*

things only to a qualified degree (they are always equal with certain qualifications, just as the portrait is a man, only a painted man); but to the degree that it is applicable to them, it is applied to them in the same sense as it is applied to the Form.

I conclude, then, that the argument leaves the Platonists asserting that the relation between 'equal' as used of the Form and as used of sensible things is one of straightforward, unembroidered, synonymy (or 'non-homonymy'). The immediate consequence of this is that they are left wide open to the Third Man argument, which is mentioned by Aristotle in *Met.* 990b15–17 (the text in connection with which Alexander cites the argument discussed in this appendix) in the same breath as the *logoi* which produce Ideas of relatives. Had they developed an account of the model-likeness relation in terms of 'focal meaning', they might have been provided with a defence against the Third Man; they might also have succeeded in rendering more plausible the application of the language of model and likeness to cases like that of the predicate 'equal'. But as it is, they do not seem to have taken this step. In *Met.* 991a2–8 Aristotle accordingly closes the pincers: 'if Forms and the things that participate in them have the same character (*eidos*), there will be something common to them (*sc.* so that the Third Man will apply); ... on the other hand, if they do *not* have the same character, they would be homonymous, and it would be just as if one were to apply the predicate "man" both to Callias and to a wooden likeness (of him), without observing anything in common between them.'

Bibliography

Allen 1965. Allen, R.E. (ed.), *Studies in Plato's Metaphysics*. London/New York.

Barford 1976. Barford, R., 'A Proof from the *Peri Ideôn* revisited', *Phronesis* 21 (1976) 198–219.

Barnes 1992. Barnes, J., 'An OCT of the *EE*', *Classical Review* n.s.42/1 (1992), 27–31.

Barnes 1997. Barnes, J., 'Roman Aristotle', in J. Barnes and M. Griffin (edd.), *Philosophia Togata II*, Oxford 1–69.

Barnes and Kenny 2014. Barnes, J., and Kenny, A., *Aristotle's Ethics: Writings from the Complete Works, Revised, edited, and with an introduction*, Princeton and Oxford, Princeton UP.

Bekker 1831. Bekker, I., *Aristotelis opera* [Prussian Academy edition], Berlin.

Bobonich 2023. Bobonich, C., "The Good or the Wild at Aristotle *Eudemian Ethics* 8.3?', *Classical Philology* 118/2: 172–93.

Broadie 2003. Broadie, S., 'Aristotelian Piety', *Phronesis* 48, 54–70.

Broadie-Rowe 2002. Sarah Broadie and Christopher Rowe, *Aristotle, Nicomachean Ethics: Translation, Introduction and Commentary*, Oxford.

Broadie unpublished. Broadie, S., 'Plato and Aristotle on the theoretical impulse. The theoretical adventurer, through the eyes of Plato and Aristotle.' Howison Lectures in Philosophy, Berkeley, CA 2014. URL: https://www.youtube.com/watch?v=fM4RTWvnoRU.

Burger 2008. Burger, R., *Aristotle's Dialogue with Socrates: On the Nicomachean Ethics*, Chicago.

Bywater 1890. *Aristotelis Ethica Nicomachea recognouit brevique adnotatione instruxit Bywater*, I.

Case 1910. Case, T., entry for 'Aristotle', *Encyclopaedia Britannica*, reprinted in Wians 1995.

Cherniss 1962. Cherniss, H., *Aristotle's Criticism of Plato and the Academy*, London.

Dirlmeier 1939. Dirlmeier, F., 'Die Zeit der Grossen Ethik', *Rheinisches Museum* 88, 214–43.

Dirlmeier 1962, Dirlmeier, F. *Aristoteles. Eudemische Ethik*, Darmstadt: Wissenschaftliche Buchgesellschaft.

Dirlmeier 1966. Dirlmeier, F. *Aristoteles, Magna Moralia*, Darmstadt: Wissenschaftliche Buchgesellschaft.

Donini 2005. Donini, P., *Aristotele, Etica Eudemia. Traduzione, Introduzione e Note*, Bari: Laterza.

Frede 2019. Frede, D., 'On the so-called common books of the *Eudemian* and the *Nicomachean Ethics*', *Phronesis* 64: 84–116.

Harlfinger 1971. Harlfinger, D 'Die Überlieferungsgeschichte der Eudemischen Ethik', in Moraux and Harlfinger 1971: 1–50.

Inwood and Woolf 2013. Inwood, B. and Woolf, R., *Aristotle, Eudemian Ethics*, (Cambridge Texts in the History of Philosophy), Cambridge.

Jaeger 1923. Jaeger, W., Jaeger, *Aristoteles, Grundlegung einer Geschichte seiner Entwicklung*, Berlin (tr. Richard Robinson, Oxford 1934).

Jost 2014. L. Jost, L., 'The *Eudemian Ethics* and its controversial relationship to the *Nicomachean Ethics*', in R. Polansky (ed.), *The Cambridge Companion to Aristotle's Nicomachean Ethics*, Cambridge: Cambridge University Press: 410–27.

Kenny 1978. Kenny, A.J.P., *The Aristotelian Ethics*, Oxford: Oxford University Press, 1st edition 1978; 2nd edition 2016.

Kenny 1991. Kenny, A.J.P., *Aristotle on the Perfect Life*, Oxford.

Kenny 2011. Kenny, A.J.P., *Aristotle. The Eudemian Ethics. A new translation by Anthony Kenny*. Oxford World's Classics.

Leszl 1970. Leszl, W., *Logic and Metaphysics in Aristotle*, Padua: Antenore.

Leszl 1975. Leszl, W., W. Leszl, *Il 'De ideis' di Aristotele e la teoria platonica delle idee*, Florence: Olschki.

Lorenz 2013. Lorenz, H., Review of Inwood and Woolf 2013, *Notre Dame Philosophical Reviews* (01/10).

Lorenz and Morison forthcoming. Lorenz, H. and Morison, B. (edd.), *Proceedings of the 2017 Symposium Aristotelicum*.

Montanari 1995. Montanari, F. (ed.), *The Brill Dictionary of Ancient Greek*. Leiden.

Moraux 1951. Moraux P., *Les listes anciennes des ouvrages d'Aristote*, Louvain: Éditions Universitaires de Louvain.

Müller-Goldingen 1988. Müller-Goldingen, C. (ed.), *Schriften zur aristotelischen Ethik*, Hildesheim.

Owen 1957. Owen, G.E.L., 'A Proof in the *Peri ideôn*', *JHS* 77, 103–11.

Pakaluk 2011. Pakaluk, M., 'On the unity of the *Nicomachean Ethics*', in Jon Miller (ed.), *Aristotle's* Nicomachean Ethics: *A Critical Guide*, Cambridge: Cambridge University Press: 1–44.

Penner and Rowe 2005. Penner, Terry, and Rowe, Christopher, *Plato's* Lysis, Cambridge.

Primavesi 2007. Primavesi, O., 'Ein Blick in den Stollen von Skepsis: vier Kapitel zur frühen Überlieferung des *Corpus Aristotelicum*', *Philologus* 151/1, 51–77.

Rackham 1935. Rackham, H., *Aristotle, Athenian Constitution, Eudemian Ethics, Virtues and Vices*, Cambridge, Mass.

Reeve 2021. Reeve, C.D.C., *Aristotle, Eudemian Ethics. Translated with Introduction and Notes*, Indianapolis.

Ross 1955. Ross, W.D., *Aristotelis fragmenta selecta*, Oxford.

Rowe 1975. Rowe, Christopher. 'A reply to John Cooper on the *Magna Moralia*', *AJPh* 96: 160–72 (reprinted in Müller-Goldingen. Hildesheim, 1988: 371–83).

Rowe 1971a. Rowe, Christopher, 'The EE and NE: A Study in the Development of Aristotle's Thought', Proceedings of the Cambridge Philological Society, supplement 3.

Rowe 1971b. Rowe, Christopher. 'The meaning of φρόνησις in the Eudemian Ethics', in Moraux and D. Harlfinger 1971: 73–92; reprinted in Müller-Goldingen. Hildesheim 1988: 253–72.

Rowe 1979. Rowe, Christopher, 'The Proof from Relatives in the Peri Ideôn: Further Reconsideration', Phronesis vol. 24 no.3, 270–81.

Rowe 1983a. Rowe, Christopher, 'De Aristotelis in tribus libris Ethicorum dicendi ratione: particles, connectives and style in three books from the Aristotelian ethical treatises' (four parts), LCM 8: 4–11, 37–40, 54–7, 70–4.

Rowe and Schofield 2000. Rowe, Christopher, and Schofield, M. (edd.), The Cambridge History of Greek and Roman Political Thought.

Rowe 2012. Rowe, Christopher, 'Aristotle's Eudemian Ethics on Loving People and Things', in F. Leigh, (ed.), The Eudemian Ethics on the Voluntary, Friendship, and Luck (The Sixth Keeling Colloquium in Ancient Philosophy), Leiden: 29–41.

Rowe 2013. Rowe, Christopher, 'Socrates and his Gods: From the Euthyphro to the Eudemian Ethics', in Melissa Lane and Verity Harte (edd.), Politeia [essays in honour of Malcolm Schofield], Cambridge 2013: 313–28.

Rowe 2014. Rowe, Christopher. 'The Best Life according to Aristotle (and Plato). A Reconsideration'. In Destrée, P. and Zingano, M. (eds.), Theoria. Studies on the Status and Meaning of Contemplation in Aristotle's Ethics: 273–67.

Rowe 2015. Rowe, Christopher. 'Aristotle's Other Ethics: some recent translations of the Eudemian Ethics'. In Polis. The Journal for Ancient Political Thought 32: 211–32.

Rowe 2021a. Rowe, Christopher, 'Why a new critical edition of Aristotle's Eudemian Ethics?' In Revista Circe de clásicos y modernos 2/1: 145–53.

Rowe 2021b. Rowe, Christopher. 'Aristotle and Socrates on the naturalness of goodness'. In Barbara Sattler and Ursula Coope (edd.), Ancient Ethics and the Natural World, Cambridge: 203–17.

Rowe 2022. Rowe, Christopher. 'Sophia in the Eudemian Ethics'. In Giulio di Basilio (ed.), Investigating the Relationship Between Aristotle's Eudemian and Nicomachean Ethics, London: 122–36.

Rowe 2023a. Rowe, Christopher, Aristotelis Ethica Eudemia quae edidit Christopher Rowe (Oxford: Clarendon Press, in the series Oxford Classical Texts).

Rowe 2023b. Rowe, Christopher, Aristotelica. Studies on the Text of Aristotle's Eudemian Ethics, Oxford: Clarendon Press.

Rowe 2024. Rowe, Christopher, 'Petrus Victorius and Aristotle's Eudemian Ethics', CQ 74/1: 1–11.

Rowe forthcoming a. Rowe, Christopher, 'Nous in the Eudemian and Nicomachean Ethics', to appear in I. Ramelli (ed.), Human and Divine Nous from Ancient to Byzantine and Renaissance Philosophy and Religion: Key Themes, Intersections and Developments.

Rowe forthcoming b. Rowe, Christopher, *Eudemian Ethics* Book II: Text, Apparatus and Notes, in Lorenz and Morison forthcoming.

Simpson 2013. Simpson, L.P., *The Eudemian Ethics of Aristotle Translated with Explanatory Commentary*, New Brunswick.

Simpson 2019. Simpson, L.P., 'Aristotle's EE: the Text and Character of the Common Books as found in EE mss', *CQ* 69 (2019): 1–15.

Susemihl 1884. Susemihl, F., [*Aristotelis Ethica Eudemia*] *Eudemi Rhodii Ethica* (Leipzig: Teubner), reproduced in 1967 as *Aristoteles, Ethica Eudemia*, Amsterdam.

Verdenius 1971. Verdenius, W.J., 'Human reason and God', in Paul Moraux and Dieter Harlfinger 1971: 285–97.

Walzer and Mingay 1991. Walzer, R. and Mingay, J., *Aristotelis Ethica Eudemia. Recensuerunt brevique adnotatione critica instruxerunt R.R. Walzer and J.M. Mingay* (Oxford: Clarendon Press, in the series Oxford Classical Texts).

Wians 1995. Wians, W.R., *Aristotle's Philosophical Development: Problems and Prospects*, London: Rowman and Littlefield.

Woods 1979. Woods, M., *Aristotle, Eudemian Ethics Books I, II and VIII, Translated with a Commentary* (Clarendon Aristotle series, Oxford; Second edition 1992).

Index of Terms

agathos   22*n*9, 65, 73, 91*n*52, 124*n*38–39, 125*n*44, 139
agent   23*n*12, 76, 92*n*56, 113–114, 116, 116*n*9, 118–119, 119*n*18, 120, 120*n*21, 120*n*26, 122*n*35
agrios   70*n*25, 123*n*38, 124*n*38
aisthêsis   18
akolasia   27*n*19, 67*n*16. *See* akolastos
akolastos   18. *See also* akolasia
akôn   18. *See also* akousios
akousios   18. *See also* akôn
akrasia   17, 144. *See also* akratês
akratês   18. *See also* akrasia
akribês   18. *See also* akribesteros, akribôs
akribesteros   149*n*15. *See also* akribês, akribôs
akribôs   146, 151*n*21. *See also* akribês, akribesteros
alazôn   18
Aldine   4*n*10, 6*n*12, 7, 14*n*50, 14*n*51, 15, 15*n*53, 124*n*38
alêthes   139*n*42. *See also* alêthôs
alêthôs   146. *See also* alêthes
analogy   95, 141*n*55, 143, 147*n*6
Analytics   29, 48, 58
animal   26, 29, 38*n*17, 38*n*22, 48, 51, 57, 66, 69, 69*n*22, 81, 83–84, 84*n*22, 90, 94, 96*n*71, 98–99, 102, 110
anthrôpos   149*n*11
antiquity   65*n*14
aorist   21*n*6, 119*n*17, 120*n*21, 120*n*23
apallattô   40*n*36, 41*n*36
aphrôn   78*n*48
apodotic   85*n*28
appetite   19, 26, 41, 44, 49–52, 54–55, 68, 68*n*20, 70, 82, 85, 95, 98, 114, 118–120
archetype   4, 6, 123*n*38
aretê   135, 138, 140, 142
aristocracy   100–101, 100*n*83
Aristotelian   1, 6*n*11, 12, 12*n*40, 25*n*23, 42*n*41, 66*n*15, 77, 93*n*59, 120*n*24, 132, 134–137, 139, 144. *See also* Aristotle, Aristotelianism
Aristotelianism   129. *See also* Aristotle, Aristotelian
arithmetical   91, 101–103

Athens   69*n*22, 73*n*30, 75*n*32, 76*n*36, 76*n*37, 84, 92*n*57, 103, 103*n*93, 105*n*100, 106*n*100

bashful   41, 43, 77
Bayerische Staatsbibliothek   6*n*12, 6*n*14, 15*n*53
beloved   63*n*11, 75–76, 92, 105, 107, 110, 112
benefactor   91, 99, 102, 103*n*92, 104*n*98, 107–18
beneficiary   91, 99, 102, 103*n*92, 108
Bessarion   15–16
bestow   73, 106, 125
blame   48, 54, 60, 74, 76, 78
blessed   22, 24, 24*n*16, 25
Byzantine, Byzantium   1, 3*n*6, 6, 15, 106*n*100, 116

civic   23, 63–64, 66, 99, 101, 103, 105–106, 123
cobbler   106
codex   6*n*15, 8*n*20, 8*n*21, 14
coinage   71*n*27
command, commander   37, 39–40, 63, 76*n*36
commentary   3, 9, 138
compulsion   51–53, 60
copyist   4, 4*n*8, 10, 10*n*30, 13–14, 14*n*46, 15, 40*n*36
corpus   1, 3*n*6, 6*n*11, 12, 42*n*41, 66*n*15
coward   41, 43–44, 61–65, 79
crocodile   84
cryptogram   141

daimôn   29. *See also* daimonion
daimonion   22*n*10, 138. *See also* daimôn
death   2, 8, 53, 64–65, 104, 105*n*100, 138*n*33
deceive   82, 89–90, 105
defect   44, 46, 61, 70–71, 79
deficient   42, 44, 46–47, 59, 72, 76, 139
degree   9–10, 23*n*12, 24, 32, 62, 72, 92, 96, 143–144, 150, 151*n*22, 155
dialectical   12, 31*n*35, 116*n*9, 138
dialogue   30*n*28, 80*n*30, 117, 117*n*10, 137, 137*n*33, 138, 138*n*33, 138*n*39
diathesis   18, 39*n*28
divination   11*n*37, 121, 136

INDEX OF TERMS

divine   20, 22, 24, 25*n*23, 29, 110–111, 120, 121*n*32, 122, 136, 138*n*38, 139, 140
divinity   21*n*1, 24*n*18, 76*n*39, 93*n*59, 120*n*26
doctor   34–35, 56, 58–59, 83, 83*n*18, 84, 84*n*19, 88, 88*n*39, 106, 125

Egypt   26, 81, 84
eikôn   146, 152
eirôn   18, 77. *See also* eirôneia
eirôneia   43*n*44, 77*n*42. *See also* eirôn
emphrôn   78*n*48
epieikês   18, 78*n*46, 91*n*52
epistêmê. *See* knowledge
ethical   2, 12–13*n*43, 18, 22, 24*n*14, 27, 38–39, 42, 43*n*48, 47, 66*n*15, 80*n*1, 86*n*31, 114, 120*n*26, 121, 122, 133–134, 139–140, 142*n*59, 143–144
ethics   1–3, 3*n*6, 4–8, 8*n*18, 9–12, 12*n*40, 3– 15, 15*n*52, 16–17, 27*n*25, 66, 66*n*15, 95*n*66, 129–131, 131*n*6, 133, 135, 137–141, 143, 144
etymology   40*n*32, 75*n*33
eudaimôn   29. *See also* eudaimonia
eudaimonia   19, 25, 133–134, 139–140, 140*n*47, 141–142, 142*n*60, 143. *See also* eudaimôn
Eudemian   1–4, 4*n*9, 8*m*18, 11, 11*n*38, 12, 14–15, 15*n*52, 16–17, 66*n*15, 72*n*29, 129–130, 130*n*6, 131, 131*n*6, 131, 135–137, 143
eupragia   19
Euripidean   107*n*104. *See also* Euripides
eutuchia   2, 12*n*41, 19, 136–138, 140
exoteric   30, 35, 132*n*12
expenditure   43*n*47, 44, 71–72, 75–76, 76*n*38
eye   33, 113, 115–117

faculty   126, 129–130, 141*n*55
falsehood   29, 77–78
farmer   72*n*28, 106
father   54, 91, 96, 100, 100*n*82, 101–102, 107
feast   75, 111
fight   50, 64–65, 84, 99, 110*n*113, 123
financial   29, 104, 106*n*100
fortune   19–20, 22, 24, 43*n*43, 82, 89, 111–112, 115, 116*n*8, 117–119, 119*n*16, 120, 120*n*25, 122, 122*n*35, 123, 125, 125*n*45, 137–138
friend   32*n*35, 80, 80*n*1, 80*n*5, 81–85, 85*n*26, 86, 88–99, 101–108, 108*n*107, 110, 110*n*111–112, 111–112, 126
friendship   14, 17, 32*n*35, 80, 80*n*2, 81, 81*n*8, 82–85, 85*n*26, 86, 86*n*29, 87–88, 88*n*41,

89, 89*n*44, 89*n*46, 90–91, 91*n*54, 92–98, 98*n*78, 99, 99*n*80, 100–112, 132, 144
god   21, 21*n*1, 22, 24*n*16, 25, 25*n*23, 29, 31, 48, 76*n*39, 77, 77*n*40, 80–81, 91–93, 93*n*59, 102–103, 103*n*92, 103*n*95, 104*n*97, 105, 108–109, 111, 116, 116*n*9, 120, 120*n*26, 121, 121*n*28–29, 121*n*31–32, 122, 126, 126*n*50, 126*n*51, 129, 138, 138*n*38, 139, 140, 140*n*47, 141
goddess   76*n*39, 104
godlike   20
Greek   4, 4*n*8, 10*n*32, 14, 21*n*4, 25*n*23, 34*n*44, 36*n*6, 42*n*41, 65*n*14, 67*n*16–17, 80*n*6, 97*n*72, 115*n*4, 118*n*13, 119*n*19, 137*n*33, 149*n*11, 149*n*16, 154*n*27
gymnastics   31, 33, 42, 47

harmony   51, 68–69, 81, 86, 89
health   23, 28, 32–35, 39, 47, 55, 58, 123, 125, 126*n*50, 141
heavens   26
hemlock   54, 97*n*75
Heraclea   63*n*11
hexis   19, 33*n*42, 38*n*23, 61*n*2, 116*n*8
historia, history   1–17, 84*n*23, 96*n*71, 105*n*100
historical   67*n*16, 16, 117*n*10, 131*n*6, 137*n*33, 145
homonymous   32*n*35, 83*n*17, 146–147, 147*n*6, 148, 148*n*10, 149–150, 150*n*17, 151, 151*n*23, 152–154, 154*n*28, 155
homonymy   32*n*35, 85, 146–147, 147*n*6, 149–151, 150*n*19, 151–155
honor   22, 26, 73–75, 93, 103, 107, 123
human   23, 25–26, 29, 33–34, 37–38, 38*n*21, 38*n*22, 44, 47–48, 51, 55–57, 62–64, 66*n*15, 68, 83–84, 84*n*22, 85*n*26, 86, 86*n*31, 87, 89, 91, 92*n*55, 94*n*64, 98, 99*n*80, 102, 103*n*92, 104*n*97, 108, 111, 117, 118*n*14, 119, 119*n*18, 125, 133–134, 140–142
humanity, humankind   28, 32*n*35, 73
hupographê   41*n*36, 42*n*41
husband   91, 94, 100, 102
hyparchetype   6–7
hypothesis   16, 48, 58, 143, 145

ideôn   30*n*29, 32*n*35, 33*n*38, 145, 149
illuminate   94*n*64, 152
illustration   13

inanimate 40, 51–52, 83, 88, 95, 98, 100
induction 35, 39, 42, 123
indulgent 41, 43, 67, 67n16, 68, 68n20, 69, 70, 72, 114–115, 115n5. *See also* self-indulgent
inferior 7, 13n45, 19, 29, 92, 92n55, 101, 103n94, 112
injustice 78, 113
instrument 83, 84n19, 121
intellect, intellectual 18, 20, 23n12, 24n14, 24n19, 38–39, 43n48, 45, 53, 61n1, 66n15, 106, 131, 131n6, 133–135, 135n20, 137–138, 141n55
intelligence 19, 23, 31, 87n37, 114, 116, 120n24, 133, 133n16, 136, 150n19
intemperate 67, 67n16, 68, 68n19

jealous 19, 64
judge, judgment 7, 9n28, 18–19, 21, 26, 29, 37, 57, 60, 67, 73, 78, 82, 88, 89n43, 90, 92, 95, 105, 108, 114, 125
justice 25, 27–28, 31–32, 57, 78, 79n49, 80, 84, 91, 99–102, 104–105, 113–114, 123, 131n6, 135

kalokagathia 19, 137, 139–140, 140n47, 142, 142n60, 140, 143. *See also* kalokagathos
kalokagathos 140. *See also* kalokagathia
knowledge, epistêmê 12, 18, 21, 21n5, 22, 22n8, 26–28, 35, 42, 45, 45n54, 54, 58–59, 63, 65, 105n100, 106, 109, 109n110, 113, 113n2, 114, 114n3, 115, 115n5, 117, 117n10, 119, 121, 129–130, 133, 133n16, 138145n1
kuriôs 146, 148, 148n10, 149–154

laconic 40n33, 93n60, 115n4
lacuna 8, 98n78, 136
lacunose 132
Laurentian 6n12, 8n21
law 16, 64, 80, 103–104
logos 2, 19, 139n42, 145–146, 149, 151, 151n23, 153–155
love 21, 63, 65, 80, 80n1, 81–85, 87–88, 88n40–41, 89, 90n50, 91–93, 93n60, 94, 94n64, 95, 95n65, 96, 96n70, 97, 97n75, 99–100, 105, 108, 110–112, 116, 134

lover 71, 71n27, 77–78, 82, 90, 92–93, 105, 110
luck 7, 20, 63, 105, 116n8, 118
Lyceum 27, 38n18, 96n68, 113n1

Macedonian 105n100, 106n101
manuscript 1, 4, 4n8, 6, 6n12, 7–12, 12n51, 14, 33n38, 62n7, 79n49, 116n8, 123n38, 124n38, 132, 136, 138n38
Marcianus 5, 7–8, 13–15
master 3, 94, 96, 100, 102, 125, 133
mathematics 27n25, 35, 48
medical 23, 31, 33, 35, 42, 68n19, 83, 83n18, 84n19, 115, 125
medication 23, 82, 86
medicine 56, 91, 126n50, 141, 141n55
medieval 32n35, 124n38
megaloprepes 19
megalopsuchia 43n46. *See also* megalopsuchos
megalopsuchos 19, 43n46. *See also* megalopsuchia
Megarians 84, 103, 103n93
melancholic 121
metaphor 44, 67n16, 68, 68n19, 68n20, 75, 97n75, 147n6
Metaphysica 146
metaphysical, metaphysics 16, 25n23, 27n25, 33n38, 66n15, 126n47, 132, 139, 144
mikroprepês 19
mikropsuchia 43n46. *See also* mikropsuchos
mikropsuchos 19. *See also* mikropsuchia
military 65, 76n37
model 146–147, 151n23, 152–153, 155
moderation 32, 41, 43, 67–70, 78, 123
modern 6, 13, 16, 21n2, 41n36, 122n37
modesty 43, 77, 78
monarchies 26, 100, 100n83
money 25, 27, 57, 71, 71n27, 72, 72n28, 89, 103–104, 105n99, 105n100, 106, 116, 125–126
mother 26, 76n36, 81, 96, 100, 100n82, 107, 111
movement 19, 23, 29, 31, 35, 37, 38n22, 38, 42, 52, 99n79, 120, 121n34
munificence 19, 43n47, 73

INDEX OF TERMS

music 68, 69*n*22–23, 90–91, 100, 100*n*83, 110, 100*n*112
musician 69*n*22, 88, 90, 106

natural 28, 51–53, 63, 72*n*28, 78, 80–81, 89, 95, 99, 102–103, 113, 119, 123, 123*n*38, 124, 124*n*38, 126, 131, 139, 139*n*41, 140–141
nature 22–24, 27–30, 37, 39, 44, 47–49, 52–53, 56, 58, 62, 64, 67, 69, 69*n*22, 70, 72, 75, 76*n*39, 86–87, 89, 91, 93–95, 97–98, 102*n*88, 104, 109–110, 115–116, 116*n*8, 117–119, 119*n*18, 123–124, 124*n*38, 125–126, 129–130, 131*n*6, 146, 146*n*2, 150*n*19, 151, 151*n*23, 154
nemesis 76, 76*n*38–39
Nicomachean 2–3, 4*n*9, 11–12, 12*n*40, 13*n*44, 14, 16–17, 66*n*15, 129, 131, 131*n*6, 134*n*19, 135, 137*n*33, 138*n*33, 143, 144*n*65. *See also* Nicomachus
nobility 19, 21*n*3, 122, 122*n*36–37, 124, 127
noble 66*n*15, 76*n*37, 122, 124

obsequious 18, 43–44, 77
Odyssey 80*n*7
oligarchy 73*n*30, 100, 100*n*83

papyrus 2, 17, 38*n*18, 41*n*36
philosopher, philosophoi 24, 24*n*19, 28, 77*n*42, 81, 136, 136*n*25, 139, 142 81, 136. *See also* philosophy, philosophical
philosophical 1, 6, 9–10, 11*n*36, 25, 25*n*23, 27–28, 30*n*29, 36*n*7, 66*n*15, 116*n*8, 122*n*36, 126, 129, 134*n*19, 139, 141–142, 142*n*56, 144
philosophy, philosophia 21*n*5, 24*n*19, 25, 28, 30, 110, 134, 139–140, 142. *See also* philosopher, philosophical
phronêsis 19, 43, 43*n*48, 78, 78*n*48, 129–131, 133–135, 135*n*21, 137–138, 140–141, 141*n*55, 142–144, 144*n*64
phronimos 134–136, 136*n*24
Phaedo 150*n*19, 151*n*22
Phrygian 100*n*83
Platonic 21, 30–31, 91, 137–138, 145–146, 149. *See also* Plato, Platonism, Platonist
Platonism 129. *See also* Plato, Platonic, Platonist

Platonist 31*n*35, 32*n*35–36, 84*n*20, 145, 147, 148, 148*n*10, 149, 155. *See also* Plato, Platonic, Platonism
pleasure 2*n*4, 14, 16, 16*n*56, 17, 22, 25–27, 35, 39*n*29, 41, 43*n*42, 44, 46, 52, 54, 58–59, 65, 67–68, 68*n*19, 69–71, 73, 75–78, 83–88, 90–92, 92*n*56, 93–98, 102, 104–107, 110, 112, 125, 132–133, 142, 142*n*58, 143, 144, 144*n*64
poet 65, 69*n*22, 69*n*24, 81, 103
poetry 81*n*9, 84*n*21, 110
politês 63*n*8
politics, politikê 16, 25, 27–28, 33, 33*n*42, 72*n*28, 73*n*30, 100, 100*n*83, 101, 123*n*38, 124, 133, 142, 142*n*56, 144
portrait 150, 150*n*18, 151, 152, 155
praise 37–38, 44, 48–49, 60, 62, 73, 93, 134*n*18
praiseworthy 48, 59–60, 73–74, 76, 78, 78*n*46, 79, 79*n*49, 123, 125
profit 43, 44*n*51, 79*n*49, 103
profiteer 72
provenance 137, 144*n*65

qualification 19, 46, 53, 55–57, 61*n*4, 62, 82–83, 85–86, 86*n*31, 87, 87*n*33, 89–90, 97, 124, 131, 134, 146, 149–152, 155

rage 20, 63, 63*n*10, 64–66, 70, 70*n*25, 71*n*26, 123*n*38
Renaissance 1, 3*n*6, 6, 15
reputation 11, 22, 27, 66, 75, 77

sacrifices 105, 107
science, scientific 18, 87, 87*n*37, 130
scribe, scribal 10, 16, 40*n*36, 42*n*41, 113*n*1, 124*n*38
scroll 38*n*18, 42*n*41
seer 84, 121*n*28, 121*n*30, 121*n*33
sex 26, 53, 68, 110
Sicily 1, 6
sick 23, 62, 82, 123
sing 68, 106, 118
slave 76, 92*n*55, 94, 96, 100, 102, 113*n*1, 125
slavish 26, 70–71
sleep 26, 36–37, 45, 81, 121*n*34
smell 68–69, 88

social   78n45, 80n1
society   25, 67n16, 71n26, 80n4
Socratic   43n44, 91n53, 115, 138–140. *See also* Socrates
son   2, 69, 77n43, 91, 93n61, 100–102
sophia   20, 38n26, 106n102, 129–130, 133–135, 135n20–21, 136–138, 140, 142, 142n60, 143
sophist   34, 97
Sophoclean   102n89
sophos   24n19, 134, 134n18, 135–136, 136n26
sound   11n36, 69, 77, 77n43 108n106, 136
Spartan   111, 123, 123n38, 124n38
speech   73, 105, 134–136
sphere   23, 28, 30–31, 42, 66n15, 68n20, 69, 72–75, 89, 104, 119, 126n47, 130, 139
spirit   43n46, 47, 49–50, 55, 63n10
spoudaios   20, 91n52, 125n44
Staatsbibliothek   6n12–13, 15n53
statesman   27–28, 27n24–25, 33, 80, 80n3, 86
steersmanship   42, 115–116, 116n7
suffer   9, 24, 26, 44, 52–53, 64–65, 100, 112
sumbebêkos   19, 37n13, 140
sycophant   43, 77

teleia   140. *See also* teleois
teleios   20, 140, 140n50. *See also* teleia
theôi   138n38
theology   4n10, 66n15
theôrein   20, 68n21, 98nn77, 126n50, 139–141
theôreisthô   42n41
theôrêtikos   20, 35n5, 45n54, 126n47, 126n50, 140–141, 141n55 143
theôria   110n112, 122n36, 139–140, 140n47, 141, 143, 144n64
therapeia   140n47, 141

therapeuein   139
translate   17, 25n0, 33n40, 35n2, 40n35–36, 41n37, 42n41, 55n55, 56n41, 63n10, 66n15, 86n31, 121n28, 126n47, 135–136, 146n2, 147
translation   4, 9n23, 9n28, 13n45,18, 18, 21n6, 25n23, 31n32, 68n19, 72n29, 76n39, 77n44, 114n3–4, 122n37, 123n38, 126n47, 130n6, 139n41, 145, 148
translator   4, 18, 40n36, 67n17, 98n78, 114n3, 122n37, 132, 144n65
triangle   48, 59

universal   31n35, 32n35, 84
universe   26, 120, 138, 138n38, 139

virtue, aretê   10, 13n43, 18, 22, 24, 30, 37, 43n48, 70, 79n49, 83, 90, 95, 109, 115–116, 117n10, 121, 123, 129, 130–131, 131n6, 132–135, 138–140, 140n47, 142, 142n59–69, 143. *See also* aretai
vulgar   25, 77–78, 110

war   31, 58
weakness   9n28 10, 30n26, 147, 152
wealth   22, 25, 29, 55, 58, 65, 72–73, 76n37, 106, 108, 108n107, 123–125, 135
weapons   64
wedding   75–76
wild   26, 63, 66, 70n25, 81, 83–84, 90, 123n38
wine   54, 63, 83, 90, 90n48, 108
witness   6n14, 7, 36, 36n9
wittiness   77n44
wolf   81
woman   45, 86, 88, 93
wooden   155

Index of Names

Aelian 145
Alexander
   of Aphrodisias 3*n*7, 145, 146–148, 149*n*15, 155
   the Great 105*n*100, 106*n*101
Anaxagoras 24*n*19, 25, 25*n*23, 26
Antileon 63*n*11
Antiphon 73, 93, 93*n*61
Apollo 21*n*1
Aristoteles 8*n*20
Aristotelicus 121*n*33. *See also* Aristotle
Aristotelis 11*n*38, 146. *See also* Aristotle
Aristotle
   ethical theories in Aristotle's *Eudemian Ethics* 18, 21*n*7, 21, 24*n*14, 24, 24*n*19, 25, 25*n*23, 27, 27*n*25, 31, 31*n*32, 33, 33*n*39, 38, 38*n*18, 38*n*19, 39, 39*n*21, 40, 40*n*32, 43, 43*n*44, 43*n*48, 61, 61*n*1, 65, 65*n*13, 66, 66*n*14, 66*n*15, 67, 67*n*17, 67*n*18, 67*n*19, 68, 68*n*20, 72, 72*n*29, 77, 77*n*42, 77*n*44, 79, 79*n*49, 81, 81*n*12, 85, 85*n*28, 86, 86*n*31, 87, 87*n*32, 88, 88*n*40, 89, 89*n*43, 90, 90*n*50, 91, 91*n*54, 93, 93*n*60, 96, 96*n*68, 96*n*70, 96*n*71, 99, 99*n*81, 100, 100*n*83, 101, 101*n*86, 104, 104*n*97, 107, 107*n*105, 122, 122*n*36, 125, 125*n*40, 138–144
   historical context of Aristotle's *Eudemian Ethics* 1–3, 4*n*10, 15, 15*n*52, 33, 33*n*42, 43, 43*n*46, 75, 75*n*32, 75*n*33, 76, 76*n*39, 84, 84*n*20, 105, 105*n*100, 106, 106*n*100, 116, 116*n*9, 117, 117*n*10, 121, 121*n*34, 137*n*33, 147*n*6, 148–149, 149*n*15
   intellectual virtues in Aristotle's *Eudemian Ethics* 129, 130, 134, 136–137
   metaphysical and theological concepts in Aristotle's *Eudemian Ethics* 113, 113*n*1, 114, 114*n*3, 118, 118*n*13, 119, 119*n*16, 119*n*18, 120, 120*n*26, 120*n*27, 121, 121*n*33, 126, 126*n*47, 126*n*50, 145, 154–155
   structure and content of Aristotle's *Eudemian Ethics* 12–13, 13*n*43, 16–17, 17*n*60
   textual transmission issues of Aristotle's *Eudemian Ethics* 4, 7*n*16, 9, 9*n*26, 10–11, 11*n*36, 30, 30*n*26, 31, 31*n*35, 33, 33*n*38, 40, 40*n*36, 41, 41*n*36, 41*n*38, 42, 42*n*41, 68, 68*n*19, 97, 97*n*75, 109, 109*n*109, 109*n*110, 115, 115*n*4, 116, 116*n*8, 122, 122*n*37, 123, 123*n*38, 124, 124*n*38, 130*n*6, 132, 144*n*64

Bekker, Immanuel 7, 7*n*16–17, 8–9, 12*n*40, 13, 13*n*45, 121*n*33

Coriscus 39, 97, 97*n*75
Cyril 12*n*40

Dirlmeier, Franz 9, 9*n*27, 9*n*28, 10, 13*n*43, 17*n*57, 90*n*47, 141*n*55

Empedocles 81
Eudemus 2–3, 3*n*6, 3*n*7, 4*n*10, 13–14, 17, 17*n*60, 32*n*35
Eunicus 92
Euripides 81*n*9, 81*n*10, 82*n*14, 89*n*45, 90*n*49, 93*n*61, 107. *See also* Euripidean
Eurystheus 111
Euthydemus 116*n*8, 117*n*10, 136, 136*n*28, 138, 138*n*37
Euthyphro 126*n*51

Fitzgerald 117*n*10, 137*n*33

Heracles 65*n*12, 110, 110*n*113, 111
Heraclitus 50, 81
Herodotus 84
Hesiod 81*n*9, 103*n*96
Hippocrates 116, 116*n*7

Iliad 65*n*14, 81*n*11, 121*n*33

Lorenz 130*n*6, 131*n*6, 144*n*65

Nicomachum 15
Nicomachus 2, 3*n*6, 17, 143*n*64. *See also* Nicomachean

Odysseus 77*n*43

Plato
Plato's ethical theories   16, 21*n*4, 21*n*6,
    27*n*24, 27*n*25, 63*n*9, 65*n*13, 77*n*42, 81*n*12,
    90*n*47, 91*n*53, 100*n*83, 104*n*97, 126*n*51,
    134*n*19, 136, 137, 138*n*33
Plato's theories of metaphysics and
    forms   30, 40*n*31, 40*n*34, 145–146, 146*n*2,
    149, 151*n*22
Plato's and Socrates' historical
    contexts   31*n*35, 32*n*35, 117*n*10, 137*n*33
Primavesi   3*n*6, 131*n*6, 144*n*65
Protagoras   90*n*47, 91*n*53, 135*n*22
Protrepticus   129
Pytho   105, 106*n*100

Socrates   22*n*8, 22*n*10, 27, 27*n*25, 43*n*44,
    63, 65, 65*n*13, 77*n*42, 81, 81*n*12, 90*n*50,
    97*n*75, 113*n*2, 116*n*8, 117, 117*n*10, 120*n*26,
    126*n*51, 136–137, 137*n*33, 138, 138*n*33,
    138*n*39, 139–140, 146, 148*n*10, 150–152,
    154. *See also* Socratic

Theodorus   27*n*25
Theognis   21, 65, 88, 104
Thrasymachus   77*n*42

Vettori   6*n*12, 8*n*21, 9, 15

Zeus   102, 107

Index of Names

Aelian 145
Alexander
   of Aphrodisias 3*n*7, 145, 146–148, 149*n*15, 155
   the Great 105*n*100, 106*n*101
Anaxagoras 24*n*19, 25, 25*n*23, 26
Antileon 63*n*11
Antiphon 73, 93, 93*n*61
Apollo 21*n*1
Aristoteles 8*n*20
Aristotelicus 121*n*33. *See also* Aristotle
Aristotelis 11*n*38, 146. *See also* Aristotle
Aristotle
   ethical theories in Aristotle's *Eudemian Ethics* 18, 21*n*7, 21, 24*n*14, 24, 24*n*19, 25, 25*n*23, 27, 27*n*25, 31, 31*n*32, 33, 33*n*39, 38, 38*n*18, 38*n*19, 39, 39*n*21, 40, 40*n*32, 43, 43*n*44, 43*n*48, 61, 61*n*1, 65, 65*n*13, 66, 66*n*14, 66*n*15, 67, 67*n*17, 67*n*18, 67*n*19, 68, 68*n*20, 72, 72*n*29, 77, 77*n*42, 77*n*44, 79, 79*n*49, 81, 81*n*12, 85, 85*n*28, 86, 86*n*31, 87, 87*n*32, 88, 88*n*40, 89, 89*n*43, 90, 90*n*50, 91, 91*n*54, 93, 93*n*60, 96, 96*n*68, 96*n*70, 96*n*71, 99, 99*n*81, 100, 100*n*83, 101, 101*n*86, 104, 104*n*97, 107, 107*n*105, 122, 122*n*36, 125, 125*n*40, 138–144
   historical context of Aristotle's *Eudemian Ethics* 1–3, 4*n*10, 15, 15*n*52, 33, 33*n*42, 43, 43*n*46, 75, 75*n*32, 75*n*33, 76, 76*n*39, 84, 84*n*20, 105, 105*n*100, 106, 106*n*100, 116, 116*n*9, 117, 117*n*10, 121, 121*n*34, 137*n*33, 147*n*6, 148–149, 149*n*15
   intellectual virtues in Aristotle's *Eudemian Ethics* 129, 130, 134, 136–137
   metaphysical and theological concepts in Aristotle's *Eudemian Ethics* 113, 113*n*1, 114, 114*n*3, 118, 118*n*13, 119, 119*n*16, 119*n*18, 120, 120*n*26, 120*n*27, 121, 121*n*33, 126, 126*n*47, 126*n*50, 145, 154–155
   structure and content of Aristotle's *Eudemian Ethics* 12–13, 13*n*43, 16–17, 17*n*60
   textual transmission issues of Aristotle's *Eudemian Ethics* 4, 7*n*16, 9, 9*n*26, 10–11, 11*n*36, 30, 30*n*26, 31, 31*n*35, 33, 33*n*38, 40, 40*n*36, 41, 41*n*36, 41*n*38, 42, 42*n*41, 68, 68*n*19, 97, 97*n*75, 109, 109*n*109, 109*n*110, 115, 115*n*4, 116, 116*n*8, 122, 122*n*37, 123, 123*n*38, 124, 124*n*38, 130*n*6, 132, 144*n*64

Bekker, Immanuel 7, 7*n*16–17, 8–9, 12*n*40, 13, 13*n*45, 121*n*33

Coriscus 39, 97, 97*n*75
Cyril 12*n*40

Dirlmeier, Franz 9, 9*n*27, 9*n*28, 10, 13*n*43, 17*n*57, 90*n*47, 141*n*55

Empedocles 81
Eudemus 2–3, 3*n*6, 3*n*7, 4*n*10, 13–14, 17, 17*n*60, 32*n*35
Eunicus 92
Euripides 81*n*9, 81*n*10, 82*n*14, 89*n*45, 90*n*49, 93*n*61, 107. *See also* Euripidean
Eurystheus 111
Euthydemus 116*n*8, 117*n*10, 136, 136*n*28, 138, 138*n*37
Euthyphro 126*n*51

Fitzgerald 117*n*10, 137*n*33

Heracles 65*n*12, 110, 110*n*113, 111
Heraclitus 50, 81
Herodotus 84
Hesiod 81*n*9, 103*n*96
Hippocrates 116, 116*n*7

Iliad 65*n*14, 81*n*11, 121*n*33

Lorenz 130*n*6, 131*n*6, 144*n*65

Nicomachum 15
Nicomachus 2, 3*n*6, 17, 143*n*64. *See also* Nicomachean

Odysseus 77*n*43

Plato
Plato's ethical theories   16, 21*n*4, 21*n*6,
    27*n*24, 27*n*25, 63*n*9, 65*n*13, 77*n*42, 81*n*12,
    90*n*47, 91*n*53, 100*n*83, 104*n*97, 126*n*51,
    134*n*19, 136, 137, 138*n*33
Plato's theories of metaphysics and
    forms   30, 40*n*31, 40*n*34, 145–146, 146*n*2,
    149, 151*n*22
Plato's and Socrates' historical
    contexts   31*n*35, 32*n*35, 117*n*10, 137*n*33
Primavesi   3*n*6, 131*n*6, 144*n*65
Protagoras   90*n*47, 91*n*53, 135*n*22
Protrepticus   129
Pytho   105, 106*n*100

Socrates   22*n*8, 22*n*10, 27, 27*n*25, 43*n*44,
    63, 65, 65*n*13, 77*n*42, 81, 81*n*12, 90*n*50,
    97*n*75, 113*n*2, 116*n*8, 117, 117*n*10, 120*n*26,
    126*n*51, 136–137, 137*n*33, 138, 138*n*33,
    138*n*39, 139–140, 146, 148*n*10, 150–152,
    154. *See also* Socratic

Theodorus   27*n*25
Theognis   21, 65, 88, 104
Thrasymachus   77*n*42

Vettori   6*n*12, 8*n*21, 9, 15

Zeus   102, 107

Printed in the United States
by Baker & Taylor Publisher Services